Hebrews

Hebrews

The Superiority of Christ

Garth Leno

CHRISTIAN PUBLICATIONS
CAMP HILL, PENNSYLVANIA

Christian Publications
3825 Hartzdale Drive, Camp Hill, PA 17011

Faithful, biblical publishing since 1883

ISBN: 0-87509-626-3
LOC Catalog Card Number: 96-85150
©by Christian Publications, Inc.
All rights reserved
Printed in the United States of America

96 97 98 99 00   5 4 3 2 1

CONTENTS

PREFACE

The mental picture most of us see when we hear the term "developing world" is one of starving children—pot-bellied, malnourished children with the saddest eyes you can imagine. But most people in *every* country of the world are undernourished. They are hungry for the majesty and the glory of God. They would not give this diagnosis of their confusion and chaos because the supremacy of Jesus Christ is an unknown cure to most of them. Furthermore, there are far more acceptable and common prescriptions on the market, but the benefit of any other remedy is temporary and trifling. Preaching that does not exalt Jesus Christ as superior to all other therapies or solutions may entertain people, but it will not touch the deepest needs of the human heart. John Piper states it well in *The Supremacy of God in Preaching*: "It does not matter if surveys turn up a list of perceived needs that does not include the supreme greatness of the sovereign God of grace. That is the deepest need. Our people are starving for God."[1]

I have earned several theological degrees, but I write this book as a preacher first, a pastor, not a scholar. What you read here were sermons before they were chapters, and as a preacher I borrowed illustrations and ideas from just about anyone who could help me communicate more effectively and expound the mystery of Hebrews. I don't claim to be overly creative or original or funny or eloquent. I want to preach and write from my heart because I have a passion for the preeminence of Jesus Christ to be lived out in the Church. Without it the deeper Christian life cannot survive.

My prayer is that this book will assist our people to acknowledge the superiority of Jesus Christ in a fresh way that
will bring lasting personal renewal.

Garth Leno

Endnotes

1. John Piper, *The Supremacy of God in Preaching* (Grand
   Rapids, MI: Baker Book House, 1990), 10-11.

ACKNOWLEDGMENTS

Here's a salute to some ordinary people who have made an extraordinary impact.

To Andy and Ethel. The seed was planted in your living room twenty years ago. I'm forever grateful to you both.

To Neill Foster and Elio Cuccaro. Thanks for spurring me on.

To my small group. You encouraged and prayed and prodded without ceasing.

To the friends in Medicine Hat. You were the first to endure my feeble attempts to unwrap the unsearchable riches of this wonderful book.

To Elva Yoder. Every pastor ought to pray for at least one person like you in the congregation. You are a gift from God to our family.

To the Glengate Church. For seven wonderful years of fruitful partnership in the gospel.

To the missionary families we have visited around the globe. If only I could live in Hebrews 11 like you do.

A special word to Bud and Marg: You have given me the best part of my life on earth.

To my children Nathan, Jamie and Kristin. You make me proud.

For my wife Patty. You are a wife of noble character, worth far more than rubies, clothed with strength and dignity. Many women do virtuous things, but you surpass them all. You make every day a dream come true.

To the Master, my life, my joy, my all.

INTRODUCTION

The Readers of the Letter

I f the title to this Bible book is accurate, then it follows
that the letter was written to a group of Jews. The traditional view is that the first readers were Christian Jews,
and the most compelling argument for Jewish recipients is
the way the book moves uniformly within the locus of the
Old Testament Scriptures and Jewish liturgy. The writer
has much to say about the tabernacle, the priests, the kind of
sacrifice they offered, the covenant that meant so much to
the Jews, and Jewish heroes like Abraham, Moses, Joshua
and a host of others mentioned in chapter 11. On the whole,
it seems best to view Hebrews as a letter written for Jewish
Christians.

As to the precise location of this group of believers or
church we cannot be sure. Some have suggested Jerusalem.
Other places in Palestine have also been named. Specifically,
some propose that these Jews had some connection with the
Qumran community. Alexandria has also been considered as
a possible destination, but Rome is the most likely location.[1]

F.F. Bruce says the recipients might possibly have belonged to a first-century house church, but were at the same
time part of the "wider fellowship of a city church, and were
tending to neglect the bond of fellowship that bound them
to other Christians outside their own inner circle."[2] This
certainly fits with the text of Hebrews 10:24-25. "And let us
consider how we may spur one another on toward love and
good deeds. Let us not give up meeting together, as some are

1

in the habit of doing, but let us encourage one another—and all the more as you see the Day approaching."

The Author of the Letter

Ever since early Christian times the writer of this epistle has remained mysteriously anonymous, but that has not ended the debate on authorship. The numerous candidates and appropriate evidence have been well surveyed in the commentaries on Hebrews and introductions on the New Testament, and it is not my intention to review them all here.

One of the earliest references to authorship is a statement of Clement of Alexandria. He said that Paul wrote the letter in Hebrew and that Luke translated the work into Greek. Some third-century Christians suggested Luke might well have been its author. Silas (1 Peter 5:12) has also been a candidate for authorship, mainly because of the similarities between Hebrews and First Peter. Reformer Martin Luther was reasonably sure in his own mind that Apollos was the author. Harnack's romantic theory was that Priscilla probably wrote it.

We have no convincing evidence about the human authorship of Hebrews. Who wrote it remains a mystery to us. We cannot improve on the words of Origen's conclusion, that "who wrote the Epistle, God only knows the truth" (*Eusebius Ecclesiastical History*, 6.25.14).

The Purpose of the Letter

This letter was intended to lead its readers from an elementary to a mature knowledge of Christian truth. They had started well (6:10; 10:32-34), but had shown a tendency to pause on the journey, if not decline spiritually (5:11-12). They had not made headway or contended for a fuller and deeper spiritual experience (6:1).

In a weighty essay on "The Dead Sea Scrolls and the Epistle to the Hebrews," which was published in 1958 and quoted by Hughes in his commentary on Hebrews, the Jewish scholar Yigael Yadin demonstrates that the members of the Dead Sea Sect were awaiting the appearance of two messianic figures. The *kingly* figure would be subordinate to the *priestly*, but both would be subject to the preeminent figure of the archangel Michael. With this in view, they patterned their manner of life closely on the idealized model of the children of Israel under Moses in the wilderness during the forty years prior to their entry into the promised land. Their withdrawal from the corrupt ministry of the temple to the wilderness near the Dead Sea was for the purpose of preparing themselves for re-entry into Jerusalem when in due course the hour for the overthrow of the false leaders and the vindication of God's true covenant people arrived. It is possible that the recipients of Hebrews may have been influenced by the beliefs of this nonconformist Jewish sect. This would explain the necessity for sending a letter insisting on the absolute and unique supremacy of Christ, and therefore His superiority to all others.

Hughes called this "undoubtedly the best theory yet advanced to explain the occasion and purpose of the Epistle to the Hebrews."[3] The Hebrew Christians to whom the letter is addressed had in one way or another felt the attraction of the teachings of this religious group. Bruce saw the recipients of the letter as "Jewish believers in Jesus whose background was not so much the normative Judaism represented by rabbinical tradition as the nonconformist Judaism of which the Essenes and the Qumran community are outstanding representatives. . . ."[4]

Since they embraced Christ they had been exposed to tyranny and persecution. They had to endure public abuse, confinement and the ransacking of their property, but they had not yet resisted to the point of shedding their blood (Hebrews 12:4). They had given testimony of their faith by serving and caring for other followers of the Way, yet their Christian growth had been arrested. Instead of pressing ahead they were inclined to come to full stop in their spiritual progress, and perhaps even slip back to a position which they had left (Hebrews 5:11-6:12). Thus, the writer sends this letter to insist that Jesus is the true Messiah, the Great High Priest, the new and living way; superior to angels, prophets, Moses, Aaron and all the rest. Supremacy rests in Him alone.

The Date of the Letter

Guthrie confessed that previous discussions on authorship and background "have not left us too sanguine about the possibility of fixing a date for this letter with any precision."[5] The truth of the matter is that we cannot be absolutely certain about the date of Hebrews. All we can hope to do is to suggest some limits within which the letter was probably written.

The mention of Timothy (13:23) shows that the writing must be early. Some regard Hebrews 10:32-34 as a reference to the Neronian persecution (A.D. 64). The words "you have not yet resisted to the point of shedding your blood" (12:4) point to a date before the persecutions, or at least before the lives of any of the recipients had been lost in the persecutions.

Nothing is said in the letter about the destruction of the temple. It leaves the impression that the Jewish sacrificial system, with its ministry of priests and all that it involved, was a continuing reality (cf. 9:6-9). Leon Morris suggested it would have been "a convincing climax had the author been able to point out that the temple and all that went with it had ceased to exist."[6] The best argument for the supersession of the old covenant would have been the destruction of the temple. The author's failure to mention this may mean that it had not yet occurred. Guthrie and Hughes favor a pre-A.D. 70 date while W.H. Griffith Thomas suggested the date of writing to be about A.D. 63-66. Barclay and Brown opt for a later date in the second half of the first century, probably A.D. 80-85.

The Message of the Letter

When we come finally to the teaching of the epistle we are standing on solid ground. Hebrews gathers all its leading ideas around one great comprehensive theme: the absolute, unconditional supremacy of Jesus Christ. The immutable dominion of Christ is established by the presentation of evidence, through the logic of Scripture, of His superiority to the angels, prophets, teachers and the great leaders of God's people in the past. He is both the fulfillment and the mediator of the new covenant. The old covenant, which was administered by prophets, priests and rulers of former times, and which by its very nature was imperfect and temporary, is now passé. In Christ the new and living way, which is perfect and eternal and by which the old is done away, has been instituted.

Jesus Christ is better than anything that was before. He is better than any Old Testament person. He is better than any Old Testament institution. He is better than any Old Testament ritual. He is better than any Old Testament sacrifice. He is better than anyone and everything else! He has the supremacy.

The Importance of the Letter

In an age of religious pluralism this letter is a constant reminder of the necessity of God's salvation through faith in Christ alone. However sensitive one chooses to be to the climate of political correctness in North America and the claims of other world religions, it is impossible for any serious student of the New Testament to escape the "scandal of exclusion" that Hebrews presents.

There are obvious, clear and uncompromising texts in the New Testament that declare that the only way we can come to God the Father is through Jesus Christ the Son (John 14:6). In a day when theologians and laypeople alike may try to detect some form of acceptable syncretism, whereby Christ and His gospel become merely one expression among others of the idea of salvation, Hebrews directs us to the uniqueness of Christ's redemptive work. "Unlike the other high priests, he does not need to offer sacrifices day after day, first for his own sins, and then for the sins of the people. He sacrificed for their sins *once for all* when he offered himself" (Hebrews 7:27, emphasis added).

This letter also helps to interpret basic human problems relevant in every generation. The letter's opening paragraph explains that by His death Jesus provided purification for sins (1:3). The issue of human guilt is as old as the race itself. Yet, for all man's sophistication, scientific discovery and psychological advances, we still suffer because of this powerful vicious force called sin. This sinister tyrant causes us to do what we hate to do, and not do what we want to do. The evil that we do not want to do—this we keep on doing (Romans 7:14-20). There is a timelessness about the message of Hebrews. It addresses its clear message of forgiveness and hope to every person weighed down by a sense of guilt. It provides clear instruction on how one may live with a clean conscience. "Let us draw near to God with a sincere heart in full assurance of faith, having our hearts sprinkled to cleanse us from a guilty conscience and having our bodies washed with pure water" (Hebrews 10:22).

Moreover, human beings also need a sense of direction, a purpose for living, and we find this in the book of Hebrews. Jesus became like us (Hebrews 2:9, 14) that we might become like Him. In Him alone can we attain our true destiny. He delivers us from selfishness and makes us holy people who are surrendered to God's purposes in the world. "But when this priest had offered for all time one sacrifice for sins, he sat down at the right hand of God. Since that time he waits for his enemies to be made his footstool, because by one sacrifice he has made perfect forever those who are being made holy" (Hebrews 10:12-14). He identifies with us and calls us His brothers and sisters. We belong to Him as God's *sanctified* children and He leads us to glory (2:10-13).

Hebrews is also a book about sanctification, the *deeper* Christian life.

Another topic of importance is the matter of death and life eternal. People today do everything they can to hide from the reality of death, but we cannot evade it. The teaching of Hebrews is that Christ has finalized an eternal deliverance. He not only came into this world as a babe in Bethlehem, but He voluntarily exposed Himself to the experience of death on a cross (Philippians 2:5-11). He suffered and tasted death (Hebrews 2:9) for everyone and passed through it victoriously, conquering the powers of sin, death and the devil. He emerged as one brought back from the dead by the God who procures and inspires peace (13:20) in the hearts and lives of all those who believe in Him. Those who take the teaching of this letter seriously can live without the fear of death. They can look death in the face and bless God that they have hope in Christ. "Since the children have flesh and blood, he too shared in their humanity so that by his death he might destroy him who holds the power of death—that is, the devil—and free those who all their lives were held in slavery by their fear of death" (Hebrews 2:14-15).

Hebrews also addresses the critical need for perseverance in the Christian life. Throughout the history of the Church, believers have been dispirited by the defection of people who were once close partners of Christ. Every church of every denomination has known the experience of receiving new members with enthusiasm and great promise, only to watch them fade and fail, even to the point of deliberately rejecting the faith they once received. Hebrews 3 and 4, and other related passages, deal with this sad possibility. Salvation is clearly portrayed in this letter as an ongoing process that does not cease once someone receives new life. The letter insists that all readers recognize their responsibility not only to believe in Jesus but to go on with Him.

Hebrews presents a direct and personal challenge to any shallow or undemanding interpretations of the gospel. Jesus said, in Luke 9:23-26:

If anyone would come after me, he must deny himself and take up his cross daily and follow me. For
whoever wants to save his life will lose it, but whoever loses his life for me will save it. What good is it
for a man to gain the whole world, and yet lose or
forfeit his very self? If anyone is ashamed of me and
my words, the Son of Man will be ashamed of him
when he comes in his glory and in the glory of the
Father and of the holy angels.

Hebrews picks up on this theme. Without some experience of denial and self-crucifixion people cannot possibly belong to the followers of Jesus. In the past, some
well-intentioned forms of the evangelistic invitation have
suffered because they have presented the benefits of the
Christian life without explaining that it is also the way of the
cross. Following Jesus means death to self. So, for that reason, Hebrews lends itself beautifully to the purpose of this
commentary series: to present the challenge of the deeper
life. I hope this book can help you experience the supremacy
of Jesus Christ in your life.

Endnotes

1. The epistle is first attested in Clement of Rome's letter.
   Also, the greeting, "Those from Italy send you their
   greetings" (13:24) is perhaps most naturally understood
   of a group of Italian origin, now living elsewhere, sending greetings back home. Many of the arguments fall
   short of proof, yet there seems to be more reasons for
   connecting the letter with Rome than with any other
   place.

2. F.F. Bruce, *The Epistle to the Hebrews* (Grand Rapids, MI:
   William B. Eerdmans Publishing Co., 1964), xxx.

3. Philip Edgcumbe Hughes, *A Commentary on the Epistle to
   the Hebrews.* (Grand Rapids, MI: William B. Eerdmans
   Publishing Company, 1977).

4. F.F. Bruce, xxix.

5. Donald Guthrie, *Hebrews* (Grand Rapids, MI: William B. Eerdmans Publishing Company, 1983), 28.

6. Leon Morris, *Hebrews*, *The Expositor's Bible Commentary*, Vol. 12, ed. Frank E. Gaebelein (Grand Rapids, MI: Zondervan, 1981), 8.

Hebrews 1:1-22

Superior to the Prophets

> *In the past God spoke to our forefathers through the prophets at many times and in various ways, but in these last days he has spoken to us by his Son, whom he appointed heir of all things, and through whom he made the universe. The Son is the radiance of God's glory and the exact representation of his being, sustaining all things by his powerful word. After he had provided purification for sins, he sat down at the right hand of the Majesty in heaven. (Hebrews 1:1-3)*

I read a story once about a man from Leeds, England, who visited his doctor to have his hearing checked. The doctor carefully removed the man's hearing aid, and the patient's hearing improved immediately. Apparently he had been wearing the device in the wrong ear for over twenty years.[1] That would be enough to cause hearing problems for anyone.

This story has stuck with me because two of my three children have serious hearing problems. At times they seem to have wads of cotton packed in their ears! They just don't hear their mother or me, especially if they're playing outside with friends when we call them in for dinner. Convenient for them, ceaselessly frustrating for Mom and Dad. The plot thickens when I announce that it's time for bed, for it is then that my youngest loves to tease her older brother. And when they get to romping around in the family room, the decibels multiply quickly. Soon I find myself screaming to catch their attention. By then *I'm* ready for bed!

At one point in His ministry, Jesus cried out, "He who has ears to hear, let him hear!" In the first few verses of this epistle, the Spirit of God is appealing to all His readers to *hear* what God says about His Son Jesus—the One who is far superior to all the prophets of old. Without parallel. Sovereign. Unique.

It is a passage that "any classical Greek orator would have been proud to write," says commentator William Barclay. "The writer of Hebrews has brought to it every artifice of word and rhythm that the beautiful and flexible Greek language could provide."[2] It takes a lot of scholars to write an encyclopedia in three volumes. It takes the Spirit of God to write an encyclopedia in three verses. The opening verses of this letter to the Hebrews form a virtual encyclopedia of truth regarding God's self-disclosure in His Son.

The Son's superiority to the prophets is advocated in eight claims. He, and He alone, is the final revelation of God, the appointed heir of God, the divine agent of creation, the radiance of God's glory, the exact representation of God the Father, the sustainer of all things, the perfect sacrifice for sins and the exalted Lord.

The Final Revelation of God

> In the past God spoke to our forefathers through the prophets at many times and in various ways, but in these last days he has spoken to us by his Son. . . .
> (Hebrews 1:1-2)

According to one newspaper report, shortly after former announcer and catcher for the St. Louis Cardinals Joe Torre was named manager of the Cardinals, New York Yankees' announcer Phil Rizzuto suggested that managing could be done better from high above the baseball field—from the level of the broadcasting booth.

Thoughtfully, Torre replied, "Upstairs, you can't look in their eyes."

In Jesus Christ, God also chose to come down on the field, look into our eyes through the eyes of His Son and speak to us.

The author of Hebrews plunges straight into the exposition of one of the wonderful themes of the epistle, namely the uniqueness and finality of the revelation of God in His Son Jesus Christ. "God spoke." This introductory declaration is basic to the whole argument of this letter to the Hebrews and to the Christian faith itself. "Had God remained silent," writes F.F. Bruce, "enshrouded in thick darkness, the plight of mankind would have been desperate indeed; but now he has spoken His revealing, redeeming and life-giving word...."[3]

"In the past God spoke through the prophets, but in these last days He has spoken to us through His Son." The contrast becomes obvious even on first reading, a contrast between the two stages of special revelation which corresponds to the Old and New Testaments respectively. It is naturally important for the author to emphasize the continuity of the Old and New Testaments, for he is writing to Jewish believers. Christ did not break the Old Testament law. He came to fulfill it. "Do not think that I have come to abolish the Law or the Prophets," he said. "I have not come to abolish them but to fulfill them" (Matthew 5:17). Without Him the Old Testament is partial, fragmentary, preparatory and incomplete. In the past God spoke at many times and in various ways, but in Christ He spoke fully, completely, finally and perfectly. Therefore, by implication, these first-century believers should listen to what He says, and so must we. He is God's final revelation.

It is a most interesting thing to see how time and again the prophets demonstrate how they are limited to a slice of the divine vision (cf. 1 Peter 1:10-12). Barclay expressed it like this:

Each prophet, out of his own experience of life and out of the experience of Israel, had grasped and expressed a fragment of the truth of God. . . . None had grasped the whole round orb of truth; but with Jesus it was different. He was not a fragment of the truth; he was the whole truth. In him God displayed not some part of himself but all of himself.[4]

Raymond Brown suggested that Ezekiel portrayed the glory of God, but Christ reflected it (Hebrews 1:3). Isaiah expounded the nature of God as holy, righteous and merciful, but Christ manifested it (1:3). Jeremiah described the power of God, but Christ displayed it (1:3). "He far surpassed the best of prophets of earlier times, and these wavering Christians must listen to his voice."[5]

No polytheism, animism, idolatry, syncretism, deception or counterfeit can stand any longer in the presence of God's final revelation of Himself. When we take Him to heart, as He reveals Himself, we simultaneously banish every other god.

The Appointed Heir of God

. . . but in these last days he has spoken to us by his Son, whom he appointed heir of all things. . . . (Hebrews 1:2)

These words echo Psalm 2:8, addressed to one who is both the Lord's Anointed and acclaimed by God as His Son: "Ask of me, and I will make the nations your inheritance, the ends of the earth your possession." However, by stating emphatically and forcefully that Jesus is heir of all things, He has in mind not only this planet, but the entire universe.

Now that we are God's children, the Scripture tells us we are also heirs—heirs of God and co-heirs with Christ. I marvel at that. God is so generous. I have done absolutely nothing to merit my position in Christ. God's grace secured it all for me. As long as I have been a follower of Jesus, I still have trouble comprehending His extravagant commitment to "graciously give us all things" (Romans 8:32). "How great is the love the Father has lavished on us, that we should be called children of God" (1 John 3:1).

My heart echoes the sentiment of Peter:

> Praise be to the God and Father of our Lord Jesus Christ! In his great mercy he has given us new birth into a living hope through the resurrection of Jesus Christ from the dead, and into an inheritance that can never perish, spoil or fade—kept in heaven for you, who through faith are shielded by God's power until the coming of the salvation that is ready to be revealed in the last time. (1 Peter 1:3-5)

God's appointed heir of heaven and earth is willing to share His inheritance with you. Amazing grace! How sweet the sound. . . .

The Divine Agent of Creation

> . . . whom he appointed heir of all things, and through whom he made the universe. (Hebrews 1:2)

With that statement we move from the future to the distant past; from Christ's future position as "heir of all things" to His role in the very beginning of the world.

Through Christ, God made the world. "Through him all things were made; without him nothing was made that has been made" (John 1:3). "He is the image of the invisible God, the firstborn over all creation. For by him all things were created: things in heaven and on earth, visible and invisible, whether thrones or powers or rulers or authorities; all things were created by him and for him" (Colossians 1:15-16). Therefore, He is God's agent or delegate in creation.

The Scripture goes to great pain to make sure we miss nothing of the intended purpose: Jesus is not merely a Galilean preacher whose time had come for a well-rehearsed discourse. He had actually executed the creative work of the Almighty God. He brings out the stars one by one on parade and "calls them each by name. Because of his great power and mighty strength, not one of them is missing" (Isaiah 40:26). Surely the One who had shaped the universe and summons the galaxies at His command could care for these Jewish Christians in their days of testing. This same Jesus can guide us through times of tribulation and stress. If the chaos of creation can be overcome, certainly He can control our destiny and provide for our needs.

The Radiance of God's Glory

> The Son is the radiance of God's glory. . . . (Hebrews 1:3)

To understand the nuance of this phrase we must return again to the Old Testament, and particularly to Exodus 24:

> When Moses went up on the mountain, the cloud covered it, and the glory of the LORD settled on Mount Sinai. For six days the cloud covered the mountain, and on the seventh day the LORD called to Moses from within the cloud. To the Israelites the glory of the LORD looked like a consuming fire on top of the mountain. Then Moses entered the cloud as he went on up the mountain. and he stayed on the mountain forty days and forty nights. (24:15-18)

After the incident of the golden calf in Exodus 32, Moses had another face-to-face with the Lord:

> Then Moses said, "Now show me your glory."
> And the LORD said, "I will cause all my goodness

to pass in front of you, and I will proclaim my name, the LORD, in your presence. I will have mercy on whom I will have mercy, and I will have compassion on whom I will have compassion. But," he said, "you cannot see my face, for no one may see me and live."

Then the LORD said, "There is a place near me where you may stand on a rock. When my glory passes by, I will put you in a cleft in the rock and cover you with my hand until I have passed by. Then I will remove my hand and you will see my back; but my face must not be seen." (33:18-23)

The glory of the Lord became the visible sign of His presence among the people. So when the ark of the covenant was captured they lamented, "The glory has departed from Israel" (1 Samuel 4:21-22). Now the author of this letter suggests that in these last days this same glory, the glory of the Lord, can be seen in the person of Christ who is, quite literally, the "radiance of God's glory." In Christ all the dignity and grandeur and majesty and magnificence and beauty and brilliance and splendor and glory and honor of God is revealed. A return to the old covenant, the old way of worship, is utterly unnecessary and absolutely retrogressive.

Just as the radiance of the sun reaches the earth, so the brilliance of God's glory in Jesus Christ reaches into the hearts of people like us, illuminating, dispelling the darkness, stimulating hope and happiness, prompting our growth and service for God, even to taking the good news to the ends of the earth. For this gospel of the kingdom must be "preached in the whole world as a testimony to all nations, and then the end will come" (Matthew 24:14).

The Exact Representation of God the Father

How can the author help his readers understand? How can he drive the message home about the nature and character of Christ? He insists that Jesus is "the exact representation" of the Father's being. (Hebrews 1:3)

Jesus—not merely an image or reflection of God—is the absolutely authentic representation of God's being, which explains why He could say, "Anyone who has seen me has seen the Father" (John 14:9).

Just as the image and superscription on a coin exactly correspond to the die, so the Son of God "bears the very stamp of his nature" (RSV). The Greek word used here, *charakter*, occurs only here in the New Testament, and originally it denoted an instrument for engraving and then a mark stamped on that instrument.[6] Jesus bears the stamp of God. He exactly and perfectly matches the Father. Want to see God? Then look at Christ.

Here the author of Hebrews meticulously and masterfully builds his argument for the superiority of Christ. Yes, God spoke through the prophets. They have a valid and authentic place in the history of God's people and in the nation of Israel. They're an important part of the heritage we possess in the Judeo-Christian tradition. However, God has now spoken through His Son, and what the Son says, God says, and what God says, the Son says. All because the Son is the exact representation of the Father. A definitive portrait. We must keep our eyes fixed on Jesus.

On March 6, 1987, Eamon Coghlan, the Irish world record-holder at 1,500 meters, was running in a qualifying heat at the World Indoor Track Championships in Indianapolis. With two-and-a-half laps left, he was tripped. He fell, but he got up and with great effort managed to catch the leaders. With only twenty yards left in the race, he was in third place. This would have been good enough to qualify for the finals.

He looked over his shoulder to the inside, and, seeing no one, he let up. But another runner, charging hard on the outside, passed Coghlan a yard before the finish, thus eliminating him from the finals. Coghlan's great comeback effort was rendered worthless because he took his eyes off the finish line.

It's tempting to let up when the sights around us look favorable. But we finish well in the Christian race only when we fix our eyes on Jesus Christ who is the exact representation of the Father.

The Sustainer of All Things

> The Son is the radiance of God's glory and the exact
> representation of his being, sustaining all things by
> his powerful word. (Hebrews 1:3)

The One who called all things into being is here viewed as the One who sustains all things by the word of His power. The creative utterance that brought the worlds into being must now function as the sustaining voice by which they are maintained.

The creation is not self-sufficient. Some people, like deists, would like us to believe that God's work ended with creation and that all things hold together by virtue of natural laws. Scripture rejects this point of view by stating clearly that the origin and the preservation of all things are a matter of divine will and exercise. God both sustains and overrules nature.

With great skill, commentator Raymond Brown brings this majestic doctrine down to a practical level:

> Possibly our vision of Christ is limited. We are in
> danger of confining him to our restricted experience
> or limited knowledge. We need a vision of Christ
> with these immense cosmic dimensions, a Christ who
> transcends all our noblest thoughts about him and all
> our best experience of him. These first-century read-
> ers would be less likely to turn from him in adversity
> if they had looked to him in adoration. The opening
> sentences of the letter are designed to bring them and
> us to our knees; only then can we hope to stand
> firmly on our feet.[7]

Could your vision of Christ use a little boost?

The Perfect Sacrifice for Sins

> After he had provided purification for sins, he sat
> down at the right hand of the Majesty in heaven.
> (Hebrews 1:3)

The author of Hebrews now turns the reader's attention
away from who Christ is to what He did on our behalf. "Christ
himself was like God in everything. He was equal with God.
But He did not think that being equal with God was something
to be held on to. He gave up His place with God and made
Himself nothing. He was born to be a man and became like a
servant. And when He was living as a man, He humbled Himself. Fully obedient and submissive to the Father's will. He
obeyed even when that caused His death—death on a cross"
(Philippians 2:6-8, NCV). He shed His blood. He endured the
cross. He purged His people of their sins. He died to sterilize
their hearts and pour out His forgiveness and mercy.

On March 5, 1994, Deputy Sheriff Lloyd Prescott was
teaching a class for police officers in the Salt Lake City Library. As he stepped into the hallway he noticed a gunman
herding eighteen hostages into the next room. With a flash
of insight, Prescott (dressed in street clothes) joined the
group as the nineteenth hostage, followed them into the
room and shut the door. But when the gunman announced
the order in which hostages would be executed, Prescott
identified himself as a cop. In the scuffle that followed,
Prescott, in self-defense, fatally shot the armed man. The
hostages were released unharmed.[8]

God dressed Himself in street clothes, entered our hostile
world, identified Himself with our condition, assumed the
full burden of our sin and provided a Savior. On the cross
Jesus Christ set us free from the power and dominion of sin.

A Perfect Sacrifice

Notice the contrast in the biblical text of Hebrews 1:3.

Jesus is perpetually the "radiance of God's glory" and continuously the "exact representation of his being." Eternally He sustains all things "by his powerful word." Yet, when He offered Himself up to death on a cross, He did it once for all. At a single point in time. Never to be repeated. No recurrence or duplication of this act will ever be necessary, nor could it occur. No replicas allowed in this arena. For after He had provided purification for sins, "he sat down." This figure of speech is used to indicate that the work of Christ the Savior is finished, the victory won and the blood of Jesus "purifies us from all sin" forever (1 John 1:7). Praises!

The Exalted Lord

> . . . he sat down at the right hand of the Majesty in heaven. (Hebrews 1:3)

The picture of the Son now being seated signifies the completion of His work of purification, "conveying the notion of rest after the fulfillment of a mission."[9] More than completion, and much more than rest, His position "at the right hand of the Majesty in heaven" indicates that He was at the highest place of honor and authority, exalted to the right hand of God. Elevated and glorified, He sits not merely on a seat, but on a throne, the King of kings and the Lord of lords (1 Timothy 6:15). This is one of the earliest affirmations of the Christian faith.

When I preached on this passage in a church some time ago, one man, who had been deeply influenced by unorthodox teaching, fiercely challenged what he thought I said. He forcefully maintained that Jesus did not literally sit down at God's right hand. "God does not have hands," he insisted, his bushy, dark eyebrows raised. I explained that the author of Hebrews never intended his readers to understand this as a literal location. That was well understood by Christians in the apostolic age. "God has no physical right hand; no material throne where the ascended Christ sits beside Him," I said. "This language effectively symbolizes the exaltation, honor and supremacy of Christ." His eyebrows came down and my answer seemed to satisfy him, at least for the moment.

In the Church we exalt Christ as Savior, Sanctifier, Healer and Coming King. Committed to communicating the deeper life from the Word of God and to increasing the pace of world evangelization, we are planting and growing churches by the grace of God. This is possible *not* because of the methods we use, the church-growth principles governing what we do or even the excellent oversight and supervision from church leaders, but only because Jesus provided purification for sins, and then He sat down at the right hand of the Majesty in heaven.

We must not lose sight of the basis and foundation of this movement and the power behind it. If Jesus had not been crucified to make purification for sin and if He had not been exalted to the place that is above every name on heaven and earth, we would not be here. There would be no church to grow. And you wouldn't be reading this book.

In three short verses the Spirit of God inspired a substantial encyclopedia of truth regarding God's self-disclosure in His Son. The Son's superiority to the prophets is advocated in eight claims in Hebrews 1:1-3. Christ is the final revelation of God, the appointed heir of God, the divine agent of creation, the radiance of God's glory, the exact representation of God the Father, the sustainer of all things, the perfect sacrifice for sins and the exalted Lord.

It has been well observed in other places that in these opening verses of the letter to the Hebrews, we have the Son set before us in His threefold messianic office: (1) as the Prophet through whom God's final word has been spoken to us; (2) as the Priest who made purification for our sins; (3) as the King who is enthroned on high, seated at the right hand of the Majesty in heaven.

A.B. Simpson said it very well:

Jesus only is our message, Jesus all our theme shall
      be;
We will lift up Jesus ever, Jesus only will we see.
Jesus only, Jesus ever, Jesus all in all we sing.
Savior, Sanctifier, and Healer, Glorious Lord and
      coming King.

Jesus is the sovereign Lord over the universe. But does He reign and rule in your heart? He is the radiance of God's glory, the exact representation of God's nature and character, and He upholds all things by the word of His power, but do we trust Him with problems of the heart? He made purification for your sins and mine and then sat down at the right hand of God the Father. But is He exalted in all you do and say?

Superior to the Angels

So he became as much superior to the angels as the name he has inherited is superior to theirs.
   For to which of the angels did God ever say,

  "You are my Son;
    today I have become your
      Father"?

Or again,

  "I will be his Father,
    and he will be my Son"?

And again, when God brings his firstborn into the world, he says,

  "Let all God's angels worship him."

In speaking of the angels he says,
  "He makes his angels winds,

his servants flames of fire."
But about the Son he says,

> *"Your throne, O God, will last for ever*
> *and ever,*
> *and righteousness will be the scepter*
> *of your kingdom.*
> *You have loved righteousness and hated*
> *wickedness;*
> *therefore God, your God, has set you*
> *above your companions*
> *by anointing you with the oil of joy."*

He also says,

> *"In the beginning, O Lord, you laid the*
> *foundations of the earth,*
> *and the heavens are the work of your*
> *hands.*
> *They will perish, but you remain;*
> *they will all wear out like a garment.*
> *You will roll them up like a robe;*
> *like a garment they will be changed.*
> *But you remain the same,*
> *and your years will never end."*

To which of the angels did God ever say,

> *"Sit at my right hand*
> *until I make your enemies*
> *a footstool for your feet?"*

Are not all angels ministering spirits sent to serve those
who will inherit salvation? (Hebrews 1:4-14)

Two little boys were standing in the school yard arguing.

"My dad's bigger 'n your dad."

"Oh yeah, well my dad could whup your dad any day."

"My dad drives a brand new car. You only got a old truck."

"No he don't. He owns a whole fleet o' trucks."

"My dad can eat a steak, a whole dozen eggs and a loaf of bread for breakfast!"

"Oh yeah, well he sure looks like it, too."

Demonstrating superiority on the playground. Kids are good at that. We don't even have to teach them how—it seems to be part of human nature. Yet, there *are* times when demonstrating superiority is crucial. Such a case is under consideration in this passage.

From Hebrews 1, it appears as if the Christians were beginning to think of the angels as intermediaries between God and man. The Jews had a vast angelology, and under religious pressure and social ostracism some of these Jewish Christians were in danger of compromising their faith. So the writer of Hebrews spends considerable time proving that Jesus Christ is far superior to all the angels.

His argument has already cemented the fact that Jesus is better than the prophets of old. Now he sets out to prove that we do not need angelic intermediaries between us and God. Because of Jesus and what He did, we have direct access to God with this confidence: "There is one God and one mediator between God and men, the man Christ Jesus, who gave himself as a ransom for all men" (1 Timothy 2:5-6a).

The first-century background for this text is mirrored today in the unusual interest in spirit beings. On a recent day-trip to a funky little town in southern Ontario, my wife and I discovered a shop called "Angel Treasures." The entire store was filled with books, trinkets, pictures, plaques, pillows, necklaces and tapes about angels. They even sold California Angels baseball caps, and the after-sale bags were gold in color. Interest in angels runs high, but as we shall see from this text, we do not need angels to contact God on our behalf. We have a superior intermediary in Jesus Christ.

This is one of those cases when demonstrating superiority is critical, but the author doesn't stand on the church's playground screaming. He carefully, logically and vigorously presents us with the facts inspired by the Holy Spirit of God. In ten verses the author uses seven Old Testament quotations showing that, as the Son of God, Jesus is superior to angels on account of five distinct factors: His Sonship, His nobility, His nature, His immutability and His Lordship. Of the seven quotations used here, five are from the Psalms, one is taken from Second Samuel 7 and one from Deuteronomy 32:43.

His Sonship

> So (Jesus) became as much superior to the angels as the name he has inherited is superior to theirs. For to which of the angels did God ever say, "You are my Son; today I have become your Father"? Or again, "I will be his Father, and he will be my Son"? (Hebrews 1:4-5)

The name "angel" means "messenger," and at times they were wonderfully used as God's heralds. They were prominent not only in the Old Testament Scriptures, but also in New Testament experience (Luke 1:19, 26-37; 2:13-14; Matthew 4:11; Luke 22:43). Jesus Himself was strengthened by angels. They were sent by God to release prisoners, to instruct preachers, to encourage believers. Yet as inspiring as all these events were, angels remained only messengers. That was their name and title.[10]

Christ has a title superior to the best of angels because He is far more than a messenger. For to which of the angels did God ever say, "I will be his Father, and he will be my Son"? None of them. No angel ever had the title of *Son*. To which of the angels did God say, "You are my Son, whom I love; with you I am well pleased" (Mark. 1:11)? None. Whom did He exalt to the highest place and to whom did He give the name that is above every name? It was the name of Jesus, the Son of God. "That at the name of Jesus every knee should bow, in heaven and on earth and under the earth, and every tongue confess that Jesus Christ is Lord, to the glory of God the Father" (Philippians 2:10-11).

Titles do not always mean something important. However, in the case of Jesus, the Son of God, it most certainly is profound. Jesus is the only Son of God come in the flesh, full of grace and truth. He is the eternal Logo ever with God (John 1:1). He is very God of very God, "of one nature with the Father," "the only begotten of God" (John 1:14, KJV). And because he is the Son, he can lead us by adoption into our own sonship with the Father (Romans 8:14-17; Galatians 4:4-7).

His Nobility

> . . . when God brings his firstborn into the world, he says, "Let all God's angels worship him." (Hebrews 1:6)

As a title of superiority and nobility, the designation "firstborn" belongs to Christ both as the eternal Son and also as the incarnate Redeemer who, after humbling Himself for our salvation, has been exalted to the highest place of honor. To Him the angels pay homage.

The two previous quotations from Psalm 2:7 and Second Samuel 7:14 have marked Jesus out as the Son of God; this one marks Him out as the One worshiped by angels.

Called the "firstborn" because He exists before all creation and because all creation is His heritage, Jesus has priority, precedence, preeminence and sovereignty (cf. Colossians 1:15-20). The angels were messengers, but Christ is the Son. The angels were worshipers; Jesus the One they worshiped.

Therefore, His dignity, His fame, His worthiness and His nobility are much superior to that of any of the angels. It was their duty to worship Him, and ours as well.

In *Touch and Live*, George Vandeman wrote about a young stranger to the Alps who was making his first climb, accompanied by two stalwart guides. Apparently it was a steep, hazardous ascent. But he felt secure with one guide ahead and one behind. For hours they climbed. Up and over, carefully making their way to the top. And now, breathless, they reached for those rocks protruding through the snow above them—the summit.

The guide ahead wished to let the stranger have the first glorious view of heaven and earth, and moved aside to let him go first. Forgetting the gales that would blow across those summit rocks, the young man leaped to his feet. But the chief guide dragged him down. "On your knees, sir!" he shouted. "You are never safe here except on your knees."[11]

Good advice. The best place for a believer is on his or her knees, bowed in reverent worship of the awesome God of the universe. If the angels worship the exalted One, how much more should we who have been saved by His glorious grace?

His Nature

> In speaking to the angels he says, "He makes his angels winds, his servants flames of fire." But about the Son he says, "Your throne, O God, will last for ever and ever, and righteousness will be the scepter of your kingdom. You have loved righteousness and hated wickedness; therefore God, your God, has set you above your companions by anointing you with the oil of joy." (Hebrews 1:7-9)

Angels are described here as servants in the likeness of wind and fire. Christ is exalted as the Sovereign, the King, the One who reigns forever and ever. Wind and fire are temporary. God's throne is eternal ("forever and ever"). Angels do have a place in the divine administration of the universe, but as high as their place may be, it is still far inferior to the position of supremacy given to the Son. So the conclusion must be that the unending reign of Christ is far superior to the temporal service of angels.

Our author thinks it worthwhile and worth His time to prove the superiority of Christ over the angels. This confirms the place that belief in angels had in the thought of the Jews of his day. It was on the increase. "The reason was that men were more and more impressed with what is called the transcendence of God. They felt more and more the distance and the difference between God and man. The result was that they came to think of the angels as intermediaries between God and man."[12]

With this vast angelology there was a very real danger that people would come to believe that angels intervene between God and them. It was necessary to expose the true nature of angels and Christ; it was critical to show that the Son was greater by far than any angels, and that he who knew the Son needed no one else.

His Immutability

> In the beginning, O Lord, you laid the foundations of the earth, and the heavens are the work of your hands. They will perish, but you remain; they will all wear out like a garment. You will roll them up like a robe; like a garment they will be changed. But you remain the same, and your years will never end. (Hebrews 1:10-12; see also Psalm 90:2; James 1:17)

The advocate of the superiority of Christ adds yet another argument to His case. The angels were created. But Christ is God's appointed agent in creation. Angels were made for God's purposes. They are only creatures. Yet "through [Christ] all things were made; without him nothing was made that has been made" (John 1:3).

The Creator always maintains superiority over His creation, and the day will come when Jesus shall roll up the present heaven and earth and create new ones. Like a garment they will all be changed. They will all perish, but Jesus remains the same, yesterday, today and forever.

His Lordship

> To which of the angels did God ever say, "Sit at my right hand until I make your enemies a footstool for your feet"? Are not all angels ministering spirits sent to serve those who will inherit salvation? (Hebrews 1:13-14; cf. Philippians 2:9-11; 1 Corinthians 15:24-28)

The writer of Hebrews takes the words of prophecy from Psalm 110 and applies them to Christ to show that His authority will finally subdue all opposition and bring all of the created order under His unified dominion.

The angels never even appear to sit before God. They always stand before Him as Luke 1:19 and Revelation 8:2 illustrate. The Son is enthroned forever (Daniel 7) as Lord of all. After all, angels are only ministering spirits sent to serve those who will inherit salvation, but from whom do these people inherit salvation? From Christ!

This letter began with a reference to the work of Christ as Redeemer and Creator. He "sat down at the right hand of the Majesty in heaven" (1:3). No angel was ever invited to sit at the right hand of God, because no angel could feel for the people; no angel could ever atone for man's sin; no angel could intercede for us as Christ does. Angels can serve us, but they cannot save us. They gladly hurried on God's errands, but their work could only be supportive because they did not understand, let alone decide, the grand redemptive outcome (1 Peter 1:12). Therefore, the achievement of Jesus is far superior to that of the angels. They are servants, but Jesus is Lord!

Sometimes demonstrating superiority is critical, and this is one of those times. But the author doesn't stand on the church's playground screaming. He carefully, logically and vigorously presents us with the facts inspired by the Holy Spirit of God. He presents Jesus as the Son of God, superior to angels on account of five distinct factors, as stated earlier: His Sonship, His nobility, His nature, His immutability and His Lordship.

A number of principles present themselves for our consideration as we close this section of the chapter. First, God's angelic servants may interest us and pique our curiosity, but let's remember that only God's Word can truly enlighten, illumine and edify us. "Calming crystals" or palm readings do not offer greater revelation. God's Word provides all the insight and wisdom needed to live a life pleasing to Him.

Furthermore, God's angels are gracious, ministering spirits and they do minister *to* the saints of God, but only God's Holy Spirit can minister effectively *in* us at the deepest level of our greatest need. One of our dearest friends in all the world prays for our handicapped daughter in this way: "Lord, please let Jamie sense your Spirit working *in* her." Angels can't accomplish that kind of ministry in Jamie's life or my life or yours. But God's Spirit of revelation and truth can!

Finally, God's heavenly helpers may protect us physically for awhile, but only God's Son can save us spiritually for all eternity. They do not fully understand this great gift of salvation that we enjoy through faith in Jesus. "Even angels long to look into these things" (1 Peter 1:12). Jesus Christ— superior to the prophets and the angels—and this is another of those cases demonstrating when superiority is critical.

Endnotes

1. Warren W. Wiersbe, *Be Confident* (Wheaton, IL: Victor Books, 1982), 7.

2. William Barclay, *The Letter to the Hebrews* (Philadelphia, PA: The Westminster Press, 1976; rev. ed., Edinburgh: The Saint Andrew Press, 1955), 11.

3. F.F. Bruce, *The Epistle to the Hebrews* (Grand Rapids, MI: William B. Eerdmans Publishing Co., 1964), 1.

4. William Barclay, 13.

5. Raymond Brown, *The Message of Hebrews* (Downers Grove, IL: InterVarsity Press, 1982), 28.

6. Leon Morris, *Hebrews, The Expositor's Bible Commentary,* Vol. 12, ed. Frank E. Gaebelein, (Grand Rapids, MI: Zondervan, 1981), 14.

7. Ibid., 32.

8. Leadership (Summer 1994): 48. Used by permission.

9. Ibid., 47.

10. Raymond Brown, 39-40.

11. Leadership (Summer 1990): 49. Used by permission.

12. William Barclay, 16.

Discussion Questions for Further Study

Hebrews 1 begins with eight claims about the superiority of Jesus Christ to the prophets. Can you find other passages that teach the same things about Christ? As you find them, jot down the references:

Claim	Related References
The final revelation of God	
The appointed heir of God	
The divine agent of creation	
The radiance of God's glory	
The exact representation of God	
The Father	
The sustainer of all things	
The perfect sacrifice for sins	
The exalted Lord	

1. How would you summarize the author's main point in 1:1-3? How would you like this truth to affect your life—your thoughts, attitudes, habits and priorities?

2. Jesus is the sovereign Lord over the universe. But does He reign and rule in your heart? How would you honestly answer that question today? What needs to change in your life in order for you to respond with a strong "yes"?

3. Some of the early Jewish Christians were in danger of compromising their faith by placing confidence in angelic intermediaries. What evidence can you provide from this chapter that we do not need any intermediary other than Christ?

4. Why do you think the author makes such a point of Christ's deity to these Jewish Christians?

5. In 1:4-14 the author uses seven familiar Old Testament passages to draw explicit contrasts between Christ and the angels. List these contrasts, and then explain what you think the cumulative effect of these contrasts would have been on a Jewish Christian who was contemplating lapsing back into the externals of Judaism.

2

Hebrews 2:1-18

Warning Against Neglect

> *We must pay more careful attention, therefore, to what
> we have heard, so that we do not drift away. For if the
> message spoken by angels was binding, and every violation
> and disobedience received its just punishment, how shall we
> escape if we ignore such a great salvation? This salvation,
> which was first announced by the Lord, was confirmed to
> us by those who heard him. God also testified to it by signs,
> wonders and various miracles, and gifts of the Holy Spirit
> distributed according to his will. (Hebrews 2:1-4)*

When elderly Adele Gaboury turned up missing,
concerned neighbors in Worcester, Massachu-
setts, informed the police. A brother told police
she had gone into a nursing home.

Satisfied with that information, Gaboury's neighbors began watching her property. One man noticed her mail, delivered through a slot in the door, piling high. When he
managed to get the door open, hundreds of pieces of mail
drifted out. He notified police, and the deliveries were
stopped.

Gaboury's next-door neighbor, Eileen, started paying her
grandson $10 twice a month to mow Gaboury's lawn. Later

Eileen's son noticed Gaboury's pipes had frozen, spilling water out the door. The utility company was called to shut off the water.

What no one guessed was that while they had been trying to help, Gaboury had been inside her home. When police finally investigated the house as a health hazard, they were shocked to find her body. The newspaper reported that police believe Gaboury died of natural causes four years earlier.[1]

The respectable, external appearance of Gaboury's house had hidden the reality of what was on the inside. Something similar can happen to people like you and me. We may appear like we have it all together while spiritually we are dying.

Hebrews 2:1-4 is the first of five admonitions found in this book written to believers. The author encourages Christians to pay close attention to the great salvation they have received in order to prevent a slow, but certain spiritual death if they neglect it. Apparently, some believers were in the early stages of spiritual neglect.

The Possibility of Neglect

> We must pay more careful attention, therefore, to what we have heard, so that we do not drift away. (Hebrews 2:1)

The writer asked the question in 1:14, "Are not all angels ministering spirits sent to serve those who will inherit salvation?" The word "therefore" in 2:1 looks back to the ministry of the angels. Because angels are dispatched by God to minister to those who have been saved, certain consequences follow. But since the Son is so far superior to the angels, we must listen to what He says. His message, methods and motives are superior to theirs. So we must "pay more careful attention . . . so that we do not drift away."

Despite its appealing constitution, attractive character and vivid presentation in Scripture, this very great eternal salvation can still be ignored by thoughtless and careless Christians. It was happening in the first century, and it happens today. Ours is a generation of drifters. Christians are quickly moving away from important truths such as moral purity, marital commitment, ministerial integrity and biblical fidelity. The possibility of spiritual drift confronts us on every side. The Holy Spirit, through the human author of Hebrews, pleads for closer attention to vital Christian living.

Believers drift because of a general lack of spiritual insight and biblical understanding. Some of us don't perceive how remarkable this salvation is simply because we do not grasp the total depravity of mankind.

> As for you, you were dead in your transgressions and sins, in which you used to live when you followed the ways of this world and of the ruler of the kingdom of the air, the spirit who is now at work in those who are disobedient. All of us also lived among them at one time, gratifying the cravings of our sinful nature and following its desires and thoughts. Like the rest, we were by nature objects of wrath. (Ephesians 2:1-3)

Dead in transgressions and sins. By nature objects of wrath. Oh, the depth of sin and its pervasive nature! If only believers had better understanding, we would have a greater appreciation for our salvation and therefore, neglect would not come to pass so easily.

Some believers do not fathom the greatness of this salvation because they believe in a dangerous and false doctrine of a second chance for people who die without Christ. Therefore, the magnitude of this great salvation is diminished. One theologian who has recently declared himself in support of such a view is Clark H. Pinnock. Pinnock believes that "the unevangelized are given an opportunity to encounter Jesus Christ as Savior after death if not before it."[2] If people have a second chance after death, why pay closer attention to this salvation now? Also, the biblical doctrine of hell loses all meaning.

In addition, some Christians begin drifting spiritually because they don't comprehend their freedom in Christ. Jesus said, "If you hold to my teaching, you are really my disciples. Then you will know the truth, and *the truth will set you free*" (John 8:31-32, emphasis added).

According to a story in the *Daily Bread*, at a special chapel service in a state penitentiary the governor was to grant a pardon to several convicts. The suspense mounted as it came time for the governor to announce the names of those selected. "Reuben Johnson, come forward and receive your pardon!" No one responded.

The chaplain directed his attention toward Johnson and said, "Reuben, it's you, come on!" But the man looked behind him, supposing there must be someone else by that name. Then, pointing directly at him, the chaplain exclaimed, "That's right, Reuben, you're the man!"

After a long pause, he slowly approached the governor to receive his pardon. Later when the other prisoners marched to their cells, Johnson fell in line and began to walk with them.

The warden called, "Reuben, you don't belong there any more. You're a free man!"

Many Christians are like that man—no comprehension of the nature of their forgiveness, little awareness of their total emancipation in Christ. He has set us free from *all* the powers of sin and *all* the powers of darkness and *all* the powers of death. Released us from the dominion of sin. Rescued us from the principalities that are ruled by Satan and his cohorts. He opened the door. Turned on the light. Invited us to leave the darkness behind. Why would anybody want to fall in line again and go back to the old life after experiencing this great salvation? But some do. That mystery still puzzles me.

Loss of memory is the second chief reason for neglect. We soon forget who we were and what we were like before Jesus saved us. We soon forget what He did for us, and as a result spiritual neglect settles in.

Moses had to remind the people of Israel not to forget the Lord's blessing. In Deuteronomy 8 he says, "Be careful to follow every command I am giving you today, so that you may live and increase and may enter and possess the land that the LORD promised. . . ." Then he says, "Remember how the LORD your God led you all the way in the desert those forty years . . ." (1-2).

Remember. Remember. Remember. Sometimes the reason for spiritual neglect is loss of memory. We forget too soon all that God has done for us, and we sin against God because of ingratitude. When was the last time you knelt down just to thank the Lord? Instant recall may not be your spiritual gift, but spiritual drift, caused by a loss of memory may have been triggered by a lack of appreciation. Got a minute to reminisce? Better take it now while you have the chance.

The Result of Neglect

> For if the message spoken by angels was binding, and every violation and disobedience received its just punishment, how shall we escape if we ignore such a great salvation? (Hebrews 2:2-3)

The divinely given law, "the message," was given through angels, which stresses the importance of the truth that the law came from God Himself. The Old Testament does not speak of angels in connection with the giving of the law. However, their presence is mentioned in other New Testament passages such as Acts 7:53 and Galatians 3:19.

Apparently, the rabbis also thought of angels as being there on that magnificent occasion. So the author makes his case: If the law came through angels, how much more honor should be given the message that came, not through angels or Moses, but through the Son?[3]

Furthermore, the law demonstrates that where God is involved, He has very strict standards for faith and conduct. This makes it critical for those who have been offered this very great salvation to do something about the offer. Notice the disaster that threatens. It's brought on by nothing more than neglect, not disobedience or rebellion or defiance. All you have to do is neglect it. Disregard it. Shake it off as if it wasn't there. Ignore it.

Then what happens? First of all, ignoring this salvation results in perilous spiritual drift. The word that is translated "drifting" in the NIV is a word of many meanings. It is used of something flowing or slipping past; it can be used of a ring that has slipped off the finger, of a particle of food that has slipped down the wrong way, of a topic that has slipped into the conversation, of a point which has escaped someone in the course of a discussion.[4]

In every case where the word is used in classical or *Koine* Greek, carelessness or thoughtlessness is attached to it. That is why Hebrews 2:1 says, "We must pay more careful attention, therefore, to what we have heard, so that we do not drift away." For most of us, the threat of life is not so much that we should plunge into disaster, but that we should drift into sin ever so slowly.

Few Christians deliberately and in a moment turn their backs on God, but many day by day drift farther and farther away from Him. Few in a single moment of time commit some disastrous sin; yet many almost imperceptibly involve themselves in some situation and then awaken to find that they have ruined life for themselves and broken someone else's heart also.[5]

Certain kinds of ants have a passion for a sweet, glandular substance given off by a particular caterpillar. These little creatures can become so addicted to the stuff that they seek out the supplier and carry him to their nest with delight. Unwittingly, they are bringing home an enemy in disguise, for this caterpillar's diet is exclusively ant larvae. This kind of threat to the colony would normally be repelled with great vigor. But the adults enjoy the tasty secretions of their "guest" so much that they are oblivious to the fact that their young are being devoured.

Believers in Christ can become absorbed in delightful practices that are dangerous to their fellowship with Jesus. Spiritual drift takes place very slowly, subtly and over an extended period of time. Could it be that you may be drifting slowly away from your mooring in Christ?

Remember, there are two results of this neglect. Drifting away from Christ is the first; spiritual judgment by God the second. In verse 3 the author asks, "How shall we escape if we ignore such a great salvation?" The obvious answer is that judgment is inevitable. The writer of Hebrews is arguing from the lesser to the greater. He probably has in mind two revelations.

One is the revelation of the "message spoken by angels" (v. 2), which refers to the Ten Commandments. Any violation or fissure of that law was followed by a strict and just punishment.

The other is the revelation which came through the Son, the Lord Jesus Christ. Because it came in and through the Son it was magnificent and infinitely greater than the revelation of God's truth brought by the angels. Therefore, any violation of it must be followed by a far more terrible punishment.

So, if men cannot escape the judgment which results from neglecting the revelation which came through the angels, how much less can they escape judgment if they neglect the revelation which came through the Son?[6] Neglect carries an enormous price for believers.

The Remedy for Neglect

This salvation, which was first announced by the Lord, was confirmed to us by those who heard him. God also testified to it by signs, wonders and various miracles, and gifts of the Holy Spirit distributed according to his will. (Hebrews 2:3-4)

Of course the good news had been proclaimed by the prophets, but not until the coming of the Lord Jesus Christ did promise give way to fulfillment. Salvation came near through the message brought by Christ. The author did not hear the message of liberation directly from the lips of the Savior, but rather it was confirmed by those who heard Him. So the author depended on the sure testimony of those who had listened carefully to all that Jesus said. But this witness was also confirmed by "signs, wonders and various miracles, and gifts of the Holy Spirit" (Hebrews 2:4).

Therefore, neglect can be treated in part by pondering the wonders and miracles of God. God gave strong testimony to this salvation through signs, wonders and various miracles. He gave gifts of the Holy Spirit and distributed them according to His will (Acts 2:1-4). "Everyone was filled with awe, and many wonders and miraculous signs were done by the apostles" (Acts 2:43). "The apostles performed many miraculous signs and wonders among the people" (Acts 5:12).

So the remedy for neglect can be found in recognizing the need to change our thinking and asking God to forgive us for any spiritual indifference. We must get right with God and quit pretending.

Next, we should pay more careful attention to God's Word. Disregard for the Scriptures is a fundamental cause of spiritual drift. Take notes on the pastor's sermon to keep your mind engaged and logically in tune with what God is saying in every passage. Keep your finger on the text.

You can also follow a daily Bible reading schedule. Your local bookstore should have one in stock. When you read the Bible at home ask yourself what it says, what it means and how you can apply it to your life.

Also, you would be wise to join a small group Bible study where you can be accountable to other Christians for the application of biblical truth to your life. You can fool a lot of people if you have contact only once a week on Sunday morning. But you can't drift away easily when you have six or eight people breathing down your neck, loving you to pieces, encouraging you to walk with God in holiness and praying for you daily.

This warning against neglect was written to believers. He writes to people like us who need to learn about the possibility of neglect, the results of neglect and the remedy made possible by the grace of God.

One of the Bible study guides on Hebrews that I have used with much profit suggests that we can summarize this passage in four applications.[7]

Absorbing what we have heard is more essential than seeking something new. "We must pay more careful attention, therefore, to what we have heard" (Hebrews 2:1).

Overcoming the peril of drifting requires the discipline of application. "Do not merely listen to the word, and so deceive yourselves. Do what it says" (James 1:22).

Obeying God's deliverance plan is still the only means of lasting satisfaction in life. "Does the LORD delight in burnt offerings and sacrifices as much as in obeying the voice of the LORD? To obey is better than sacrifice, and to heed is better than the fat of rams" (1 Samuel 15:22).

Neglecting God's deliverance plan inevitably leads to inescapable consequences. "How shall we escape if we ignore such a great salvation?" (Hebrews 2:3). You can't. Period. End of story.

Remember the respectable, external appearance of Gaboury's house? It had hidden the reality of what was on the inside. Something similar can happen to us if we're not careful. We may appear outwardly proper while spiritually we are drifting away from God. And whom are we trying to fool?

It's easy for any of us to drift. Moral purity, marital commitment, personal integrity, biblical fidelity—none of them is immune to the wiles of neglect. We buy into the rationalization of our times and pursue what's cushy and cozy rather than what's right.

If you're a drifter, take this warning seriously. Get ahold of your life. Put it back into the hands of God's Spirit. Come near to God and He will come near to you, again and again and again (James 4:8). Heed the warning and pay more careful attention to what you have heard, so that you don't lose your mooring.

Attracted to the Pioneer

It is not to angels that he has subjected the world to come, about which we are speaking. But there is a place where someone has testified:

"What is man that you are mindful of him,
he son of man that you care for him?
You made him a little lower than the angels;
you crowned him with glory and honor
and put everything under his feet."

In putting everything under him, God left nothing that is not subject to him. Yet at present we do not see everything subject to him. But we see Jesus, who was made a little lower than the angels, now crowned with glory and honor because he suffered death, so that by the grace of God he might taste death for ev-eryone.

In bringing many sons to glory, it was fitting that God, for whom and through whom everything exists, should make the author of their salvation perfect through suffering. Both the one who makes men holy and those who are made holy are of the same family. So Jesus is not ashamed to call them brothers. He says,

"I will declare your name to my brothers;
in the presence of the congregation I
will sing your praises."

And again,

"I will put my trust in him."
And again he says,

"Here am I, and the children God has given me."
(Hebrews 2:5-13)

Several years ago two young Canadian banks, the Canadian Commercial Bank and Northlands Bank of Canada, both went broke. Since their assets were frozen by the government, money was tied up for months while investigators tried to untangle the mess in their ledgers.

A trustee was called in to settle the claims. Although most people were covered by the Canadian Deposit Insurance Corporation, many common shareholders lost their life savings. The collapse of these two banks triggered other banking disasters across the country because people no longer trusted the system.

Once trust is broken it is very difficult to rebuild. However, trust in the Lord Jesus Christ leads to significant dividends. You will never go broke; all of God's riches are yours in Christ Jesus. He is the Author of our Salvation—our Pioneer. *The Revised Standard Version* translates Hebrews 2:10 like this: "For it was fitting that he, for whom and by whom all things exist, in bringing many sons to glory, should make *the pioneer of their salvation* perfect through suffering" (emphasis added).

The Greek word *archegos* ("author" in the NIV) may be used in more than one sense. It can denote a leader, a ruler or one who begins something as the first founder, the one who leads the way. Here it is surely the idea of origin that is stressed. However, the choice of words helps us to see Jesus as one who trod this earth before us as He established the way of salvation, making it clear for all who follow. Jesus Christ is both the Author and the Pioneer of our salvation.[8]

We shall examine three components of this great theme which will lead us to trust Him more fully.

The Pioneer's Humanity

The apostle Paul tells us in Philippians 2 that when Jesus Christ came to earth, He left the glory of heaven and "made himself nothing, taking the very nature of a servant, being made in human likeness" (2:7).

When Jesus assumed human nature He willingly took upon Himself our limited humanity.

> But there is a place where someone has testified: "What is man that you are mindful of him, the son of man that you care for him? You made him a little lower than the angels; you crowned him with glory and honor and put everything under his feet." In putting everything under him, God left nothing that is not subject to him. Yet at present we do not see everything subject to him. (Hebrews 2:6-8)

Psalm 8 reminds us that man was intended to be a creature of supreme favor, a creature of special privilege, "a little lower than the heavenly beings." Moreover, he was meant to be a creature of unique dignity, the treasured head of God's creation, "crowned . . . with glory and honor" (Psalm 8:5), the recipient of God's special favor. Man was initially marked out as a creature of unrivaled dominion with "everything under his feet" (8:6).

Yet, this is not man as we now see him living out his life in the modern world. Rather, we see him scorning God's favor, prostituting his privileges, disregarding his dignity and restricting his dominion. However, what comforts us most of all is to know that Jesus Christ understands all the hindrances of our humanness and every limitation because He willingly took upon Himself our imperfect humanness.

Furthermore, when Jesus assumed human nature He willingly took upon Himself our afflicted humanity. "But we see Jesus, who was made a little lower than the angels, now crowned with glory and honor because he suffered death . . ."

(Hebrews 2:9). Becoming man, Jesus entered immediately into the realm of our anguish and pain. When Christ assumed our humanity He became like us, exposed to all the hazardous perils of our life and death. He was not protected from trouble and adversity. He comprehends suffering and pain and rejection and scorn and mocking. You can trust Him! He's been there before, the Pioneer.

Our tormented humanity became His also. He suffered death (Hebrews 2:9). He went through the psychological, physical and material conditions, and He did it for everyone (2:9).

Death is a terrifying problem. It threatens us daily. It can be a grim experience. It carries much pain for those who are left to mourn, and it never waits for your emotions to catch up to your thoughts. But Jesus lived under the threat of death, too, and He has gone through all of this in advance for us. His feet have moved through the lonely terrain of pain and death, and He has conquered its power for everyone who believes.

Jesus took on our afflicted, tormented and limited humanity. He did it for you and for me. You can't trust just anybody these days, but you can sure trust a Savior who paid it all for you!

The Pioneer's Assignment

> In bringing many sons to glory, it was fitting that God, for whom and through whom everything exists, should make the author of their salvation perfect through suffering. (Hebrews 2:10)

Christ came not only to assume our humanity and share in its essence, but He came also to transform it. Sin has marred the original blueprint God had for our lives, and now, because of sin, man is not crowned with glory; he is degraded. When Christ entered the world He advanced with a divine mission: to bring many sons to glory through His own suffering.

It was an assignment initiated by the wisdom of God. Man's salvation begins in the heart and mind of God. "For the message of the cross is foolishness to those who are perishing, but to us who are being saved it is the power of God" (1 Corinthians 1:18). It was an assignment which also affects the destiny of every person who believes in Him: He is bringing us to glory.

Also, it was an assignment that completed the perfection of Christ. God the Father made His Son "perfect through suffering." But if the Holy Son of God is the radiance of the Father's glory and the very representation of His being, how can He be less than perfect? F.F. Bruce gives us a beautiful answer:

> The perfect Son of God has become His people's perfect Savior, opening up their way to God; and in order to become that, He must endure suffering and death. The pathway to perfection which His people must tread must first be trodden by the Pathfinder; only so could He be their adequate representative and high priest in the presence of God.[9]

Although Christ was morally perfect and sinless, His incarnation was completed or perfected when He experienced suffering. Through suffering Jesus was made fully able for the task of being the Pioneer of our salvation. His assignment was an unlimited success. Therefore, He is able to save completely those who come to God through Him.

The Pioneer's Significance

> Both the one who makes men holy and those who are made holy are of the same family. So Jesus is not ashamed to call them brothers. (Hebrews 2:11)

Here the author emphasizes the significant link between Jesus and those He saves. The one who makes men holy is, of course, Jesus Christ. He makes them holy through the blood sacrifice He offered on Calvary. He is qualified to be our Priest and Savior and Pioneer because He shares our nature, because He is truly one of us.

Believers in Christ are moving day by day closer to glory. But something else is happening in us—or should be. By His death on the cross, our Pioneer has not only prepared our way to glory, He has also set us apart for God. He made us holy and He made us family. There is a sense in which Jesus is Brother to all who call God their Father. That is why it is important to identify the "them" in "Jesus is not ashamed to call them brothers." It is not people as such He calls brothers but only those who are sanctified.

Sanctification demands some attention. It's distinct from regeneration, but it's nothing to be afraid of. A.B. Simpson explains it well:

> Regeneration is the beginning. It is the germ of the seed, but it is not the summer fullness of the plant. The heart has not yet gained entire victory over the old elements of sin. It is sometimes overcome by them. Regeneration is like building a house and having the work done well. Sanctification is having the owner come and dwell in it and fill it with gladness, and life and beauty.[10]

Sanctification means separation from sin, dedication to God, conformity to the likeness of Christ and the will of God. It means love, supreme love to God and all mankind, according to Simpson.

How does one get sanctified? It is part of the fruit of Calvary. "We have been made holy through the sacrifice of the body of Jesus Christ once for all" (Hebrews 10:10). Jesus purchased it for us with His own blood, and He secured it with the truth of God (John 17:19). It does not come to us by our own efforts, but it is offered to us by His grace to be received as one of the free gifts God desires to bestow upon

us by faith (Acts 26:18). It comes through the personal indwelling of Jesus.[11] Without the significant ministry of the
Pioneer, we would have no hope of being sanctified.

In this passage the author has proven that the Pioneer of
our salvation can be trusted. Because of His own humanity
He is able to sympathize with our feebleness. His assignment, initiated by the wisdom of God, brings us to glory.
His significance is seen in the fact that He alone makes men
holy through the power of His Spirit. He set us apart for
God and made us a part of the family of God, His family.
He sanctified us by becoming one of us and by making us
one with Him. Christ is not ashamed to call us brothers. Jesus makes us holy and Jesus makes us "family."

The Canadian Commercial Bank and the Northland Bank
of Canada both went broke. However, if you put your trust
in the Pioneer of eternal life, all of heaven's riches are at
your disposal, and you need never stay broke. That's a
promise written in heaven for each one of us who are sanctified by His blood.

When we choose to follow Christ we must deny ourselves
and take up our cross daily (Luke 9:23). There's a cost. A
price to pay. But the ones who choose Christ over the world
are the real winners. "Whoever finds his life will lose it, and
whoever loses his life for my sake will find it" (Matthew
10:39). Losers become keepers in Christ. Choosing self, on
the other hand, always results in false hope, emphasizing
man's dignity but ignoring God's glory. Do you know what
it is to have Christ sanctify you and fill you with His Spirit?
Do you know what it is to be wholly dedicated to God?

> Until we have seen ourselves as God sees us, we
> are not likely to be much disturbed over conditions
> around us as long as they do not get so far out of hand
> as to threaten our comfortable way of life. We have
> learned to live with unholiness and have come to look
> upon it as the natural and expected thing.[12]

In what areas have you chosen Christ as your Pioneer, as the leader, the ruler, the one who leads the way? Think about your home and your work. Where have you chosen to make Jesus Lord of all?

In what areas are you still trying to be lord? Open the closet of your mind, the closed recesses of your heart. Allow the Father to reveal where you have maintained control to the exclusion of the Spirit's dominion.

Now ask the Lord to help you put *everything* into His hands. Be specific and concrete. This is the road to holiness, my friend. The deeper life in Christ awaits. Trust in the Pioneer with all your heart, and do not lean on your own understanding. In all your ways acknowledge Him and He will make your spiritual bank rich forever!

Freedom Fighter

> Since the children have flesh and blood, he too shared in their humanity so that by his death he might destroy him who holds the power of death—that is, the devil—and free those who all their lives were held in slavery by their fear of death. For surely it is not angels he helps, but Abraham's descendants. For this reason he had to be made like his brothers in every way, in order that he might become a merciful and faithful high priest in service to God, and that he might make atonement for the sins of the people. Because he himself suffered when he was tempted, he is able to help those who are being tempted. (Hebrews 2:14-18)

Flanked by his parents, his two sisters, his brother and his two Winnipeg lawyers, David Milgaard stood outside the Stony Mountain prison one morning in April 1992 and gazed at the Manitoba prairie that stretched endlessly to the horizon under overcast skies. The thirty-nine-year-old Milgaard savored the view because, for the first time in almost twenty-three years, he was a free man.

His mother Joyce had always believed he was innocent of the 1970 rape and murder of a Saskatoon nursing assistant named Gail Miller, and she fought for her son's freedom. This freedom fighter would not give up until she won her son's freedom. She wrote letters, visited members of Parliament, chased down new leads in the case and worked tirelessly for the release of her son.

Jesus Christ has proven that He is the supreme freedom fighter. This third and final section of the chapter celebrates Jesus as the freedom fighter who, through His death, destroyed the power of the devil, atoned for our sins and helps those who are tempted.

He Destroyed the Enemy

> Since the children have flesh and blood, he too shared in their humanity so that by his death he might destroy him who holds the power of death. . . . (2:14)

Jesus shared "flesh and blood" with the children of God. He came to where we are in order to cancel the power of the devil, who is described as the one who "holds the power of death." This raises a problem because God alone is the One who controls the issues of life and death (Job 2:6; Luke 12:5). "But it was through Adam's sin, brought about by the temptation of the devil, that death entered the world" (Genesis 2:17; 3:19; Romans 5:12).

"From this it is logical to assume that the devil exercises his power in the realm of death. But the death of Christ is the means of destroying the power of the devil."[13] Satan is not an independent sovereign who inflicts death and destruction upon people whenever and wherever he chooses. Scripture does teach, however, that in opposition to the kingdom of light where Christ rules there is a realm of darkness in which people are enslaved to Satan, sin, self and death (Ephesians 6:12; 1 John 2:9-11; 3:12, 14; Colossians 1:13).

Thus Satan exercises the power of death in that he promotes sin and rebellion against God, slanders God's people and calls for their death from God (Job 1-2). But Christ destroyed the devil at the cross. He satisfied fully the claims of God's outraged righteousness. No more could Satan slander a believer before God. No more could he impugn God's righteousness because the sinner had not paid with his own life. No more. The penalty was paid in full in Christ.[14]

Jesus set us free from the power and authority of the devil. Scripture describes the devil as the father of lies (John 8:44), the accuser of the brethren (Revelation 12:10) and the ruler of this world. He prowls about "like a roaring lion seeking someone to devour" (1 Peter 5:8). He has power; therefore, freedom from the vice-grips of Satan is a compelling need for all people of all nations.

He Made Atonement for Sins

> For this reason he had to be made like his brothers in every way, in order that he might become a merciful and faithful high priest in service to God, and that he might make atonement for the sins of the people. (Hebrews 2:17)

The salvation God planned for His people involved a genuine incarnation. "He had to be made like his brothers" means "He owed it" (the verb can be used of financial debts), "He ought."[15] There is a sense of moral duty. Heavenly obligation. The nature of His work demanded the incarnation, which was not aimless; it was for the specific purpose of Jesus becoming a High Priest to save men.

The death of Jesus on the cross not only destroys him who holds the power of death, it also atoned for our sins. It brings those who are estranged from God into unity with God when they express their personal faith in Jesus Christ (Ephesians 2:8-9).

We are handicapped and impaired by sin (Romans 3:23).

But instead of allowing God to deal with sin in His way, we try to cover it up. Yet no matter how hard we try to cover or deny our sinful nature, it's fool's work. Sin will eventually awaken from sleep and shake off its cover. Were it not for the saving grace of the Master's hand, sin would eat us alive.

Transgression shatters our relationship with God. Sin splinters intimacy with the Holy Spirit. So we need to be freed from the power of sin, and that can happen only when we yield our lives fully to Jesus Christ.

He Helps the Tempted

> Because he himself suffered when he was tempted, he is able to help those who are being tempted. (Hebrews 2:18)

Temptation must have been one of the immediate problems faced by the first-century readers. As Jewish Christians they were continually confronted by pressure from their fellow Jews to repudiate Christ or face persecution. There was also the hostility of the Gentiles. To such people Christ ministers as a faithful and merciful High Priest because He is fully acquainted with human grief.

A significant proof of the genuineness of the humanity of Jesus and of His true likeness to us is apparent in that He Himself suffered when He was tempted. "He Himself" (*autos*) is emphatically placed in the Greek text. *Jesus* suffered. Not a phantom. Not a spirit. Not an apparition. He *Himself* suffered when He was tempted. And because of that, He is able to help those who are being tempted, because only one who has truly suffered *can* help in this way

The author of this letter is deeply persuaded that the conquest of sin, self, death and the devil by Christ took place once and for all in history. However, He knows that victory is a lingering procedure, a day-to-day affair. Jesus helps us when we face temptation, first of all, by limiting the amount of temptation to that which we can bear.

Temptation often comes not at our strongest, but at our weakest moments. Yet, by His abounding grace, Jesus limits those moments to what we can tolerate. Then He provides a way out. Finally, He gives us strength to stand up under that temptation and not give in, therefore enabling believers to maintain their freedom and dignity.

Martin Luther was often very graphic in his description of the activities of Satan and his tempters. Asked one time how he overcame temptation, he replied, "Well, when the devil comes knocking upon the door of my heart, and asks, 'Who lives here?' the dear Lord Jesus goes to the door and says, 'Martin Luther used to live here but he has moved out. Now I live here.' The devil, seeing the nail-prints in His hand and the pierced side, takes flight immediately." Jesus helps those who are being tempted.

A navy submarine on patrol one night had to remain submerged for several hours. When it finally returned to the harbor, a friend asked the captain, "How did you fare in that terrible storm last night?"

The officer looked at him in surprise and asked, "What storm? We didn't even know there was one!" The submarine had been so far down that it had reached the area known to sailors as "the cushion of the sea." Although the ocean's surface had been whipped into huge waves by high winds, the submarine was not affected because the waters below remained calm and tranquil.

Our freedom in Jesus Christ is an accomplished fact, but we need to sink deep into Christ, deep into the cross, deep into the grace of God. Then, when the huge waves of trouble roll and the high winds of hardship blow, we will stand firm because our anchor holds.

Come to the throne of mercy today. Find grace to help you in your time of need.

Jesus is waiting for you there!

Endnotes

1. *Leadership* (Summer 1994): 48. Used by permission.

2. Clark Pinnock, "The Finality of Jesus Christ in a World of Religions," in *Christian Faith and Practice in the Modern World: Theology from an Evangelical Point of View*, ed. Mark A. Noll and David F. Wells (Grand Rapids, MI: Eerdmans, 1988), 160-64, as quoted in William V. Crockett and James G. Sigountos, *Through No Fault of Their Own?* (Grand Rapids, MI: Baker Book House, 1991), 30.

3. Leon Morris, *Hebrews*, *The Expositor's Bible Commentary*, vol. 12, (Grand Rapids, MI: Zondervan, 1981), 21-22.

4. William Barclay, *The Letter to the Hebrews*, rev. ed., (Philadelphia, PA: The Westminster Press, 1976), 21.

5. Ibid.

6. Ibid., 20-21.

7. Charles R. Swindoll, *Hebrews Bible Study Guide, Vol. I*.

8. Leon Morris, 27.

9. F.F. Bruce, *The Epistle to the Hebrews* (Grand Rapids, MI: Eerdmans, 1964), 43.

10. A.B. Simpson, *The Fourfold Gospel* (Harrisburg, PA: Christian Publications, 1925), 28.

11. Ibid., 37-39.

12. A.W. Tozer, *The Knowledge of the Holy* (San Francisco, CA: Harper & Row Publishers, 1961), 110.

13. Leon Morris, 28-29.

14. See Homer Kent, *The Epistle to the Hebrews: A Commentary* (Grand Rapids, MI: Baker Book House, 1972), 58-60, for other helpful comments on this passage.

15. Leon Morris, 29.

Discussion Questions for Further Study

1. According to 2:3-4, the message of salvation came to this group of believers with a threefold authority and validation. Explain each in your own words.

2. How can a person ignore the great salvation while still saying and thinking that he or she believes in Christ?

3. Sin marred man's intended glory. Instead of being God's vice-regent on earth, man became enslaved to sin, fear of death and Satan (2:15). What did Christ do to make it possible for all men to be restored to glory and honor (2:9)?

4. What purposes for Christ's death do you see in 2:14-17?

5. Make a list of some reasons why you personally consider God's salvation to be so great. Then give praise to God for what He has accomplished for you.

3

Hebrews 3:1-19

Greater than the Greatest

> *Therefore, holy brothers, who share in the heavenly call-
> ing, fix your thoughts on Jesus, the apostle and high priest
> whom we confess. He was faithful to the one who ap-
> pointed him, just as Moses was faithful in all God's house.
> Jesus has been found worthy of greater honor than Moses,
> just as the builder of a house has greater honor than the
> house itself. For every house is built by someone, but God is
> the builder of everything. Moses was faithful as a servant
> in all God's house, testifying to what would be said in the
> future. But Christ is faithful as a son over God's house.
> And we are his house, if we hold on to our courage and the
> hope of which we boast. (Hebrews 3:1-6)*

It was a fog-shrouded morning, July 4, 1952, when a
young woman named Florence Chadwick waded into
the water off Catalina Island. She intended to swim the
channel from the island to the California coast. Long-distance swimming was not new to her; she had been the first
woman to swim the English Channel in both directions.

The water was numbing cold that day. The fog was
thick—so thick that she could hardly see the boats in her
party. Several times sharks had to be driven away with rifle

fire. She swam for more than fifteen hours before she asked
to be taken out of the water. Her trainer tried to encourage
her to swim on since they were so close to land. But when
Florence looked, all she saw was fog. So she quit—only one-
half mile from her goal.

Later she said, "I'm not excusing myself, but if I could
have seen the land I might have made it." It wasn't the cold
or fear or exhaustion that caused Florence Chadwick to fail.
It was the fog. She couldn't see the land, and she lost sight of
her goal. Perhaps the same thing was happening for the first
readers of Hebrews. They were losing sight of their preeminent goal: Jesus Christ.

In chapter 1 the writer argued that Jesus Christ is superior
to the prophets of old (Hebrews 1:1-3), and to the angels
(1:4-14). The second chapter begins with a warning to pay
more careful attention to what we have heard, so that we do
not drift away (2:1-4), but it concludes with a wonderful
word of encouragement. The Superior One is able to help
those who are being tempted because He is both merciful to
us and faithful to God in dealing with the sins of the people.
However, membership in God's family carries both privileges and responsibilities. Therefore, in chapter 3 we are exhorted to fix our thoughts on Jesus, the apostle and high
priest whom we confess (3:1) to keep focused on the goal of
knowing Christ.

Superior to prophets. Superior to angels. Now, in chapter
3, superior to Moses. The author approaches this delicate
topic carefully. For a first-century Jew, Moses held a place
that was utterly unique, regarded by Jews as the greatest of
men. "The LORD would speak to Moses face to face, as a
man speaks with his friend" (Exodus 33:11). He was the revered recipient of the Ten Commandments at holy Mount
Sinai (Exodus 19-20).

So, for a Jew, Moses was one of the greatest figures in the religious world; a distinguished, celebrated, honored, heroic man.
Perhaps, then, he was greater than Jesus? In response to this hypothetical question, the writer of this letter declares that nothing

could be further from the truth. When we fix our thoughts on Jesus we will see that He is much greater than the greatest. "The writer does nothing to belittle Moses. Nor does he criticize him. He accepts Moses' greatness but shows that as great as he was, Jesus was greater by far."[1]

Jesus Is Greater Than Moses Because of His Office

> Therefore, holy brothers, who share in the heavenly calling, fix your thoughts on Jesus, the apostle and high priest whom we confess. (Hebrews 3:1)

Jesus Christ is both the "apostle" and "high priest" whom we confess. The word *apostle* literally means "one who is sent forth," and this is the only place in Scripture where Jesus is called an apostle. Thus, the author gives it unique significance here.

In the Greek world it was a word frequently used to describe an ambassador who usually possesses all the rights, power and authority of the ruler who sends him. So the implication is clear: Jesus came in the power of God, with all of God's grace, all of God's love, all of God's mercy, all of God's justice and all of God's power in His control.

An ambassador also speaks completely and decisively on behalf of the one who sent him. Jesus said, "I did not speak of my own accord, but the Father who sent me commanded me what to say and how to say it" (John 12:49). Jesus Christ was the perfect Ambassador, the impeccable Apostle sent from God to speak on the Father's behalf.

The term "high priest" brings forth the idea of sacrifice and opens up a storehouse of precious truth. It is an idea the writer returns to again and again. The Latin word for priest is *pontifex*, which means "bridge-builder." The priest is the person who builds a bridge between God and man. Jesus is the flawless High Priest because He is perfectly man and perfectly God; He can irreproachably represent man to God and God to man—the one person through whom man comes to God and God comes to man. "For there is one God and one mediator between God and men, the man Christ Jesus" (1 Timothy 2:5).

Moses was a prominent figure—none would deny that—a faithful spokesman for God. However, "Jesus has been found worthy of greater honor than Moses" (Hebrews 3:3). Furthermore, Moses' office came to an end when he died in Moab, and his bones were buried in the valley opposite Beth Peor. The Scripture says, "Moses was a hundred and twenty years old when he died, yet his eyes were not weak nor his strength gone" (Deuteronomy 34:7). Jesus, on the other hand, is a priest forever (Hebrews 7:15-17). Consequently, Jesus is greater than the greatest because of His unchanging office of Apostle and High Priest.

Jesus Is Greater Than Moses Because of His Work

> [Jesus] was faithful to the one who appointed him, just as Moses was faithful in all God's house. Jesus has been found worthy of greater honor than Moses, just as the builder of a house has greater honor than the house itself. For every house is built by someone, but God is the builder of everything. (Hebrews 3:2-4)

Here we find a brief comparison of the work of Jesus with the work of Moses. Keep in mind that Moses was a very important figure for the Jewish people. Almost everything of importance connected with God is connected with Moses. Moses was the one who received the revered Torah (the Law) from the hand of God while he was on Mount Sinai, the one in whose presence the bush burst into flames.

The text declares that Moses was faithful. That's good. But so was Jesus Christ. The writer implies that Moses was worthy of honor, yet it so happens that Jesus Christ "has been found worthy of greater honor than Moses" (Hebrews 3:3). He gives Moses the credit for managing the household of God. Nevertheless, "God is the builder of everything."

In other words, the work Moses did was very good work. We commend him for it. Three cheers for his efforts and achievements. Yet, the work of Jesus is so much greater than the greatest. Why? Partly because Moses never finished his work. He did not achieve his aim of leading the people into the Promised Land. He died before that happened.

Jesus, on the other hand, fulfilled His work upon the cross. "It is finished. With that, he bowed his head and gave up his spirit" (John 19:30). That is why He is able to say, "I will build my church, and the gates of Hades will not overcome it" (Matthew 16:18).

His work is greater than the greatest, and I can think of no better place to invest my time and energy than in the work of God.

Jesus Is Greater Than Moses Because of Who He Is

Moses was faithful as a servant in all God's house, testifying to what would be said in the future. But Christ is faithful as a son over God's house. And we are his house, if we hold on to our courage and the hope of which we boast. (Hebrews 3:5-6)

The author of Hebrews consistently approaches a delicate subject with caution. Moses was the national historical hero of the Jews, God's friend and spokesman. Miracle worker during the plagues. Leader of the Exodus. Perhaps some of the Jewish Christians to whom this letter was addressed were turning in reverence back to Moses instead of to Jesus.

In the midst of their pain and turmoil, were they tempted to look back to the familiar? In careful anticipation of the answer to those questions, the writer meticulously highlights the similarities between Moses and Messiah; then he underscores their differences, showing Christ to be greater than the greatest.

Both were appointed by the Lord God. Both proved faithful. Both were related to God's house, a term which refers more to God's people than a building. However, the differences are even more striking than the similarities. Moses was part of the house; Christ was its architect. Moses knew God personally; Christ is God permanently. Moses was a temporary servant in the house; Christ is the eternal Son over the house.

Moses was no more than a member of the house, even though he was a very distinguished one. He was essentially one with all the other members of God's house. That would appear later in time, whereas Christ is the revelation itself (Hebrews 1:1-13). Moses loved God, but Jesus is God. "The implication is plain. To forsake the way of Christ for the way of Moses is to go from the greater to the lesser. It is to abandon the permanent in favor of the temporary."[2]

The passage ends with a verse that has been debated for centuries: "And we are his house, if we hold on to our courage and the hope of which we boast" (3:6). Here the writer gives a very enlightening definition of the house of which he has been speaking. It is we, persons who are born again, believers in Jesus, who are His house. He also couples the status of the Christian with an "admonitory proviso: we are God's house if, on condition that, we hold fast our confidence and pride in our hope."[3]

F.F. Bruce contributes to the discussion:

> The conditional sentences of this epistle are worthy of special attention. Nowhere in the New Testament more than here do we find such repeated insistence on the fact that continuance in the Christian life is the test of reality. The doctrine of the final perseverance of the saints has as its corollary the salutary teaching that the saints are the people who persevere to the end.[4]

Note the perfect balance in Hebrews 3:1-6, and throughout the letter, between the believer's promised security and his necessary perseverance. At first reading, on the surface, the word "if" in verse 6 seems to indicate that if you do not hold fast until the end, you are not really part of God's forever family. However, continuance is the test of reality. In the parable of the sower (Mark 4:1-20), the seed sown on the rocky places sprang up quickly, because the soil was shallow. It made a good showing at first, but when the sun came up, the plants were scorched. They withered because they had no root.

This is precisely what the author of Hebrews fears may happen with his readers. Several times in Hebrews, statements are made with the intention of getting people like us off the fence. That explains his repeated emphasis on the necessity of maintaining constant courage and the hope of which we boast (Hebrews 3:6). The person who is truly born again perseveres, abides and continues until the end. Jesus underscored the divine side of the equation when He said:

> All that the Father gives me will come to me, and whoever comes to me I will never drive away. For I have come down from heaven not to do my will but to do the will of him who sent me. And this is the will of him who sent me, that I shall lose none of all that he has given me, but raise them up at the last day. For my Father's will is that everyone who looks to the Son and believes in him shall have eternal life, and I will raise him up at the last day. (John 6:37-40)

However, sometimes we get sidetracked, don't we? So many stresses and strains, tensions and temptations, perfidious as well as conspicuous, can seduce us and lure us away from Christ and our faith. One day as we look out through the window of our hearts, our view of God is clear and crisp. Then, suddenly, a pebble of pain strikes the window and it cracks.

Maybe the stone was thrown when you were just a little child. Maybe the rock hit when you were a teenager. Maybe you made it into your adult years before the window shattered. But then the pebble came. A phone call? A letter? Diagnosis from the doctor? A court document titled "divorce"? A pink slip that spells "reject"?

Whatever the form the result is the same. A broken pane of glass. And suddenly your vision of God is not so clear. He seems removed, distant, aloof, unconcerned, unreachable, harder to understand. Your pain distorts the view and the emotional storms attack your faith.

Those who truly possess eternal life and find themselves in the crucible of God's workmanship will experience trials of various kinds. That comes as no surprise to me or to you. James said, "Consider it pure joy, my brothers, whenever you face trials of many kinds, because you know that the testing of your faith develops perseverance" (James 1:2-3).

Trials are inevitable, and the Greek word translated "many kinds" (*poikilois*) is the term from which we get the idea of "polka dots." In other words, believers are destined to face trials of all kinds that spatter their lives like polka dots. However, the Lord Jesus Christ has been appointed as the apostle and high priest. A bridge-builder.

He came to construct an eternal link between us and God that is not prone to mechanical failure of any description. He ministers to us like no one else can. He's superior to the prophets, the angels and even the greatest figure in Jewish history, old man Moses. Jesus helps us to understand and accept the fact that trials are meant to perfect us, make us complete, deficient in nothing.

What should we do, then, when the pebbles hit the windows of our hearts and we become disappointed with God? The message of Hebrews is this: When you can't see Him, trust Him. Authentic Christians turn to Christ when the bottom falls out. The Holy Spirit still woos us and pursues us, drawing us closer and closer to the Father's heart when we cling to the cross. Such a response in the midst of trials and pain proves that I am His and He is mine. Hallelujah! Praises to the King!

Florence Chadwick figured she would make it across the channel. She didn't. The water was cold. The fog was thick. The sharks were looking for lunch. But it wasn't the cold or the fog or the sharks that made her quit. Remember, she simply lost sight of her goal. And you should be careful that you don't lose sight of *your* goal, the Lord Jesus Christ. It can happen to the best of them. Fix your thoughts on Jesus, the Apostle and High Priest whom you confess, and you'll stay firm to the end.

Warning Against Unbelief

So, as the Holy Spirit says,

"*Today if you hear his voice,*
  do not harden your hearts
as you did in the rebellion,
  during the time of testing in the desert,
where your fathers tested and tried me
  and for forty years saw what I did.
That is why I was angry with that
      generation,
  and I said, 'Their hearts are always
      going astray,
  and they have not known my ways.'
So I declared on oath in my anger,
  'They shall never enter my rest.' "

See to it, brothers, that none of you has a sinful, unbelieving heart that turns away from the living God. But encourage one another daily, as long as it is called Today, so that none of you may be hardened by sin's deceitfulness. We have come to share in Christ if we hold firmly till the end the confidence we had at first. As has just been said:

"Today, if you hear his voice,
  do not harden your hearts
  as you did in the rebellion."

Who were they who heard and rebelled? Were they not
all those Moses led out of Egypt? And with whom was he
angry for forty years? Was it not with those who sinned,
whose bodies fell in the desert? And to whom did God
swear that they would never enter his rest if not to those
who disobeyed? So we see that they were not able to enter,
because of their unbelief. (Hebrews 3:7-19)

Max Lucado tells a touching story about a tender, loving mother named Theresa Briones and her daughter, Alicia.

One day Theresa used a stout left hook to punch a lady in a coin laundry because some kids were making fun of Alicia.

Alicia is bald. Her knees are arthritic and her nose is pinched. Her hips are creaky. Her hearing is bad. She has the stamina of a seventy-year-old, but she's only ten.

"Mom," the kids taunted, "come and look at the *monster!*"

Alicia weighs only twenty-two pounds and she is shorter than most preschoolers. She suffers from progeria—a genetic aging disease that strikes one child in 8 million, according to Lucado's article. The life expectancy of its victims is twenty years, and there are only fifteen known cases of the disease in the world.

"She is not an alien or a monster," Theresa defended. "She is just like you and me."

Mentally, Alicia is a bubbly, fun-loving third grader. She has a long list of friends. She watches television in a toddler-sized rocking chair and plays with Barbie dolls and teases her younger brother. Sounds just like my own kids!

Theresa has grown accustomed to the glances and questions. She is patient with the constant curiosity. Genuine inquiries she accepts, insensitive slanders she does not.

The mother of the finger-pointing children came to investigate. "I see 'it,' " she told the kids.

"My child is not an 'it,' " Theresa stated. Then she decked the woman. Wham! Right in the chops.

"Who could blame her?" asks Lucado. "Such is the nature of parental love. Mothers and fathers have a God-given ability to love their children regardless of imperfections. Not because the parents are blind. Just the opposite. They see vividly."[5]

Theresa sees all of Alicia's inabilities and imperfections. But she also sees her worth, her significance, her value. And when God looks at you and me, He sees great potential for today and tomorrow and the day after that. He's cheering for us to cross the finish line with our heads held high. That's why we need ceaselessly to "fix [our] thoughts on Jesus" (Hebrews 3:1).

"We have come to share in Christ if we hold firmly till the end the confidence we had at first" (Hebrews 3:14). Life in Christ requires repentance and faith, but perseverance and fortitude are necessary also. Holding firmly till the end. That can happen only when we follow God's Word.

The apostle Paul, the first church theologian, resoundingly affirmed the truth of Scripture. Irenaeus, brilliant second-century apologist whose writings stemmed the early tides of heresy, argued that the Scriptures were perfect since they were spoken by the Word of God. Augustine wrote, "I have learned to hold the Scriptures alone inerrant."

In the sixteenth century, Luther spoke movingly of the Word of God as "greater than Heaven and earth, yea, greater than death and Hell, for it forms part of the Power of God and endures everlastingly." His fellow reformer John Calvin argued: That which distinguishes Christianity is the knowledge that God has spoken to us and so "we owe to the Scriptures the same reverence which we owe to God."[6]

With that strong affirmation of the Scriptures in mind, let's explore what the passage before us says about standing firm till the end through the Word of God.

A Caution from the Past: "Do Not Harden Your Hearts"

So, as the Holy Spirit says,

"Today if you hear his voice,
    do not harden your hearts
as you did in the rebellion,
    during the time of testing in the desert,
where your fathers tested and tried me
    and for forty years saw what I did.
That is why I was angry with that
        generation,
    and I said, 'Their hearts are always
        going astray,
    and they have not known my ways.'
So I declared on oath in my anger,
    'They shall never enter my rest.' "
        (Hebrews 3:7-11)

Some members of this first-century community of faith were in danger of turning back and giving up. Quoting from Psalm 95:7-11, which in turn refers to history recorded in the books of Exodus and Numbers, the writer of Hebrews summarizes the chronicle of Israel under Moses' leadership in the desert. He reminds them of Israel's unbelief, disobedience and fatal mistakes in the wilderness, and in doing so he brings a serious warning to us today.

"So, as the Holy Spirit says: 'Today, if you hear his voice, do not harden your hearts as you did in the rebellion, during the time of testing in the desert . . .' " (Hebrews 3:7-8). The urgent warning against hardening of the heart is attributed directly to the Holy Spirit, and the emphatic positioning of the word "today" adds to the urgency of this statement. Immediate action is critical. The voice of God is ringing now. It must not be ignored or overlooked.

Arteriosclerosis is commonly called hardening of the arteries. It can cause strokes and heart attacks and claims many lives every year. Fats and cholesterol cling to the inside lining of the arteries and restrict the flow of blood. If the artery completely clogs up, you're in big trouble! Hardening of the arteries can cause critical health problems, but hardening of the heart against the voice of God can produce spiritual paralysis. If believers hear the voice of God and ignore it, they will suffer spiritually. So, today, if you hear His voice, do not harden your hearts.

The Holy Spirit also warns us against testing God. Hebrews 3:9-10a says, "Your fathers tested and tried me and for forty years saw what I did. That is why I was angry with that generation. . . ." This faithlessness was no mere passing fad or a moment of spiritual weakness. The Israelites had rejected God for forty years, and it was now nearly forty years since their descendants had rejected Jesus—a reason for serious concern.

A God who is perpetually and continually tested will never be accepted for who He is. Most people don't need more evidence or confirmation of truth. They simply need to repent of their sin and turn to God in faith and obedience.

I have observed the signs and wonders movement for several years. As I write this book, the "Airport Revival" is several months along. It's taking place in an industrial building close to Pearson International Airport in Toronto. Most, if not all, of the people involved seem sincere, dedicated to Christ and determined to follow His blueprint for their lives. Devotees have transported "the blessing" to other countries like England and Australia and Germany.

Some of the teaching has been a welcomed correction to a sleepy generation of believers who enjoy the comforts of the church, and the focus on personal worship has been wonderfully refreshing. Yet, the constant call (or is it demand?) for signs and wonders, the incessant request for visual demonstrations of God's infinite power, the incredible lack of repentance and the presumptuous declaration that confrontations with the demonic world are necessary for truly effective evangelism at times sound like a dare or a test or at best a fleece. If this movement is of God, then of course I stand aside and say, "Let God be God."

I'm sure God is in this thing somewhere. But I'm not anxious to put God to the test by demanding that He show me through signs and wonders that He is the God of the Bible and the Lord of salvation. Personally, I am more inclined to follow the advice of the same Psalm from which our author of Hebrews quotes: "Come, let us bow down in worship, let us kneel before the LORD our Maker; for he is our God and we are the people of his pasture, the flock under his care" (Psalm 95:6-7).

It may be helpful to remember that only once in all of Scripture does God invite His people to test Him. You'll find it in Malachi 3:7-12.

> "Ever since the time of your forefathers you have turned away from my decrees and have not kept them. Return to me, and I will return to you," says the LORD Almighty.
>
> "But you ask, 'How are we to return?'
>
> "Will a man rob God? Yet you rob me.
>
> "But you ask, 'How do we rob you?'
>
> "In tithes and offerings. You are under a curse—the whole nation of you—because you are robbing me. Bring the whole tithe into the storehouse, that there may be food in my house. Test me in this," says the LORD Almighty, "and see if I will not throw open the floodgates of heaven and pour out so much blessing that you will not have room enough for it. I will prevent pests from devouring your crops, and the vines in your fields will not cast their fruit," says the LORD Almighty. "Then all the nations will call you blessed, for yours will be a delightful land," says the LORD Almighty.

The consequences of testing the Lord outside of His prescribed will certainly lead to disastrous results. "That is why I was angry with that generation, and I said, 'Their hearts are always going astray, and they have not known my ways.' So I declared on oath in my anger, 'They shall never enter my rest' " (Hebrews 3:10-11).

The seriousness with which God looked at the nation's sin is shown by the divine oath. God is not passive or indifferent to sin. Our God is a consuming fire, and His reaction to sin is wrath or "anger," which "points to the strong and settled opposition of God's holy nature to all that is evil."[7] He did not allow the sinning Israelites to enter the rest.

God has done so much for us. Do we really need more proof that He is who He said He is? We should walk in faith and trust Him, not test Him. Do we need signs and wonders to prove that Jesus is faithful and able to keep us safe in the palm of His nail-pierced hand? Missionaries affirm the need for power evangelism in areas where the gospel has never been preached. But in the United States? In Canada? This serious warning is for us: Do not harden your hearts. Do not test the Lord your God. Open your ears and listen to what He says, and do not let your heart go astray.

A Petition for the Present: "Encourage One Another"

See to it, brothers, that none of you has a sinful, unbelieving heart that turns away from the living God. But encourage one another daily, as long as it is called Today, so that none of you may be hardened by sin's deceitfulness. We have come to share in Christ if we hold firmly till the end the confidence we had at first. As has just been said:

"Today, if you hear his voice,
    do not harden your hearts
as you did in the rebellion."

Who were they who heard and rebelled? Were
they not all those Moses led out of Egypt? And with
whom was he angry for forty years? Was it not with
those who sinned, whose bodies fell in the desert?
And to whom did God swear that they would never
enter his rest if not to those who disobeyed? So we
see that they were not able to enter, because of their
unbelief. (Hebrews 3:12-19)

It's not enough for the author to remind his readers of the
warning from God's word in the past. He presses home his
message with compelling devotion and tender concern in
verse 12. "See to it, brothers, that none of you has a sinful,
unbelieving heart that turns away from the living God."
This characterization stands in marked contrast to the faithfulness ascribed to both Jesus and Moses. Leon Morris suggests that "turn away" is perhaps not strong enough; the
meaning is rather "rebel against."[8]

The people of Moses' day failed to enter God's rest because of their hardened hearts. "Their hearts had crossed
over into territory where choice is extinct. They fell victim
to their questioning natures and experienced the inevitable
and depressing consequences of sustained unbelief."[9]

A reader cannot escape the grim description in these
verses of the human condition without God's revolutioniz-
ing, transforming grace. Our hearts can become rebellious,
wayward, ignorant, undiscerning, evil, faithless, hardened,
deceived and disobedient. "The heart is deceitful above all
things and beyond cure. Who can understand it?" (Jeremiah
17:9).

Furthermore, God is described in Romans 1 as the Holy
One who allowed sin to run its course as an act of judgment.
After mankind had "exchanged the glory of the immortal

God for images made to look like mortal man and birds and animals and reptiles," then "God gave them over in the sinful desires of their hearts to sexual impurity for the degrading of their bodies with one another. They exchanged the truth of God for a lie, and worshiped and served created things rather than the Creator—who is forever praised" (Romans 1:23-25).

Perhaps you're asking the same questions I am asking: How can we keep this from happening to others? How can I keep this from happening to me? The answer has vertical and horizontal dimensions. "But encourage one another daily, as long as it is called Today, so that none of you may be hardened by sin's deceitfulness. We have come to share in Christ if we hold firmly till the end the confidence we had at first" (Hebrews 3:13-14).

Encouragement and endurance stand side by side, hand in hand. I can't make it on my own! I need my brothers and sisters walking beside me, encouraging me, provoking me to love and good deeds—admonishing, advising, exhorting, scolding, counseling, loving, rebuking—and the need is urgent because "today" does not last forever.

We need each other. The consistent encouragement and support we give to others may stimulate and motivate them to hold firmly till the end the confidence they had at first. But I also need to persevere in the midst of my own trials, remembering that continuance is the proof of reality.

When I approach barriers in my own life, I need to turn them over to the Lord, accepting them as tests from Him and asking Him to show me His power in the eye of the storm. His grace is sufficient.

Furthermore, in order to hold firm till the end, I need to focus more intently on the Scriptures. For emphasis, in verse 15 the writer of Hebrews repeats what he said earlier: "Today, if you hear his voice, do not harden your hearts as you did in the rebellion." I can avoid being hardened by sin's deceitfulness when I continually and willfully hear the Word of God, personally and publicly. I must meditate on its life-changing message. Every day demands a fresh appointment with God. Every day requires an accurate application of what I hear.

Anyone who has ever painted a house knows that the hardest work is preparing the surface, not the actual painting. The better the preparation, the better the results. As in painting, preparation is necessary for receiving the truth of God's Word. Without adequate preparation, we simply whitewash our lives with knowledge, which will quickly peel, revealing an unchanged character underneath. So if you really want to hear the voice of God as you read His Word or listen to your pastor preach, then get ready. Be prepared.

Next, believe the Word, and encourage others to believe the Word with you. It's one thing to hear the Word, it is quite another to accept its message in responsive faith. Hebrews 3:19 says, "So we see that they were not able to enter, because of their unbelief." The people of Israel did not enter God's rest because of their unbelief. Let's not make the same mistake.

Then comes obedience. "And to whom did God swear that they would not enter his rest if not to those who disobeyed?" (Hebrews 3:18). One interesting thing to watch from the window of an airplane is the winding path of a river below. No two waterways are alike, but they all have one thing in common. They are all crooked. Have you ever seen a straight river? No, and the reason is simple—rivers always follow the path of least resistance. They flow around anything and everything that blocks their eroding work.

Believers in Jesus Christ cannot expect to stand firm to the end if they always follow the path of least resistance. Your Christian friends and family need the encouragement daily to walk that pathway to victory. Obedience is not easy. It can be a long road, but it's necessary if we want to enter God's eternal rest.

James gives his wise counsel on the matter:

> Anyone who listens to the word but does not do what it says is like a man who looks at his face in a mirror and, after looking at himself, goes away and immediately forgets what he looks like. But the man who looks intently into the perfect law that gives freedom, and continues to do this, not forgetting what he has heard, but doing it—he will be blessed in what he does. (James 1:23-25)

Oswald Chambers once wrote, "We presume that we would be ready for battle if confronted with a great crisis, but it is not the crisis that builds something within us—it simply reveals what we are made of already." Do you ever find yourself saying, "If God calls me to the front lines, of course I will rise to the occasion?" Yet you won't rise to the occasion unless you have done so on God's training ground which is the personal study of His Word.

If you are not doing the task that is closest to you now, which God has engineered into your life, when the crisis comes, instead of being fit for battle, you will be revealed as being unfit. Crises always reveal a person's true character, and a consistent private life of personal study and prayer is the greatest element of spiritual fitness. Study and obey. There's no other way to be fit for battle on a daily basis.[10]

Finally, we can share the Word. "But encourage one another daily, as long as it is called Today, so that none of you may be hardened by sin's deceitfulness" (Hebrews 3:13). We need to share the Word with others so they will be encouraged to stand firm. Sin is so deceitful, and we need to capture every opportunity to encourage our brothers and sisters with the Word of God.

A few years ago a magazine article about Chuck Colson's prison ministry concluded that "prison radicalized the life of Chuck Colson." Colson responded by saying,

> It is understandable that the reporter might have thought that, but it is simply not so. I could have left

prison and forgotten it; I wanted to in fact. But while every human instinct said, "Put it out of your mind forever," the Bible kept revealing to me God's compassion for the hurting and suffering and oppressed; His insistent Word demanded that I care as He does. What "radicalized" me was not prison, but taking to heart the truths revealed in Scripture. For it was the Bible that confronted me with a new awareness of my sin and need for repentance; it was the Bible that caused me to hunger for righteousness and seek holiness; and it was the Bible that called me into fellowship with the suffering. It is the Bible that continues to challenge my life today.[11]

Would you like the Spirit of God to "radicalize" your Christian life and fill it with power, insight and blessing? Would you like to see the honor of God advanced through your life? It may mean that you yourself must suffer temporary dishonor or loss. That's what it takes to be a fully devoted follower of Jesus.

May I encourage you to hear the Holy Spirit making His appeal to you today through the Bible? Learn to live for God's honor by a kind of spiritual reflex. Hear the Word, believe the Word, obey the Word and then share the Word with others. Long for God's holiness to be real in your life.

The person God uses is the one who desires holiness more than happiness. He gasps for the glory of God as a suffocating man gasps for air. She wants to carry her cross with full knowledge of the consequences. A man or woman who goes out to be crucified doesn't come home for dinner! We choose to obey Christ and by so doing choose to carry the cross.

Tozer once wrote, "The yearning after happiness found so widely among Christians professing a superior degree of sanctity is sufficient proof that such sanctity is not indeed present." God wants us holy, sometimes at the expense of happiness, but that requires a radical commitment to obeying what God says in His Word. Are you willing to make that kind of commitment today? To say "yes" to all that God has for you?

Theresa saw all of her daughter Alicia's inabilities and imperfections. But she also saw her worth, her significance, her value. And when God looks at you and me, He sees great potential for today and tomorrow and for every single day after that. He's cheering for us to cross the finish line with our heads held high. That's why we need to ceaselessly fix our thoughts on Jesus (Hebrews 3:1).

Endnotes

1. Leon Morris, *Hebrews, The Expositor's Bible Commentary*, Vol. 12, ed. Frank E. Gaebelein, (Grand Rapids, MI: Eerdmans, 1981), 31.

2. Raymond Brown, *The Message of Hebrews* (Downers Grove, IL: InterVarsity Press, 1982), 79.

3. Philip Edgcumbe Hughes, *A Commentary on the Epistle to the Hebrews* (Grand Rapids, MI: Eerdmans, 1977), 138.

4. F.F. Bruce, *The Epistle to the Hebrews* (Grand Rapids, MI: Eerdmans, 1964), 59.

5. Max Lucado, *In the Eye of the Storm* (Dallas, TX: Word Publishing, 1991), 41-42. Used by permission.

6. Charles Colson, *Loving God* (Grand Rapids, MI: Zondervan, 1983), 71. Copyright 1983, 1987 by Charles W. Colson. Used by permission of Zondervan Publishing House.

7. Leon Morris, 35.

8. Ibid., 36.

9. Charles Swindoll, *Bible Study Guide: Hebrews, Vol I*, (Fullerton, CA: Insight for Living), 30.

10. This devotional is taken from *My Utmost for His Highest* by Oswald Chambers, edited by James Reimann, copyright ©1992 by Oswald Chambers Publications Assn.,

11. Charles Colson, *Loving God*, 40. Copyright 1983, 1987 by
    Charles W. Colson. Used by permission of Zondervan
    Publishing House.

Discussion Questions for Further Study

1. Notice that 3:1 begins with "Therefore." Briefly summarize the doctrinal truth in 2:5-18 that is the basis for the
   application in 3:1.

2. Why is it important to "fix your thoughts" on your
   Apostle and High Priest?

3. What do you think is the significance of the "if" clause at
   the end of Hebrews 3:6?

4. The author has demonstrated Christ's superiority over
   the prophets (1:1-4), the angels (1:5-2:18) and Moses (3:1-
   6). What, then, is the significance of beginning 3:7-19
   with "so"?

5. How might believers harden their hearts after hearing
   God's voice? What actions and attitudes might this involve?

6. In view of the seriousness of the warning in 3:7-12, why
   is it so important to encourage one another daily (3:13)?
   What might happen if we fail to encourage one another?

4

Hebrews 4:1-5:10

Entering God's Rest

Therefore, since the promise of entering his rest still stands, let us be careful that none of you be found to have fallen short of it. For we also have had the gospel preached to us, just as they did; but the message they heard was of no value to them, because those who heard did not combine it with faith. Now we who have believed enter that rest, just as God has said,

> *"So I declared on oath in my anger,*
> *'They shall never enter my rest.' "*

And yet his work has been finished since the creation of the world. For somewhere he has spoken about the seventh day in these words: "And on the seventh day God rested from all his work." And again in the passage above he says, "They shall never enter my rest."

It still remains that some will enter that rest, and those who formerly had the gospel preached to them did not go in, because of their disobedience. Therefore God again set a certain day, calling it Today, when a long time later he spoke through David, as was said before:

> *"Today, if you hear his voice,*
> *do not harden your hearts."*

For if Joshua had given them rest, God would not have spoken later about another day. There remains, then, a Sabbath-rest for the people of God; for anyone who enters God's rest also rests from his own work, just as God did from his. Let us, therefore, make every effort to enter that rest, so that no one will fall by following their example of disobedience.

For the word of God is living and active. Sharper than any double-edged sword, it penetrates even to dividing soul and spirit, joints and marrow; it judges the thoughts and attitudes of the heart. Nothing in all creation is hidden from God's sight. Everything is uncovered and laid bare before the eyes of him to whom we must give account. (Hebrews 4:1-13)

In one scene of a movie titled *Robin Hood, The Prince of Thieves*, Kevin Costner as Robin came to a young man taking aim at an archery target. "Can you shoot amid distractions?" Robin asked.

Just before the boy released the bow, Robin poked his ear with the feathers of an arrow. The boy's shot went high by several feet. After the laughter of those watching died down, Maid Marian, standing beside the boy, asked Robin, "Can you?"

Robin Hood then raised his bow and took aim. His eyes focused on the bull's-eye. Just as he released the arrow, Maid Marian leaned beside him and flirtatiously blew into his face. The arrow missed the target, glanced off the tree behind it and scarcely missed a bystander[1]

Distractions come in all types, all shapes and sizes. And whether they are painful or pleasant the result is the same: We miss God's mark. The writer of Hebrews does not want his readers distracted from their primary goal in life. "See to it, brothers, that none of you has a sinful, unbelieving heart that turns away from the living God" (3:12). "Let's throw off everything that hinders us from running this race of faith with perseverance. Ditch the sins that entangle you. Fix your eyes on Jesus! Don't be distracted" (loose paraphrase of Hebrews 12:1-2).

Those who could have been healthy, wealthy and wise in the land flowing with milk and honey were strewn and spread about the wilderness because of unbelief and disobedience. In essence, the advice in Hebrews 4:1-13 is "Don't be like them! Rest is available for you to enjoy now and forever. But it's not automatic, and you need to be careful!" Before he examines the rest that remains, he presents the promise of rest and the danger of falling short.

The Promise of Rest

> Therefore, since the promise of entering his rest still stands, let us be careful that none of you be found to have fallen short of it. (Hebrews 4:1)

Jesus Christ is supreme. He is greater than the prophets. Greater than the angels. Greater than Moses. And greater in the rest He gives. The warning section now proceeds to another emphasis: the danger of missing the rest which God provides. Yet the writer of Hebrews is at pains to emphasize that such a rest was not limited to the historical circumstance of Israel going into Canaan under Joshua's leadership. A Sabbath-rest for the people of God still remains.

Hughes helps put this verse and this passage in perspective:

> In the passage which this verse introduces, our author's purpose is to apply (*therefore*) to his readers still more insistently the solemn lesson which the history of their forefathers in the wilderness teaches, and in doing so he makes it plain that the scope of the promise of entering into God's rest extends far beyond the historical event of the entry of the Israelites into Canaan under Joshua's leadership. The possession of the land of Canaan was indeed a fulfillment of

the promise, but only in a proximate, this-worldly sense. The perspective of faith discerns its ultimate fulfillment in the entry into a heavenly country (11:16) and a heavenly Jerusalem (12:22), in an eternal consummation effected through the redemptive mediation of the incarnate Son.

Hughes also explains why this is so significant to the overall structure of the epistle:

It is the key to the understanding of the priestly order of Melchizedek which is realized in the person and work of Christ, our High Priest forever (chapters 8-10), and to the understanding of the outlook of Abraham and other men of faith in the Old Testament period, who in their lifetime did not see the fulfillment of the divinely given promises but fixed their expectation on a heavenly consummation hereafter (chapters 11-13).[2]

So here, too, readers are advised that "the promise of entering his rest still stands."

God's promises mean a great deal to the writer. The word *epangelia* ("promise") occurs more often in Hebrews than in any other New Testament book. Over and over we discover the word "promise" flowing from his pen.

"When God made his *promise* to Abraham, since there was no one greater for him to swear by, he swore by himself" (Hebrews 6:13).

"And so after waiting patiently, Abraham received what was *promised*" (6:15).

"Because God wanted to make the unchanging nature of his *purpose* very clear to the heirs of what was *promised*, he confirmed it with an oath" (6:17).

"For this reason Christ is the mediator of a new covenant, that those who are called may receive the *promised* eternal inheritance . . ." (9:15).

"You need to persevere so that when you have done the will of God, you will receive what he has *promised*" (10:36).

"By faith he (Abraham) made his home in the *promised* land like a stranger in a foreign country; he lived in tents, as did Isaac and Jacob, who were heirs with him of the same *promise*" (11:9).

"These were all commended for their faith, yet none of them received what had been *promised*" (11:39).

In Hebrews 4:1 the *promise* of entering God's rest remains open. But the danger of falling short of that rest is real. Christian pilgrims in the contemporary world must realize that, in light of a passage such as this, it will not do to confess a merely nominal allegiance to Christian truth, or pay occasional lip service in meetings and worship services to faith in Christ. Our commitment must be genuine and sincere.

The Danger of Falling Short

Let us be careful that none of you be found to have fallen short of it. For we also have had the gospel preached to us, just as they did; but the message they heard was of no value to them, because those who heard did not combine it with faith. (Hebrews 4:1-2)

The author of Hebrews urges his readers to press on until they attain that goal. But it won't be reached automatically. "Let us be careful" might be better translated, "Let us fear." It's an emphatic exhortation. Danger ahead! Proceed with caution!

The driver of CTA Bus Number 22 in Chicago gave a warning the day that Dean Niferatos rode that bus. It brimmed with dozing office workers, restless punkers and affluent shoppers. At one stop, two men and a woman climbed aboard. The driver, a seasoned veteran, immediately bellowed, "Everybody watch your valuables. There are pickpockets on board." Women clutched their purses tightly.

Men put their hands on their wallets. All eyes fixed on the trio, who, looking insulted and harassed, didn't break stride as they promptly exited through the middle doors.[3]

The Spirit of God is telling us in Hebrews 4:1 to be careful. Don't allow yourselves to get ripped off. Hang on to the promise tightly! Nothing comes automatically. Some Christians would do well to fear the possibility of missing it, much like the Israelites missed their goal when they came out of Egypt.

Remember, a whole generation died off before God let them into the Promised Land, because they were disobedient. He swore "that they would never enter his rest" (Hebrews 3:18). And they didn't. Unbelief led to disobedience. Disobedience led to distress. Distress led to the desert. The desert led to death. A whole generation vanished through a lack of faith.

It is evident from this text that true believers are the only ones who enter God's rest, not members of physical Israel nor card-toting members of a church. If you don't have the right attitude of faith and trust, you can't enter. "For we also have had the gospel preached to us, just as they did" (Hebrews 4:2).

The pressure is on the readers. They have the message. They must act on it in order for it to have value. Previously, those who heard "did not combine it with faith" (4:2). They disqualified themselves. Their injury was self-inflicted.

If the people of God in an earlier day, with all their advantages, failed to enter that rest, Christians ought not to think there will be automatic acceptance for them. They must take care lest they, too, fall short of the blessing.

The Rest That Remains

> Therefore, since the promise of entering his rest still stands, let us be careful that none of you be found to have fallen short of it. . . . There remains, then, a Sabbath-rest for the people of God; for any-

one who enters God's rest also rests from his own
work, just as God did from his. Let us, therefore,
make every effort to enter that rest, so that no one
will fall by following their example of disobedience.
(Hebrews 4:1, 9-11)

The question then arises whether the rest takes place here
and now, or after death, as seen in Revelation 14:13.
"Blessed are the dead who died in the Lord. . . . They will
rest from their labor, for their deeds will follow them."

F.F. Bruce thinks it is "an experience which they do not
enjoy in their present mortal life, although it belongs to
them as a heritage, and by faith they may live in the good of
it here and now."[4]

Leon Morris reverses the order that Bruce sets out: "They
live in it here and now by faith, but what they know here is
not the full story. That will be revealed in the hereafter."[5]

First, let's examine the rest we have access to now.

In Hebrews 4:4-6 the writer takes us all the way back to
Genesis and the story of creation. He uses this as a basis for
his discussion of Sabbath-rest. "For somewhere he has spoken about the seventh day in these words: 'And on the seventh day God rested from all his work.' "

Entering into this creative rest of God is critical for busy
laypeople, pastors and missionaries. In the clear-sighted
book *Ordering Your Private World*, author Gordon MacDonald says, "If my private world is in order, it will be because I
have chosen to press Sabbath peace into the rush and routine
of my daily life in order to find the rest God prescribed for
Himself and all of humanity."[6]

When I first read those words in 1986, my wife had given
birth to our second child only weeks before. My life as a pastor was out of control. Days were too short and the nights
too long. I was weary, worn and frazzled at the edges, and I
decided that I too must press some Sabbath peace into the
rush and routine of my daily life. Nice thought, but soon
forgotten.

Eight years later I am starting to write this book. Eight years later I'm struggling again with the tyranny of the urgent. Eight years later I'm beginning to believe another shocking insight. Being a Christian, more often than not, seems to get in the way of working as a pastor. And working as a pastor, with surprising frequency, seems to put me at odds with living the Christian life.[7] The urgent squeezes out the important and I've no time left for God.

God Himself is the first rester. "By the seventh day God had finished the work he had been doing; so on the seventh day he rested from all his work. And God blessed the seventh day and made it holy, because on it he rested from all the work of creating that he had done" (Genesis 2:2-3).

Then Moses makes this ordinary comment in Exodus 31:17 that had an extraordinary effect on me: "In six days the LORD made the heavens and the earth, and on the seventh day he abstained from work and rested." *Abstain from work and rest*. As a driven, stereotypical Type-A personality, I desperately needed to abstain from work and rest once a week. Quit trying to be Super Pastor. Stop knocking myself out trying to please people. Rest from my work, just as God rested from His (Hebrews 4:10).

God chose to rest. The Almighty doesn't have to recuperate. But He submitted the creation to a rhythm of work and rest that He Himself modeled for us. On the seventh day He rested. "In this way, He showed us a key to order in our private worlds."[8] This creative-rest is not a luxury for me any longer. It's a necessity. "The Sovereign LORD has given me an instructed tongue, to know the word that sustains the weary" (Isaiah 50:4).

That explores the "doing" part of my ministry as a preacher, pastor and writer. "He wakens me morning by morning, wakens my ear to listen like one being taught. The Sovereign LORD has opened my ears, and I have not been rebellious; I have not drawn back" (Isaiah 50:4-5).

This informs the "being" part of my life as a pilgrim making progress. In order to do and be what God wants for me,

I need to follow His pattern: abstain from work one day in seven and rest.

What accomplisheth ye by this? I interpret my work and press significant meaning into it during this Sabbath time. I make sure I dedicate it all to Jesus. Second, it helps to recalibrate my spirit, measuring the interior life with the unchanging, uncompromising standard of God's truth.

> "We are daily the objects of a bombardment of messages competing for our loyalties and labors. We are pushed and pulled in a thousand different directions asked to make decisions and value judgments, to invest our resources and our time. By what standard of truth do we make these decisions?[9]

Sabbath rest helps me grapple with that portentous question and recalibrate my spirit according to Scripture rather than pop psychology. Finally, during Sabbath I affirm my intentions to pursue personal holiness and a Christ-centered tomorrow.

The pastoral vocation in America is embarrassingly banal. It is banal because it is pursued under the canons of job efficiency and career management. It is banal because it is reduced to the dimensions of a job description. It is banal because it is an idol—a call from God exchanged for an offer by the devil for work that can be measured and manipulated at the convenience of the worker. Holiness is not banal. Holiness is blazing.[10]

As I read Eugene Peterson's words, I had to reckon with myself. "Is this what's happening in my life and ministry, Lord?"

Pastors commonly give lip service to the vocabulary of a holy vocation, but in our working lives we more commonly pursue careers. Our actual work takes shape under the pressure of the marketplace, not the truth of theology or the wisdom of spirituality.[11]

I am seeking to change that in my own life with a refusal to be distracted from entering creative rest when I need it. One day in seven. Care to join me in the pursuit?

The second type of rest that remains is the eternal rest with God. The term "Sabbath-rest" (*sabbatismos*) does not occur before this passage in the New Testament, and Morris states it "looks like the author's own coinage."[12] He didn't have a word to convey what he was thinking, so he made one up! Sabbath-rest. There are various kinds of "rest." The rest the post-Moses generation of Israel enjoyed when they finally made it into the Promised Land. The rest we have when we take a vacation. The rest from wars (Deuteronomy 25:19).

But none of these fit the need of the moment (Hebrews 4:9-11). So he makes up a new word for a new idea. Sabbath-rest. The reality of God's rest was not exhausted by the conquest of Canaan. The spiritual counterpart of the earthly promised land is still the goal of the people of God today.

Entering God's rest takes the right equation: hearing + believing = rest. "For we also have had the gospel preached to us, just as they did; but the message they heard was of no value to them, because those who heard did not combine it with faith. Now we who have believed enter that rest . . ." (Hebrews. 4:2-3).

Remove one part of the equation and the whole thing falls apart. Bees and honey, love and marriage, hearing and faith. They all go together. You can't have one without the other. And when hearing and faith work in tandem, you get rest.

"There remains, then, a Sabbath-rest for the people of God . . ." (Hebrews 4:9). How can we be sure the blessing is for us? Believe in *the promise of God's Word*! "The word of God is living and active. Sharper than any double-edged sword, it penetrates even to dividing soul and spirit, joints and marrow; it judges the thoughts and attitudes of the heart" (Hebrews 4:12).

What God says he will do. That's a promise (Hebrews 4:1)! Second, trust in *the promise of God's character*. "Nothing in all creation is hidden from God's sight. Everything is uncovered and laid bare before the eyes of him to whom we must give account" (Hebrews 4:13).

Think about that for a moment: Nothing is hidden from God's sight. Everything is uncovered and laid bare before His watchful eye. God sees the true picture. He is omnipotent, omniscient and omnipresent. All-powerful. All-knowing. God's character backs up God's Word. All of the attributes of God stand behind His promises for the future. They cannot fail. God's Word will accomplish the purpose for which it was sent.

A little girl from a very poor family was in the hospital. The nurse brought her a glass filled to the brim with cold, fresh milk. This was the first time the girl had a whole glass of milk of her own. At home she always had to share with her brothers and sisters. When the nurse returned to the room, she found the glass of milk still full.

"Why didn't you drink it?" she asked. "Do you need some help?"

"No, ma'am," replied the little girl. "You did not tell me how deep I could drink."

The nurse, who knew how poor the family was, fought back the tears. "Drink all of it," she said tenderly. "Drink all of it. I brought this whole glass just for you."

God wants every true believer to thirst for His Word and "drink all of it." Today, if you hear His voice, do not harden your hearts. Listen carefully to His counsel about rest.

Enter the creative-rest that God offers you, and don't miss the joy of Sabbath activities with your family. Choose to rest and follow the Savior's lead in this. He often withdrew to a quiet place. He sought solitude and seclusion. "While others were lulled to the rest of sleep, Jesus was drawn to the rest of gaining strength and direction for His next phase of ministry."[13]

If you cannot take a full day of rest or if you're a pastor or missionary whose responsibility includes helping others enjoy their Sabbath, then budget part of another day. Totally withdraw if you are able, even if it's only for a few hours.

Hire a babysitter and jealously guard the opportunity for spiritual restoration and renewal. Read Scripture. Listen to music. Write in your journal. Go for a walk with someone and talk about the work of Christ in your lives. Reflect, recalibrate and reaffirm. In other words, rest.

Furthermore, let nothing distract you from the hope of God's eternal rest that awaits you. The Lord sees all your imperfections, but He likes you for always and loves you forever. He knows your great potential for service in the kingdom of God. Layperson, pastor, student, missionary—we are people of the promise—and we will stand firm to the end if we stand on the promises of God. He's put His own name on the contract!

> Standing on the promises of Christ, my
>   King,
> Through eternal ages let His praises ring;
> Glory in the highest, I will shout and sing,
> Standing on the promises of God.

Jesus, the Great High Priest

Therefore, since we have a great high priest who has gone through the heavens, Jesus the Son of God, let us hold firmly to the faith we profess. For we do not have a high priest who is unable to sympathize with our weaknesses, but we have one who has been tempted in every way, just as we are—yet was without sin. Let us then approach the throne of grace with confidence, so that we may receive mercy and find grace to help us in our time of need.

Every high priest is selected from among men and is appointed to represent them in matters related to God, to offer gifts and sacrifices for sins. He is able to deal gently with those who are ignorant and are going astray, since he himself is subject to weakness. This is why he has to offer sacrifices for his own sins, as well as for the sins of the people.

No one takes this honor upon himself; he must be called by God, just as Aaron was. So Christ also did not take upon himself the glory of becoming a high priest. But God said to him,

"You are my Son;
    today I have become your Father."

And he says in another place,

"You are a priest forever,
    in the order of Melchizedek."

During the days of Jesus' life on earth, he offered up prayers and petitions with loud cries and tears to the one who could save him from death, and he was heard because of his reverent submission. Although he was a son, he learned obedience from what he suffered and, once made perfect, he became the source of eternal salvation for all who obey him and was designated by God to be high priest in the order of Melchizedek. (Hebrews 4:14-5:10)

A pair of Gulf-coast fishermen decided to take their boat to a favorite fishing spot several miles offshore. They plotted their course and even carried a depth finder to identify the spot. When they arrived at what they thought was the right area, they turned on the depth finder. They were shocked to discover that they were nowhere near their target. After a quick check, they found out why. One of them had laid a flashlight near the ship's compass, and the magnet in the flashlight had thrown the compass needle way off.

Many people plot their course in life and later discover that they are nowhere near their target. Believers, however, have someone to help them find their way. Jesus Christ is the way and the truth and the life. No one comes to the Father except through Him.

Jesus Christ is our Great High Priest. He has built a bridge between us and God. We need to examine some of the delightful statements in this passage that describe Christ as the Great High Priest—triumphant, gracious, submissive and sufficient for every need!

Our Great High Priest Is Triumphant

> Therefore, since we have a great high priest who
> has gone through the heavens, Jesus the Son of God,
> let us hold firmly to the faith we profess. (Hebrews
> 4:14)

The paragraph beginning at this point is somewhat of a
transition leading to a discussion of Christ's ministry as
High Priest. It is a fitting climax to a chapter on resting, but
perhaps it is best understood as a summary of the previous
passage and a resumption of the thought of Hebrews 3:1-6
which was interrupted by the warning passage.

The sounds of triumph, mastery and conquest are heard
throughout this beautiful letter to the Hebrews that exalts
the superiority of Jesus Christ as Lord. Yet perhaps the first-
century readers were yearning for the Jewish priesthood. So
let them understand that Christians have a High Priest. His
name is Jesus, and they need no other. He has gone through
the heavens (Hebrews 4:14), thus He is out of sight, but He
is actually performing for us what Aaron could accomplish
only in the most limited and largely symbolic and ceremonial way.

The fact that Christ has passed through the heavens and
has figuratively "sat down at the right hand of God" (Acts
2:32-33; Romans 8:34; Colossians 3:1; Hebrews 10:12; 1 Peter 3:22) means that His saving work is complete and successful. He is the superior Priest, since all other priests come
from the ranks of men.

The ascension of Christ was not just a dramatic end to
His earthly ministry. It was God's visible act of vindication,
exaltation and glorification. The fight is over. The battle is
finished. "Thanks be to God! He gives us the victory
through our Lord Jesus Christ" (1 Corinthians 15:57). The
victory is won.

The writer of Hebrews returns to one of his favorite
themes: the exaltation of Jesus. In light of this victory, the

author says, there is no time for cowardice. "Let us hold firmly to the faith we profess" (Hebrews 4:14).

In the town of Stepanavan, Armenia, lives a woman whom everyone calls "Palasan's wife." She has her own name, of course, but townspeople call her by her husband's name to show her great honor.

When the devastating 1988 earthquake struck Armenia, it was nearly noon, and Palasan was at work. He rushed to the elementary school where his son was a student. The facade was already crumbling, but he entered the building and began pushing children outside to safety. After Palasan had managed to help twenty-eight children out, an aftershock hit that completely collapsed the school building and killed him.

So the people of Stepanavan honor his memory and his young widow by calling her Palasan's wife. Sometimes a person's greatest honor is not who he or she is but to whom he or she is related. The highest honor of my life is to be called a disciple of the triumphant "great high priest who has gone through the heavens, Jesus the Son of God."

Our Great High Priest Is Gracious

> For we do not have a·high priest who is unable to sympathize with our weaknesses, but we have one who has been tempted in every way, just as we are— yet was without sin. Let us then approach the throne of grace with confidence, so that we may receive mercy and find grace to help us in our time of need. (Hebrews 4:15-16)

The negative way in which this statement is set forth may suggest that rebuttal is being made to an objection, perhaps by the Jews. Was it being implied that having a high priest in heaven was no substitute for a priest on earth to whom one could go with one's problems?

The author's point here, at any rate, is that Christ's presence in heaven, and His identity as the Son of God, did not remove Him from an understanding of humanity. He knows what it's like! Matthew supports this when he records Jesus' reaction to the crowds one day. "He had compassion on them, because they were harassed and helpless, like sheep without a shepherd" (Matthew 9:36). I am so grateful to the Lord for His gracious compassion!

On Monday, August 9, 1993, a thirty-one-year-old woman, Sophia Mardress White, burst into the hospital nursery at USC Medical Center in Los Angeles brandishing a .38-caliber handgun. She had come gunning for Elizabeth Staten, a nurse whom she accused of stealing her husband. White fired six shots, hitting Staten in the wrist and stomach.

Staten fled, and White followed her into the emergency room, firing once more. There, with blood on her clothes and a hot pistol in her hand, the attacker was met by another nurse, Joan Black, who did the unthinkable. Black walked calmly to the gun-toting woman—and hugged her. The assailant said she didn't have anything to live for, that Staten had stolen her family.

"You're in pain," Black said. "I'm sorry, but everybody has pain in their life. I understand, and we can work it out." As they talked, the hospital invader kept her finger on the trigger. Once she began to lift the gun as though she would blast her brains out. Nurse Black pushed her arm down and continued to hold her. At last Sophia White gave the gun to the nurse. She was disarmed by a hug, by understanding, by compassion.

Black later told an AP reporter, "I saw a sick person and had to take care of her."

Jesus Christ looks upon us in a similar fashion—persons sick and broken inside, in need of His care. His grace and His compassionate embrace disarm us.

Is there anyone today who does not need a compassionate Savior? The Bible says, "The Lord is full of compassion and mercy" (James 5:11), and He offers us true understanding.

Max Lucado tells the story about a boy who went into a pet shop, looking for a puppy:

The store owner showed him a litter in a box. The boy looked at the puppies. He picked each one up, examined it, and put it back into the box.

After several minutes, he walked back to the owner and said, "I picked one out. How much will it cost?"

The man gave him the price, and the boy promised to be back in a few days with the money. "Don't take too long," the owner cautioned. "Puppies like these sell quickly."

The boy turned and smiled knowingly, "I'm not worried," he said. "Mine will still be here."

The boy went to work—weeding, washing windows, cleaning yards. He worked hard and saved his money. When he had enough for the puppy, he returned to the store.

He walked up to the counter and laid down a pocketful of wadded bills. The store owner sorted and counted the cash. After verifying the amount, he smiled at the boy and said, "All right, son, you can go get your puppy."

The boy reached into the back of the box, pulled out a skinny dog with a limp leg, and started to leave.

The owner stopped him.

"Don't take that puppy," he objected. "He's crippled. He can't play. He'll never run with you. He can't fetch. Get one of the healthy pups."

"No, thank you, sir," the boy replied. "This is exactly the kind of dog I've been looking for."

As the boy turned to leave, the store owner started to speak but remained silent. Suddenly he understood. For extending from the bottom of the boy's trousers was a brace—a brace for his crippled leg.[14]

Why did the boy want that dog? Because he knew how it felt. He knew it was very, very special. What did Jesus know that enabled Him to do what He did? He knew how the people felt, and He knew that they were special. When you and I come to our Priest who is in the heavens and call on His name for all our needs, there is an immediate identification with us in the stress and pressure of what we're experiencing. He can sympathize with our weaknesses. All of them. He knows our pain, rejection, loneliness and fear.

Jesus offers you compassion, true understanding and *grace*. Oh, I love to sing about grace! I enjoy preaching about grace. Grace gives people a "Yes" face, a look that summons us closer. I have never seen it, but I can imagine that Jesus had a "Yes" face, too. When we look at Him, He invites us to approach His throne of grace with confidence, so that we may receive mercy and find grace to help us in our time of need. Shall we?

Our Great High Priest Is Submissive

The author of Hebrews indicates that a high priest must be a man who represents man to God and God to man. A "spiritual umpire" of sorts. He must offer sacrifices for sins and be able to deal gently with those he represents. He must be called by God, divinely appointed to his office and not self-made; a submissive, obedient agent for God.

Having made clear what is required of high priests, the author now shows that Jesus has all the right qualifications to be the Great High Priest because He was submissive to the Father's will.

Every high priest is selected from among men and is appointed to represent them in matters related to God, to offer gifts and sacrifices for sins. He is able to deal gently with those who are ignorant and are going astray, since he himself is subject to weakness. This is why he has to offer sacrifices for his own sins, as well as for the sins of the people.

No one takes this honor upon himself; he must be called by God, just as Aaron was. So Christ also did not take upon himself the glory of becoming a high priest. But God said to him,

"You are my Son;
   today I have become your Father."

And he says in another place,

"You are a priest forever,
   in the order of Melchizedek."

During the days of Jesus' life on earth, he offered
up prayers and petitions with loud cries and tears to
the one who could save him from death, and he was
heard because of his reverent submission. Although
he was a son, he learned obedience from what he suffered. . . . (Hebrews 5:1-8)

Jesus demonstrated His submission to the will of the Father
over and over again. In Gethsemane He fell with His face to
the ground and prayed, "My Father, if it is possible, may this
cup be taken from me. Yet not as I will, but as you will" (Matthew 26:39). "He went away a second time and prayed, 'My
Father, if it is not possible for this cup to be taken away unless I
drink it, may your will be done' " (Matthew 26:42).

"During the days of Jeaus' life on earth, he offered up
prayers and petitions with loud cries and tears" to God the
Father, and the text says, "he was heard because of his reverent submission" (Hebrews 5:7).

The word used here for *cry* is *krauge*. Barclay tells us that
it is a cry "which a man does not choose to utter but is
wrung from him in the stress of some tremendous tension or
searing pain."[15] The genuineness of Christ's humanity and
His submission to the Father comes through loud and clear,
wrung from Him in stress. Gethsemane! What a comfort to
know that our Lord fully understands what it's like to cry
out from the bottom of our hearts.

"Although he was a son, he learned obedience from what
he suffered" (Hebrews 5:8). It is not entirely unintelligible
that sons learn obedience by what they suffer at the hands

of earthly fathers. But with Christ it is very different. His Sonship was perfect. So why did He have to learn obedience?

As Guthrie points out, "Here we are faced with the mystery of the nature of Christ. In considering the divine Son it may be difficult to attach any meaning to the learning process . . . but in thinking of the Son as perfect man it becomes at once intelligible."[16]

By a progressive process of submission to the Father's will, Jesus showed His obedience, reaching its climax in death. We are treading now on the holy ground of divine mystery, but the fact of it makes our High Priest's understanding of us unquestionably more real. And if the Lord of lords submitted His heart and mind to the Father above, how much more should we?

In the midst of our dark and foggy times, all sorts of voices are shouting orders into the night, telling us what to do, how to adjust our lives. Out of the darkness, one voice signals something quite opposite to the rest—something almost absurd. But the voice happens to be the Light of the World, and we ignore it at our peril.

Jesus lived a life of reverent submission to the Father. A great example to follow.

Our Great High Priest Is Sufficient

> . . . (Jesus) became the source of eternal salvation for all who obey him and was designated by God to be high priest in the order of Melchizedek. (Hebrews 5:9-10)

We have already been told in Hebrews 2:10 that it was through sufferings that Jesus was made perfect. This perfection was progressively achieved as He moved on toward the cross, which marked the culmination of His suffering and obedience. Christ is fully qualified to be the Savior and High Priest of His people.

The perfection of the Savior's unstained manhood certified Him to endure the incomparable suffering of the cross for us, who, because of our sin, are stained, defeated and in need of salvation. Thus He became the source of eternal salvation for all who obey Him.

In a book titled *Peace Child*, Don Richardson records the moving account of how the Sawi people of Irian Jaya came to understand salvation through Jesus Christ. For many months he and his family sought for some way to communicate the gospel to this tribe. Then they discovered the key for which they had been praying.

All demonstrations of kindness expressed by the Sawi were regarded with suspicion. All except one. If a father gave his own son to his enemy, his sacrificial deed showed that he could be trusted! Furthermore, everyone who touched that child was brought into a friendly relationship with the father. The Sawi were then taught that in a similar way God's beloved Son could effectively bring them eternal peace through His blood.

The writer of Hebrews has made his point forcefully. Jesus shared our human life. Now the author returns to the thought that Jesus was made High Priest by God. He became the source of eternal salvation . . . and, we might add, the only sufficient source of eternal salvation.

In Acts 4:12 we read, "Salvation is found in no one else, for there is no other name under heaven given to men by which we must be saved." As a missionary church, we are deeply concerned about the eschatological fate of unevangelized people. However, Clark Pinnock comments, "Although this is a question that weighs heavily on our minds, Acts 4:12 does not say anything about it." He suggests that "there have been and are lesser instances of saving power at work in the world where Jesus' name is unknown."

In the closing paragraph of the article, Pinnock says:

> Acts 4:12 makes a strong and definitely exclusive claim about the messianic, holistic salvation Jesus has

brought into the world. It is a salvation that is incomparable and without rival. It is available through no other name than Jesus the incarnate Son of God. But the text does not exclude from eternal salvation the vast majority of people who have ever lived on the earth. I myself do not believe they are automatically excluded. . . .[17]

Yet, Jesus Christ Himself said, "I am the way and the truth and the life. No one comes to the Father except through me" (John 14:6). That's hard to argue with. Sounds exclusive to me! How do you read it? Did He mean there might be another way? Is there room for someone else to provide eternal salvation for all who obey?

Acts 4:12, John 14:6 and Hebrews 5:9 seem to indicate that people need to hear about Jesus in order to be saved. There is no other way. Therefore, Jesus' last command to "go and make disciples of all nations, baptizing them in the name of the Father and of the Son and of the Holy Spirit" (Matthew 28:19), must continue to be our first concern.

Hebrews 7 says, ". . . because Jesus lives forever, he has a permanent priesthood. Therefore he is able to save completely those who come to God through him, because he always lives to intercede for them" (7:24-25).

One could easily digress here into a discussion about eternal security. I shall resist the temptation; however, I am happy to know that our salvation is abiding, eternal, forever. "It is something which keeps a man safe both in time and in eternity," wrote William Barclay. "With Christ a man is safe forever. There are no circumstances that can pluck him from Christ's hand."[18]

"Jesus will bring people a salvation that is eternal in its scope and efficacy, a salvation that brings them into the life of the world to come. It is a nice touch that he who learned to obey brought salvation to those who obey."[19]

Somewhat like those fishermen with empty nets (John 21:3), many people plot their course in life and later discover that they are nowhere near their target. But as a Christian, you have a bridge-builder, an intercessor, a High Priest who lives forever. His name is Jesus Christ, and He is forever triumphant, gracious, submissive and sufficient.

He is triumphant because He has already won the war for us, gracious in allowing us to approach Him with confidence in our time of need, submissive to the highest will of the Father and forever sufficient as the source of eternal salvation for all who obey Him.

But you are facing situations in your own life that are bewildering and confusing. Wondering where God is in all this mess. Physical problems, emotional problems, financial problems, family problems. Sometimes counseling helps. Sometimes talking with another Christian believer helps. Reading a good book may bring relief. But often the only solution is reverent submission. We don't understand it, and we don't have all the answers, but we trust *Him* to work it out.

Elisha Hoffman said it well:

> You have longed for sweet peace,
>   and for faith to increase,
> And have earnestly, fervently prayed;
> But you cannot have rest,
>   or be perfectly blest,
> Until all on the altar is laid.
> Is your all on the altar of sacrifice laid?
> Your heart, does the Spirit control?
> You can only be blest and have peace
>   and sweet rest,
> As you yield Him your body and soul.

To one who asked him the secret of his service, George Muller said: "There was a day when I died, utterly died." As he spoke he bent lower and lower until he almost touched the floor. " . . . died to George Muller, his opinions, preferences, tastes, and will—died to the world, its approval or censure—died to the approval or blame even of my brethren and friends—and since then I have studied only to show myself approved unto God."[20]

Jesus is the great High Priest. Please don't plot your course in life according to the pattern of this world. You will soon discover that you are nowhere near the target God has set up for you. Instead, come to the secret garden of reverent submission. Taste and see that the Lord is good. Dine with Him and He will dine with you. Ascribe to the Lord glory and strength. Give Him the government of your heart today.

Endnotes

1. *Leadership* (Winter 1993): 49. Used by permission.

2. Philip Edgcumbe Hughes, *A Commentary on the Epistle to the Hebrews* (Grand Rapids, MI: Eerdmans Publishing Company, 1977), 155.

3. *Leadership* (Fall 1990): 48. Used by permission.

4. F.F. Bruce, *The Epistle to the Hebrews* (Grand Rapids, MI: Eerdmans Publishing Company, 1964), 78.

5. Leon Morris, *Hebrews, The Expositor's Bible Commentary*, Vol. 12, ed. Frank E. Gaebelein (Grand Rapids, MI: Zondervan, 1981), 43.

6. Gordon MacDonald, *Ordering Your Private World* (Nashville, TN: Thomas Nelson Publishers, 1984), 172.

7. Eugene H. Peterson, *Under the Unpredictable Plant: An Exploration in Vocational Holiness* (Grand Rapids, MI: Eerdmans, 1992), 2. © Eugene H. Peterson, 1992. Used by permission.

8. Gordon MacDonald, 176.

9. Ibid., 179.

10. Eugene H. Peterson, 5.

11. Ibid.

12. Leon Morris, 42

13. Gordon MacDonald, 182.

14. Max Lucado, *In the Eye of the Storm* (Dallas, TX: Word Publishing, 1991), 48-49. Used by permission.

15. William Barclay, *The Letter to the Hebrews*, rev. ed. (Philadelphia, PA: The Westminster Press, 1976), 47.

16. Donald Guthrie, *Hebrews* (Grand Rapids, MI: Eerdmans, 1983), 130-131.

17. Clark Pinnock, "Acts 4:12—No Other Name Under Heaven" in *Through No Fault of Their Own?*, eds. William V. Crockett and James G. Sigountos (Grand Rapids, MI: Baker Book House, 1991), 107-115.

18. William Barclay, 48.

19. Leon Morris, 50.

20. Paul Lee Tan, *Encyclopedia of 7700 Illustrations* (Chicago, IL: R.R. Donnelley and Sons, Inc., 1979), 1366.

Discussion Questions for Further Study

1. What four exhortations does the author give his readers in Hebrews 4:1-16?

2. The Israelites failed to enter God's rest. But how do we know that the promised rest is still available to those with faith?

3. The statement that "anyone who enters God's rest also rests from his own work" (4:10) has been interpreted as having a present application, a future application or both. What do the following cross references reveal about the rest that is available both now and in the future? (Matthew 11:28-30, Romans 5:1-2, Revelation 14:13, 21:1-4)

4. As an eternal High Priest, Christ achieved eternal atonement and salvation (5:9). Why is this salvation available only to those who "obey him"?

5. What aspect of this chapter of the book seems most personally relevant to you? How would you like this truth to affect your life?

5

Hebrews 5:11-6:20

Evidence of Immaturity

We have much to say about this, but it is hard to explain because you are slow to learn. In fact, though by this time you ought to be teachers, you need someone to teach you the elementary truths of God's word all over again. You need milk, not solid food! Anyone who lives on milk, being still an infant, is not acquainted with the teaching about righteousness. But solid food is for the mature, who by constant use have trained themselves to distinguish good from evil.

Therefore let us leave the elementary teachings about Christ and go on to maturity, not laying again the foundation of repentance from acts that lead to death, and of faith in God, instruction about baptisms, the laying on of hands, the resurrection of the dead, and eternal judgment. And God permitting, we will do so. (Hebrews 5:11-6:3)

Bertoldo de Giovanni. A name even the most enthusiastic lover of art is unlikely to recognize. He was the pupil of Donatello, the greatest sculptor of his time, and he was the teacher of Michelangelo, probably the greatest sculptor of all time.

Michelangelo was only fourteen years old when he came to Bertoldo, but it was already obvious that he was gifted.

Bertoldo was wise enough to realize that people are often tempted to coast rather than to grow, and therefore he pressured and pushed Michelangelo to work seriously at his art—pressured him to do his best—pressured him to grow instead of coast.

One day, he came into the studio to find Michelangelo toying with a piece of sculpture far beneath his abilities. Bertoldo grabbed a hammer, stomped across the room and smashed the work into tiny pieces, shouting this unforgettable message, "Michelangelo, talent is cheap. Dedication is costly!"

It is always easier to coast than to grow, and that's why the writer of Hebrews seeks to encourage his readers. He wants them to grow in maturity, to grow in their walk with God, to grow in their understanding of the Word of God. We must never be satisfied with the status quo. Instead, we should press on to better things in the Lord.

There are five specific warnings peppered throughout the letter to the Hebrews. This is the third of that series and it seems to interrupt the main discussion. Included is some of the severest language in Scripture directed against God's people. Most commentators agree that the warning begins at 5:11 and continues throughout most of chapter 6. The author approaches his goal by exposing several deadly characteristics of immaturity.

Indolence

> We have much to say about this, but it is hard to explain because you are slow to learn. (Hebrews 5:11)

The writer of Hebrews implies that spiritual immaturity stems from spiritual neglect. Simply put, these people were lazy. Their original eagerness to hear and respond to the Word of God had cooled. How can the writer begin to explain the deeper things of God when they have lost their appetite for Christian truth? It would be impossible for them to comprehend what it means for Christ's ministry to be "in the order of Melchizedek" (Hebrews 5:10) when they had misplaced their passion for the complex truth of God's resplendent revelation!

Slow to learn. The word literally means "sluggish, or lazy," and it was used of lazy men who refused to tackle hard work. He uses the word again in 6:12. "We do not want you to become lazy, but to imitate those who through faith and patience inherit what has been promised."

Picture a person who has developed a "couldn't care less" attitude toward the study and application of God's Word in his day-to-day life, and you'll have the right idea. It means slow-moving in mind. Torpid in understanding. Dull of hearing. Witlessly forgetful.

It can be used of the numbed limbs of an animal which is ill. It can be used of a person who has the imperceptive nature of a stone.[1] They were not naturally slow learners or developmentally delayed. No diagnosed learning disabilities. They just got lazy. That's a *learned* behavior. Other interests and distractions had captured their attention.

The writer points his Holy Spirit-inspired finger into the faces of his adult readers and says to them, "Grow up!" The scene is pathetic and pitiful. Lazy, sluggish adults playing with ABC building blocks in the nursery of theology ought to be ashamed of themselves. These people ought to know better (and so should we!). Yet they do not seem to connect with the deeper things of God.

They were born again, but they were immature because they were spiritually lazy and they failed to grow up as they grew older. This is a peril that many believers fall into, and woe to the preacher or the missionary who does so. Our people will forgive us for many mistakes, but they will not forgive us for laziness in the Word or sluggishness in our walk with the Lord.

It happens when we dodge teaching something because it is demanding or difficult to teach, unpalatable or distasteful to our audience. We may defend ourselves by saying,

"Those teens cannot grasp this anyway," "This will never increase attendance" or "Our people aren't ready for this yet."

Even though the old story has been told and retold, I'm always encouraged by one part of the *Mutiny on the Bounty*— the part about the transformation brought on by the Word of God. Nine mutineers with six men and twelve women (Tahitians) put ashore on Pitcairn Island in 1790.

One sailor soon began distilling alcohol and the little colony was plunged into debauchery and vice. Ten years later, only one white man survived, surrounded by native women and children of mixed race.

In an old chest from the *Bounty*, this sailor one day found a Bible. He began to read it and then to teach it to the others. The result was that his own life and ultimately the lives of all those in the colony were changed. Discovered in 1808 by the *USS Topas*, Pitcairn had become a prosperous community with no jail, no whisky, no crime and no laziness.

You may be striving for change in your walk with the Lord; you want a transformation. However, it's much easier to coast than it is to grow spiritually. The writer of Hebrews inspires us to grow up, mature in our faith and avoid becoming sluggish. Don't be slow to learn or dull of hearing. Indolence is one of the deadly characteristics of spiritual immaturity.

Incompetence

> In fact, though by this time you ought to be teachers, you need someone to teach you the elementary truths of God's word all over again. You need milk, not solid food!" (Hebrews 5:12)

He complains that *by this time*, that is, taking into account the substantial period of time that has elapsed since their conversion, *they ought to be teachers*. That doesn't mean that they all should be in official teaching positions in the church, but rather that they ought by now to be acceptably advanced in their grasp of Christian dogma to be able to instruct and edify those who are still young in the faith.

However, they are so far from having maintained normal progress that they have slipped back into a position where they are themselves in need of a teacher to instruct them again in the first principles of God's Word. They need to repeat the pastor's Welcome Class. Like children in kindergarten who are unable to read or write, they have to start at the very beginning by learning the ABCs.[2]

Spiritual laziness leads to spiritual incompetence and ineffectiveness. The leadership potential had been neutralized. They turned their backs on strenuous study and diligent application of the truth. They remained like babies when they ought to have been adults, pupils when they could have been instructors, VDPs (Very Draining Persons) in need of help when they could have been VRPs (Very Resourceful Persons) offering help to others.

The writer says they still needed someone to teach them the "elementary truths" (*stoicheia*) of God's Word all over again. This word has a variety of meanings, according to Barclay. In grammar it means the letters of the alphabet, the ABCs; in physics it means the elements of proof like the point and the straight line; in philosophy it means the first elementary principles with which the student begins.

Sorrow has come to the heart of the writer to the Hebrews. After many years of Christianity his people have never passed the rudiments, the simple foundational truths of the Word. They are like children who don't know the difference between right and wrong, left and right, A and Z.[3]

Apparently a similar condition also appeared in Corinth. Paul writes to the brothers there: "I could not address you as spiritual but as worldly—mere infants in Christ. I gave you milk, not solid food, for you were not yet ready for it. Indeed, you are still not ready" (1 Corinthians 3:1-2). It's bad enough that they were not as far along as they should have been, but it's worse that they could not pass on what they knew. They had become spiritually impotent.

People who have had an arm in a cast for a lengthy period of time can tell you what happens when the plaster is finally removed. The muscles have shrunk and become weak because they have not been used. A lack of exercise greatly diminishes power and effectiveness. A lack of spiritual exercise in God's Word will greatly diminish our power and effectiveness, too.

On June 6, 1981, Doug Whitt and his bride, Sylvia, were escorted to their hotel's fancy bridal suite in the wee hours of the morning. In the suite they saw a sofa, chairs and table, but where was the bed?

Then they discovered the sofa was a hide-a-bed, with a lumpy mattress and sagging springs. They spent a fitful night and woke up in the morning with sore backs. The new husband went to the hotel desk and gave the management a tongue-lashing. "Did you open the door in the room?" asked the clerk. Doug went back to the room. He opened the door they had thought was a closet. There, complete with fruit basket and chocolates, was a beautiful bedroom![4]

Opening all the doors in a honeymoon suite is like obeying all the words of Jesus and becoming all He wants us to be. That's critical for all who want to become mature and productive and effective in His service. "In fact, though by this time you ought to be teachers, you need someone to teach you the elementary truths of God's word all over again. You need milk, not solid food!" Ouch! That is a stinging rebuke from God's Spirit today. Our churches are plagued by people who refuse to grow up. Professional weaker brothers contaminate the religious scene.

It may be easier to coast than it is to grow spiritually, but that should not prevent us from opening the doors and walking into the throne room of grace. Trust the Lord for all you need. He's an eager Father who seeks those who will worship Him in spirit and in truth.

Carelessness

> Anyone who lives on milk, being still an infant, is not
> acquainted with the teaching about righteousness.
> But solid food is for the mature, who by constant use
> have trained themselves to distinguish good from evil.
> (Hebrews 5:13-14)

Here the author explains his reference to milk and solids. This is the way it is: Anyone occupied with elementary truths is spiritually still an infant and must be treated as such. These people were indifferent to the deeper things of God and they had developed some careless habits that prevented healthy development. They perfected a thirst for milk rather than a hunger for solid meat. They emphasized information without application. They preferred to remain babies under a protected shelter rather than to move out and live as soldiers for Jesus Christ.

The writer says the mature believer trains herself to "distinguish good from evil." Spiritual faculties have to be trained. The Greek word for "trained" is *gegymnasmena*, from which we get the word gymnasium. Discernment demands training and discipline, not indifference, nonchalance or carelessness, because carelessness carries consequences. Just ask Julie.

When Julie bought Bandit she thought he was irresistible. No raccoon that ever existed had more natural cuteness than this ninety-day-old bundle of mischief. Julie was sure they would be lifelong friends. Everywhere she went, he perched on her shoulder. Bandit's habit of holding Julie's cheeks in his paws and looking into her eyes with sparkling curiosity always melted her.

And he grew. Eighteen months passed and Bandit became a strapping twenty-five-pound adolescent raccoon, still full of the dickens and only slightly less playful. He still loved affection, rode on her shoulders and seemed to be a glowing advertisement that raccoons make great pets.

Why don't more people keep raccoons as pets? According to a zoo veterinarian, "they undergo a glandular change at about twenty-four months. After that, they become unpredictable, independent and often attack their owners."

Someone broke the news to Julie. "It will be different for me. Bandit is different." She smiled as she added, "Bandit wouldn't hurt me. He just wouldn't." Three months later, Julie underwent plastic surgery for facial lacerations sustained when her adult raccoon attacked her for no apparent reason. Bandit was released into the wild.

Maybe you've heard Julie's careless reply, too. "It will be different for me."

Rob, a sixteen-year-old boy, said, "I know what I'm doing. It's different for me. I know all about dosages and stuff. My dad's a pharmacist." Rob overdosed six months later and spent two months in a psychiatric ward.

Judy, a young woman who should have known better, argued: "I know he's been around, but it's different with us. He really loves me. He really does." Judy is now twenty-five and living at home with her nine-year-old son. The son never met his father.

Pat is a thirty-five-year-old woman. "My kids are different. They will be able to handle the divorce fine. I'll spend more time with them. Besides, my lover is great with kids." Pat divorced her husband and got remarried to her lover. She divorced again after he tried to kill her. The children haven't slept well for years and need to see a counselor weekly.[5]

Carelessness. Heavy consequences, no? Lack of training diminishes the ability to distinguish good and evil. Olympic athletes do not work out once a month or once a week. They train every single day, for several hours every day. They eat wholesome, nutritious food.

Maturity in the Christian life also requires good food. We need more than a bottled formula supplied by someone else. With our own utensils, we need to reach into the full plate of God's Word.

In this section of Hebrews, the author has published the ugly portrait of spiritual immaturity. With the power of an inspired artist, he illustrates what indolence, incompetence and carelessness do to the life of Christ in us.

Spiritual immaturity takes practice, though. It doesn't happen overnight. Maturity also requires practice. Application. Training. Exercise. Too much of what we hear stays only in our heads. If the input exceeds the output, then the upkeep becomes our downfall. It is easier to coast than it is to grow. Talent is cheap. Dedication is costly, but that's exactly what the Lord expects from us.

Mark Reed tells a beautiful story that illustrates what I've been trying to say:

> Eating lunch at a small cafe, I saw a sparrow hop through the open door and peck at the crumbs near my table. When the crumbs were gone, the sparrow hopped to the window ledge, spread its wings and took flight. Brief flight. It crashed against the window pane and fell to the floor.
>
> The bird quickly recovered and tried again. Crash. And again. Crash.
>
> I got up and attempted to shoo the sparrow out the door, but the closer I got the harder it threw itself against the pane. I nudged it with my hand. That sent the sparrow fluttering along the ledge, hammering its beak at the glass.
>
> Finally, I reached out and gently caught the bird, folding my fingers around its wings and body. It weighed almost nothing. I thought of how powerless and vulnerable the sparrow must have felt. At the door I released it, and the sparrow sailed away.[6]

God takes us captive only to set us free. The price He paid to set us free is great—too great to ignore. Much too great to treat with contempt or neglect, laziness or carelessness. How about you, my friend? Are you growing up in the

Lord, or are you just growing older? Are you merely adding years to your life, or adding life to your years? If you teach Sunday school or preach the Word, are you meeting the challenge or giving in to apathy and indifference?

The Winter 1991 issue of *The University of Pacific Review* offers a chilling description of the 1986 Chernobyl nuclear disaster:

> There were two electrical engineers in the control room that night, and the best thing that could be said for what they were doing is they were "playing around" with the machine. They were performing what the Soviets later described as an unauthorized experiment. They were trying to see how long a turbine would "free wheel" when they took the power off it.
>
> Now, taking the power off that kind of a nuclear reactor is a difficult, dangerous thing to do, because these reactors are very unstable in their lower ranges. In order to get the reactor down to that kind of power, where they could perform the test they were interested in performing, they had to override manually six separate computer-driven alarm systems. One by one the computers would come up and say, "Stop! Dangerous! Go no further!" And one by one, rather than shutting off the experiment, they shut off the alarms and kept going. You know the results: nuclear fallout that was recorded all around the world, from the largest industrial accident ever to occur in the world.[7]

The instructions and warnings in Scripture are just as clear. We ignore them at our own peril, and tragically, at the peril of innocent others.

Let's go on to maturity. Let's face the challenges of laziness, ineffectiveness and carelessness in the church and in our own personal lives, and let's move out for God. Let's get more accomplished for the kingdom. Let's get going, and let's get growing.

The Marks of Apostasy

> *It is impossible for those who have once been enlightened, who have tasted the heavenly gift, who have shared in the Holy Spirit, who have tasted the goodness of the word of God and the powers of the coming age, if they fall away, to be brought back to repentance, because to their loss they are crucifying the Son of God all over again and subjecting him to public disgrace.*
>
> *Land that drinks in the rain often falling on it and that produces a crop useful to those for whom it is farmed receives the blessing of God. But land that produces thorns and thistles is worthless and is in danger of being cursed. In the end it will be burned. (Hebrews 6:4-8)*

The writer of this epistle has been busy exposing the deadly characteristics of spiritual immaturity, and some of us have been quivering at the prospect. Now he proceeds to underscore the seriousness of apostasy from the faith and of failure to make any spiritual progress, deeply concerned that some of his readers had become lazy, ineffective and careless, and that some of them were in real danger of falling away from the grace of God. "It is impossible for a Christian to stand still. He either progresses in the faith or slips back."[8]

Doctrinal ignorance and spiritual immaturity can lead to serious disasters. Apparently some of the recipients of this letter were not merely drifting morally or ethically. Not mere chronic invalids or spiritual casualties. They had actually become fierce opponents of the Christian gospel, "crucifying the Son of God all over again and subjecting him to public disgrace" (Hebrews 6:6). They had become apostates.

Understandably, some members of this church (not unlike some of us) had become worried about the destiny of those

who had fallen away, and the writer finds it necessary to say
something about this matter of concern. William Barclay
calls Hebrews 6:4-8 "one of the most terrible passages in
Scripture."[9]

Homer Kent says this paragraph "is one of the most dis-
puted in the New Testament."[10] It has caused many sleep-
less nights for some believers, and the misunderstanding
and misinterpretation of these verses have caused untold
havoc.

Who are these people? What are they like? What have
they done?

Spurns God's Gifts

> It is impossible for those who have once been en-
> lightened, who have tasted the heavenly gift, who
> have shared in the Holy Spirit, who have tasted the
> goodness of the word of God and the powers of the
> coming age, if they fall away, to be brought back to
> repentance.... (Hebrews 6:4-5)

The men and women in view had been "enlightened." To
be enlightened evidently corresponds to receiving "the
knowledge of the truth" (Hebrews 10:26, 32). At the beginning they had been miraculously and mercifully "enlightened," but now their vision was dimmed.

Some see in this phrase a reference to baptism, for this
verb was apparently used of baptism in the second century.
But it is not attested as early as this, and so it is better to interpret the term in connection with John 1:9, "The true light
that gives light to every man was coming into the world."
The bright light of Christ's illuminating presence had shone
into the dark corners of their hearts and the shadowy recesses of their minds.

They had "tasted the heavenly gift," the gift of God's enriching provision. This phrase, difficult to interpret in this
context, may simply refer to the blessing which God freely

and graciously bestows in Christ. Also notice how the metaphor of light is followed by that of food.

Jesus is the gift of God, the bread of heaven, the manna come down to earth, the only true satisfying food for eternal life. How sad to think that some believers could experience the goodness of God's gift in Christ Jesus to some degree and then spurn it, scorn it and reject it. Once the spiritual appetite becomes preoccupied with godless concerns, how difficult to bring it back to heartfelt repentance!

Furthermore, these people had "shared in the Holy Spirit" (Hebrews 6:4). By God's astonishing and sometimes staggering generosity these people had become partakers of the Holy Spirit. Yet now they forcefully and comprehensively disown this Spirit of grace. How can they hope to alter their ways and be led back to God if they reject the only One who can bring them home?

In the past they had also "tasted the goodness of the word of God" (6:5). So far, every chapter in this epistle to the Hebrews has had something to say about holy Scripture and our response to it. These people had experienced the Word of God in the gospel and found it good and satisfying, but now they could no longer see Christ in the pages of Scripture. They had tasted the goodness of the Lord, but now they have turned their backs on Him. As a result God's Word had become sour upon their lips.

When the gospel is received and "tasted," certain powers of the coming age are also witnessed (Hebrews 6:5). Yet now they trampled these treasures underfoot. Peter says it would have been better for such rebellious and seditious apostates "not to have known the way of righteousness, than to have known it and then to turn their backs on the sacred command that was passed on to them" (2 Peter 2:21).

Let's go back and get the full force of what the writer is saying to us. "It is impossible for those who have once been enlightened, who have tasted the heavenly gift, who have shared in the Holy Spirit, who have tasted the goodness of

the word of God and the powers of the coming age, if they
fall away, to be brought back to repentance . . . " (Hebrews
6:4-6). These men and women have been numbered among
the followers of Christ. But now they leave that company.
Such people cannot be brought back to repentance. Leon
Morris comments:

> Notice that he does not say "cannot be forgiven" or
> "cannot be restored to salvation" or the like. It is re-
> pentance that is in mind, and the writer says that it is
> impossible for these people to repent. This might
> mean that the repentance that involves leaving a
> whole way of life to embrace the Christian way is
> unique.
>
> In the nature of the case, it cannot be repeated.
> There is no putting the clock back. But it seems more
> likely that the reference is to a repentance that means
> leaving the backsliding into which the person has
> fallen. He cannot bring himself to this repentance.[11]

They despise God's gracious gifts, and genuine repentance for these people is not only difficult, but according to
the Bible it is impossible. As F.F. Bruce puts it, "God has
pledged himself to pardon all who truly repent, but Scripture and experience alike suggest that it is possible for human beings to arrive at a state of heart and life where they
can no longer repent."[12]

Repudiates God's Son

> [It is impossible] if they fall away, to be brought back
> to repentance, because to their loss they are crucify-
> ing the Son of God all over again and subjecting him
> to public disgrace. (Hebrews 6:6)

Apparently, these people had once turned to the cross in
anguish and found some sense of relief. But now they de-

nounce Christ and hold Him up to contempt, as did the law-less and godless mob who mocked Him on that first Good Friday. This highly condensed verse underscores the gravity of their offense. They disowned His deity.

It is *the Son of God* they crucified afresh, the Son who re-veals the Father and sustains the universe. These people did not simply refuse to subscribe to an essential doctrine, they abused Christ and insulted Him. They despised His beauty. They subjected Him to public disgrace. They repudiated the only One who gave His life for them.

They took their place among those who cried, "Crucify Him, crucify Him." They actively and purposely walked with those who blasphemed the Holy Spirit by attributing the works of Christ to Satan. In heart and mind they delib-erately become one with those who drove the nails through His hands and feet.

Did they drift into this lifestyle by mistake? No way! They made a knowledgeable, conscious decision to turn away from God, and as a result, they cannot be brought back to repentance. It is too late. They rejected God's Son; thus they rejected the only valid plan for salvation.

"Salvation is found in no one else, for there is no other name under heaven given to men by which we must be saved" (Acts 4:12). If you reject the Son, you reject eternal life. Jesus Christ is the way, the truth and the life. No one comes to the Father except through Him.

Between an airplane and every other form of transporta-tion there is one great contrast. The horse and wagon, the automobile, the bicycle, the diesel locomotive, the speed-boat, the greatest battleship that plies the seas—all can come to a standstill without danger. And they can all reverse their engines, or their power, and go back.

But there is no reverse about the engine of an airplane. It cannot back up. It dare not stand still. If it loses its momen-tum and forward drive, then it crashes. The only safety for an airplane is in its forward and upward motion. The only safe direction for the Christian to take is forward and Son-

ward. If he begins to repudiate the Son of God, that moment
he is in very grave danger.

Relinquishes God's Favor

> Land that drinks in the rain often falling on it and
> that produces a crop useful to those for whom it is
> farmed receives the blessing of God. But land that
> produces thorns and thistles is worthless and is in
> danger of being cursed. In the end it will be burned.
> (Hebrews 6:7-8)

The author brings this pastoral warning to a close by using a colorful parable drawn from agricultural life. It is probably dependent on some Old Testament Scripture as well.
For example, Isaiah 5:1-7 talks about the gardener who had a
vineyard on a fertile hillside. He dug it up and cleared it of
stones and planted it with the choicest vines. He built a
watchtower in it and cut out a winepress as well. Then he
looked for a crop of good grapes, but it yielded only bad
fruit. That vineyard received all the attention that any vineyard could have received, but it produced nothing but bad
fruit.

Believers who persevere in faith and commit themselves
to spiritual growth and development are like the fertile land
which produces fruit. It brings great joy to the farmer. They
enjoy God's favor. On the other hand, those who have been
touched by and then despise God's gifts, rejecting His Son
and spurning His love, are compared to land that produces
only thorns and thistles. The inevitable consequence? Judgment.

Both types of land, good and bad, genuine and apostate,
have received the rain that often falls upon it (cf. Matthew
5:45). The blessings of God's rich goodness have come to
both. However, one produces a harvest of righteousness,
peace and joy, and receives a blessing from God. The other
bears only useless and even harmful thorns and thistles.

In other words, those who turn their backs on God's gifts and God's Son will forfeit God's blessing. They will, in fact, face His judgment. Some commentators think the author of Hebrews knew very little about agriculture because the burning of a field was not a curse but rather a blessing because it got rid of all the weeds. However, his point is that land that produces nothing but weeds will face nothing but fire.

It is probably true to say that these warnings in Hebrews have caused more unnecessary anxiety to believers than almost any other verses in the New Testament. Aware of moral failure or spiritual apathy, thoughtful Christians the world over have been haunted by this passage. Some have been driven to despair at the thought that they may have forfeited forever the blessings of the gospel.

Warren Wiersbe has written, "I have received long-distance phone calls from disturbed people who have misread this passage and convinced themselves (or been convinced by Satan) that they were hopelessly lost and had committed some unpardonable sin."[13]

In a Christian magazine that comes to our home, I read this question, written to a Christian counselor:

> Our middle daughter has chosen to reject our faith and do things she knows are wrong. She's living with a twice-divorced man and apparently has no intention of marrying him. She has had at least two abortions that we know about, and her language is disgraceful. My wife and I have prayed until we're exhausted, and yet she has shown no interest in returning to the church. At times, I become very angry at God for allowing this terrible thing to happen. I have wept until there are just no more tears. Can you offer us any encouragement?[14]

Maybe you're painfully aware of people in your family or in your church who began the Christian life with fine prom-

ise and immense spiritual potential. But these professed believers, with such a rich spiritual life expectancy, have since
turned their backs on Christ. Most Christians know of people who were once warmhearted colleagues, but are now
adrift without anchor or aim. What happened? What's the
explanation for such a set of circumstances?[15]

When all is said and done, I must remember that better
theologians and people more godly than I have discussed
and dissected this passage for centuries. Since the earliest
days of its ministry, the denomination I'm affiliated with always has been made up of people holding differing doctrinal
positions.

I think I can safely say that we are all committed to the
great fundamentals of the faith, such as the inerrancy of
Holy Scripture, the deity of Christ, the lostness of those
who are not followers of Jesus, to name a few. But in some
other matters we differ.

Some are sure that Christ will rapture His Church before the Great Tribulation; others believe the Church will
go through it, and a few believe in a mid-tribulation rapture. We differ concerning worship styles, the use of
hymnbooks or overhead transparencies in a service and the
ordination of women. Some believe that anyone who receives Jesus as her Savior is eternally secure. Others feel
that a person can turn his back on Christ and lose his salvation.

As much as I enjoy debating the finer points of theology
and as much as I enjoy the intellectual pursuit of such matters, I must discipline myself to bow in the presence of
mystery and the Almighty. My purpose in this chapter
was not to demonstrate that one view is right and the other
wrong, but to warn us all with the very words of holy
Scripture and to plead with my brothers and sisters in
Christ to walk in a manner worthy of the gospel of our precious Savior.

We need to ask ourselves and our loved ones, "Are we
flirting with this danger? Have we begun to drift danger-

ously near a point of no return? What do I need to do to return to my first love? Are there more thorns than fruit being produced in my life?"

I pray that we will all heed this warning and produce a useful crop for Jesus Christ and receive the bountiful blessing of God.

Pursue the Better Things!

> *Even though we speak like this, dear friends, we are confident of better things in your case—things that accompany salvation. God is not unjust; he will not forget your work and the love you have shown him as you have helped his people and continue to help them. We want each of you to show this same diligence to the very end, in order to make your hope sure. We do not want you to become lazy, but to imitate those who through faith and patience inherit what has been promised.*
>
> *When God made his promise to Abraham, since there was no one greater for him to swear by, he swore by himself, saying, "I will surely bless you and give you many descendants." And so after waiting patiently, Abraham received what was promised.*
>
> *Men swear by someone greater than themselves, and the oath confirms what is said and puts an end to all argument. Because God wanted to make the unchanging nature of his purpose very clear to the heirs of what was promised, he confirmed it with an oath. God did this so that, by two unchangeable things in which it is impossible for God to lie, we who have fled to take hold of the hope offered to us may be greatly encouraged. We have this hope as an anchor for the soul, firm and secure. It enters the inner sanctuary behind the curtain, where Jesus, who went before us, has entered on our behalf. He has become a high priest forever, in the order of Melchizedek. (Hebrews 6:9-20)*

The preceding section carried warnings about the dangers of apostasy. We must make progress along the way or suffer disaster. There are no other possibilities. Sitting on the fence is a modern concept that has no foundation in the Word of God.

Now the writer of Hebrews goes on to say that he has confidence in his first-century readers. The warning has been necessary. But he does not think they will fall away. "Even though we speak like this, dear friends, we are confident of better things in your case—things that accompany salvation" (Hebrews 6:9).

Even though he has had some tough things to say to his readers, he speaks tenderly to them now, addressing them for the only time in this epistle as "dear friends." There's an absence of skepticism or exasperation and a movement toward affirmation.

However, he takes advantage of the opportunity to exhort them all to go forward, to keep growing, to show progress, to pursue the better things that God has in store. He turns from the ministry of warning to encourage them that God's justice is perfect and that God's promise is reliable.

God's Perfect Justice

> God is not unjust; he will not forget your work and the love you have shown him as you have helped his people and continue to help them. (Hebrews 6:10)

If God were to forget your work and love and how you have helped His people, He would be unrighteous, unjust, in conflict with His own being. God cannot possibly cast aside and disregard what has been done and is being done because of love to His name. However, God is not bound by human obligations.

Salvation is not founded on works, and God is not in the position of being our debtor here. It is clear everywhere in Scripture that there is no other fount of salvation but the free mercy of God (Acts 4:12; Ephesians 2:8-9; 1 Timothy 1:16; 1 Peter 1:3, 2:10; Jude 21).

"But when the kindness and love of God our Savior appeared, he saved us, not because of righteous things we had done, but because of his mercy" (Titus 3:4-5). The fact that God here and there promises rewards for works depends on the free promise by which He adopts us as sons and reconciles us to Himself by not imputing our sins to us.

"A reward is laid up for works not through merit but out of the sheer bounty of God, and even this gratuitous recognition of works has no place except after our reception into grace through the mercy of Christ."[16]

A masterful understatement! "God is not unjust!" The author's confidence of better things rests solely on the consistent justice of Almighty God. He will not forget your work. He will not forget the love you have shown Him as you have helped His people.

Your profession of faith in Jesus Christ has resulted in good works that glorify the Father in heaven, and this will not go unnoticed. He will remember you because He is not unjust, and His mercy is greater than you can imagine.

Lee Iacocca once asked legendary football coach Vince Lombardi what it took to make a winning team. The book *Iacocca* records Lombardi's answer:

> "There are a lot of coaches with good ball clubs who know the fundamentals and have plenty of discipline but still don't win the game. Then you come to the third ingredient: if you're going to play together as a team, you've got to care for one another. You've got to *love* each other. Each player has to be thinking about the next guy and saying to himself: 'If I don't block that man, Paul is going to get his legs broken. I have to do my job well in order that he can do his.'
>
> "The difference between mediocrity and greatness," Lombardi said that night, "is the feeling these guys have for each other."[17]

In the healthy church, each Christian learns to care for others. As we take seriously Jesus' command to love each other, we contribute to a winning team. And better yet, "God is not unjust; he will not forget your work and the love you have shown him as you have helped his people and continue to help them" (Hebrews 6:10).

We do not teach a works-salvation. We are not saved by what we do for God. "For it is by grace you have been saved, through faith—and this not from yourselves, it is the gift of God—not by works, so that no one can boast" (Ephesians 2:8-9). Yet in evangelical circles we sometimes underestimate the power of faith-filled deeds done in the name of Christ.

Major Osipovich, an air force pilot for the former USSR, planned to give a talk at his children's school about peace. But he would need time off during the day to give his talk, so he volunteered for night duty. And that's how Major Osipovich found himself patrolling the skies over the eastern regions of the Soviet Union on September 1, 1983—the night Korean Air Lines Flight KE007 strayed into Soviet air space.

Soon the Soviet pilot was caught in a series of blunders and misinformation. In the end, Major Osipovich followed orders and shot down the unidentified aircraft. The actions of an air force major preparing to talk about peace plunged 240 passengers to their deaths and sparked an international incident that pushed world powers to a standoff.

Our talk is important. But our actions carry far more weight. God says when we have helped His people and continue to help them, then we are actually showing love to Him (Hebrews 6:10). That kind of action carries a lot of weight. And because He is just, He will not forget your work. Take heart, my friend, and go another round.

"Let us not become weary in doing good, for at the proper time we will reap a harvest if we do not give up. Therefore, as we have opportunity, let us do good to all people, especially to those who belong to the family of believers" (Galatians 6:9-10). Don't quit. God will reward you for your labor of love.

God's Reliable Promise

> We want each of you to show this same diligence to
> the very end, in order to make your hope sure. We do
> not want you to become lazy, but to imitate those
> who through faith and patience inherit what has been
> promised. (Hebrews 6:11-12)

This church has known fierce opposition (10:32-34). The
promises of God are of supreme importance in crises like these.
So is perseverance and endurance to the very end. Promises
sustain us through the darkest days, it is true, but they must be
received and acted on. As essential as affirmation may be, it
doesn't negate personal responsibility.

Leon Morris tells us that "we want" (6:11) translates a
verb that refers to strong desire.[18] Guthrie says it expresses
"more than a pious wish."[19] The writer was passionately
concerned for his dear friends. He wanted all of them to
show diligence to the very end.

Their past performance had set a standard, and he looks
for it to be maintained with fervency. Steadfastness becomes
the cry of his heart once again, and it is precisely this persis-
tence that will develop our hope to its fullest potential
through the power of God's Spirit.

Furthermore, the writer tells his people to be imitators of
those who "through faith and patience inherited what was
promised" (6:12). What he is saying is this: "You're not the
first to launch out on the glories and the perils of the Christian faith. Others have braved the dangers and endured the
tribulations before you and won. You can do it too!" He's
telling them to go on in the realization that others have gone
through their struggle and won the victory.

Abraham is the best example of what the author has in
mind. Though he had God's promise, he had to live for
many years in patient expectation with nothing to go on except that God had made a promise. But that was enough for
Abraham. Is it enough for you? Can you live on promise?

"When God made his promise to Abraham, since there was no one greater for him to swear by, he swore by himself, saying, 'I will surely bless you and give you many descendants.' And so after waiting patiently, Abraham received what was promised" (Hebrews 6:13-15). The account is taken from Genesis 22.

The angel of the LORD called to Abraham from heaven a second time and said, "I swear by myself," declares the LORD, "that because you have done this and have not withheld your son, your only son, I will surely bless you and make your descendants as numerous as the stars in the sky and as the sand on the seashore. Your descendants will take possession of the cities of your enemies. . . ." (22:15-17)

Abraham is chosen as a single example, though there are many. He was not idle or lazy in the manifestation of his faith, but steadfastly maintained the full assurance of hope throughout his difficult life. Through persistent faith in a God who could not fail, and the promise that would not change, he pressed on.

It would have been easier to give up, to quit, to throw in the sandal and abandon the promise. But he trusted God and would not withdraw. God said, "I will surely bless you," and Abraham took God at His word. He held fast to the promise.

When God initially made the promise to His servant everything seemed impossibly bleak. God kept talking about descendants as numerous as the sand on the seashore, but in point of fact Abraham did not have a single child by his wife Sarah. Yet they went on believing in the promises of a faithful God. And then it happened! Isaac was born. The promise was fulfilled. Then years later, when Abraham almost lost his son, the gracious promise was renewed. God said, "I will bless you and multiply you and make you a nation."

"In his justice our love is remembered; in his generosity our faith is rewarded."[20]

Men swear by someone greater than themselves, and the oath confirms what is said and puts an end to all argument. Because God wanted to make the unchanging nature of his purpose very clear to the heirs of what was promised, he confirmed it with an oath. God did this so that, by two unchangeable things in which it is impossible for God to lie, we who have fled to take hold of the hope offered to us may be greatly encouraged. We have this hope as an anchor for the soul, firm and secure. It enters the inner sanctuary behind the curtain, where Jesus, who went before us, has entered on our behalf. He has become a high priest forever, in the order of Melchizedek. (Hebrews 6:16-20)

God not only gave Abraham a promise, but He also confirmed that promise with an oath. When a witness takes an oath in court, he is confronted with the words, "so help me God." We call on the greater to witness for the lesser.

None is greater than God, so He swore by Himself. God had no need to swear an oath. Nevertheless, He did it to make absolutely clear to His servant that His promise would be fulfilled. It's just like our heavenly Father to do something like that, isn't it! Grace upon grace.

But the Lord did not do this only for Abraham. He has also given His promise and oath to "the heirs of what was promised" (6:17). Abraham and his descendants are the first of these heirs, but all believers are included as Abraham's spiritual seed, according to Galatians 3:29; "If you belong to Christ, then you are Abraham's seed, and heirs according to the promise."

God confirmed the promise with an oath so that "we who have fled to take hold of the hope offered to us may be greatly encouraged" (Hebrews 6:18). And it is impossible for God to lie. This is the basis of our conviction and our encouragement as believers.

We know that eternal life in Christ does not depend on our stability or the strength of our faith but on the absolute trustworthiness of God's Word. We fled from the entrapments of a sinful life, and once we took hold of the hope offered to us, we were greatly encouraged.

Hebrews 6:4-8 carried heavy warnings about the dangers of apostasy. We must make progress along the way or suffer disaster. There are no other possibilities. In 6:9-20 the writer expresses a father's confidence in his first-century readers. The warning has been necessary, but he does not think they will fall away.

However, he takes advantage of the opportunity to exhort them all to go forward, to keep growing, to show progress, to pursue the better things that God has in store. He presses them to strive for the better things by reminding them that God's justice is perfect and God's promise is reliable.

Robert Robinson, author of the hymn "Come Thou Fount of Every Blessing," lost the happy communion with the Savior he had once enjoyed. In his declining years he wandered in his faith. As a result, he became deeply troubled in spirit. Hoping to relieve his mind, he decided to travel.

In the course of his journeys, he became acquainted with a young woman. They talked about spiritual matters and she asked him what he thought of a hymn she had just been reading. To his astonishment he found it to be none other than his own composition. He tried to evade her question, but she continued to press him for a response.

Suddenly he began to weep. With tears streaming down his cheeks, he said, "I am the man who wrote that hymn many years ago. I'd give anything to experience the joy I knew then." Although greatly surprised, she reassured him that the "streams of mercy" mentioned in his song still flowed. Mr. Robinson was deeply touched. Convinced that God had not forgotten him, convinced that God's justice was perfect and His promise true, he turned his wandering heart to the Lord and was restored to full fellowship.

Hebrews is a book of *en*couragement, not *dis*couragement. "We have this hope as an anchor for the soul, firm and secure" (Hebrews 6:19). That's good news! The ship firmly anchored is safe from idle drifting. Its position, safety and destiny are sure. Hope is a stabilizing force in the life of every believer in Jesus, and it "enters the inner sanctuary behind the curtain" (6:19)

The metaphor takes us back to the tabernacle, with its curtain separating the Most Holy Place from the rest of the tabernacle, making it an especially sacred place. That little room symbolized the very presence of God, but people were not allowed to enter it. But hope can, says the author.

Therefore, our hope is not exhausted by what it sees of earthly possibilities. So pursue the better things, my friend. Our hope in the justice and promise of God stretches into the very presence of the Almighty! God is just. His promise is true. He cannot lie. We will not lose. Christ does not leave. Hallelujah!

Endnotes

1. William Barclay, *The Letter to the Hebrews*, rev. ed., (Philadelphia, PA: The Westminster Press, 1976), 49.

2. See the excellent discussion of this matter by Philip Edgcumbe Hughes, *A Commentary on the Epistle to the Hebrews* (Grand Rapids, MI: William B. Eerdmans Publishing Company, 1977), 189-190.

3. William Barclay, 49.

4. Leadership (Winter 1994): 46. Used by permission.

5. Gary Richmond, *A View from the Zoo* (Waco, TX: Word Books Publisher, 1987), 115-117.

6. *Leadership* (Winter 1994): 46. Used by permission.

7. *Leadership* (Fall 1993): 56. Used by permission.

8. Leon Morris, *Hebrews, The Expositor's Bible Commentary*, vol. 12, ed. Frank E. Gaebelein (Grand Rapids, MI: Zondervan, 1981), 54.

9. William Barclay, 56.

10. Homer Kent, Jr. *The Epistle to the Hebrews: A Commentary* (Grand Rapids, MI: Baker Book House, 1972), 107.

11. Leon Morris, 10.

12. F.F. Bruce, *The Epistle to the Hebrews* (Grand Rapids, MI: William B. Eerdmans Publishing Co., 1964), 124.

13. Warren Wiersbe, *Be Confident* (Wheaton, IL: Victor Books, 1982), 63.

14. Focus on the Family, December 1994, 5.

15. There have been innumerable attempts to provide an adequate explanation of these verses. Greater minds than mine have debated this portion of God's Word, and no matter which side you come out on, you're in good company. Apostates are people who clearly despise God's gifts (Hebrews 6:4-5), reject God's Son (6:6) and thus, forfeit God's blessing (7-8). But who are these people who have fallen away? Are they saved people who have lost their salvation? Are they wolves in sheep's clothing? Who are they? Are they real Christians or impostors?

16. John Calvin, *Calvin's New Testament Commentaries, Hebrews and I and II Peter*, trans. by W.B. Johnston, eds. David W. Torrance and Thomas F. Torrance (Grand Rapids, MI: William B. Eerdmans Publishing Company, 1963), 79.

17. *Leadership* (Summer 1994): 49. Used by permission.

18. Leon Morris, 58.

19. Donald Guthrie, *Hebrews* (Grand Rapids, MI: William B. Eerdmans Publishing Company, 1983), 148.

20. Raymond Brown, *The Message of Hebrews* (Downers Grove, IL: InterVarsity Press, 1982), 120.

Discussion Questions for Further Study

1. What would you say is the main message of 5:11-6:12?

2. According to 5:11-14, what are the spiritual deficiencies of this group of believers, and what are the primary

marks of spiritual maturity? How does the deeper life relate to this?

3. What does the author mean by "solid food," and why is it only for the mature?

4. How does a person train himself or herself to distinguish good from evil? What steps can you take to improve in this area?

5. What do you think is the essential point the author wants to get across in 6:4-8?

6. What are some "things that accompany salvation" (6:9-10)?

7. One practical sign of a Christian's love for God is his commitment to helping God's people (6:10). How can you show love for God in that way this week? Pray for and act on one concrete way of doing this.

Hebrews 7:1-28

Mysterious Melchizedek

This Melchizedek was king of Salem and priest of God Most High. He met Abraham returning from the defeat of the kings and blessed him, and Abraham gave him a tenth of everything. First, his name means, "king of righteousness"; then also, "king of Salem" means "king of peace." Without father or mother, without genealogy, without beginning of days or end of life, like the Son of God he remains a priest forever.

Just think how great he was: Even the patriarch Abraham gave him a tenth of the plunder! Now the law requires the descendants of Levi who become priests to collect a tenth from the people—this is, their brothers—even though their brothers are descended from Abraham. This man, however, did not trace his descent from Levi, yet he collected a tenth from Abraham and blessed him who had the promises. And without doubt the lesser person is blessed by the greater. In the one case, the tenth is collected by men who die; but in the other case, by him who is declared to be living. One might even say that Levi, who collects the tenth, paid the tenth through Abraham, because when Melchizedek met Abraham, Levi was still in the body of his ancestor.

If perfection could have been attained through the Le-
vitical priesthood (for on the basis of it the law was given
to the people), why was there still need for another priest
to come—one in the order of Melchizedek, not in the order
of Aaron? For when there is a change of the priesthood,
there must also be a change of the law. He of whom these
things are said belonged to a different tribe, and no one
from that tribe has ever served at the altar. For it is clear
that our Lord descended from Judah, and in regard to that
tribe Moses said nothing about priests. And what we have
said is even more clear if another priest like Melchizedek
appears, one who has become a priest not on the basis of a
regulation as to his ancestry but on the basis of the power
of an indestructible life. For it is declared:

"You are a priest forever,
  in the order of Melchizedek."

The former regulation is set aside because it was weak
and useless (for the law made nothing perfect), and a bet-
ter hope is introduced, by which we draw near to God.
(Hebrews 7:1-19)

Many years ago, while I was a student at seminary, my wife was convinced I needed to read about things other than supralapsarianism, super-churches and structural criticism. She listened patiently while I talked about such elevated ideas as foreknowledge and foreordination and contextualization and consubstantiation. I warned her of the colossal dangers lurking behind annihilationism and antinomianism and Arminianism. But when I got to *formgeschichte* and *heilsgeschichte*, she gave up.

I think she was heavily influenced by those other student wives who formed a support group. "Bookworm Widows" I think they called it—women who comfort one another by sharing their common stories of lonely nights as student wives, shut away in the married students' apartments while hubbies lost themselves in study carousels in the library.

Too much Tertullian and Thielicke, she decided. So she bought me a hardback copy of *Sherlock Holmes: The Complete Illustrated Short Stories* by Sir Arthur Conan Doyle. This handsome collection contains all fifty-six short stories written by Conan Doyle about the world's most famous detective, Sherlock Holmes. The stories were originally published to widespread acclaim in *The Strand Magazine*, London's most celebrated illustrated periodical, between 1891 and 1927, and my wife made sure I read most of them!

Holmes' deductive genius enthralls every armchair sleuth, but the stories appeal no less to readers like me. I discovered that I actually *enjoy* an exciting adventure mystery. Brilliant, egotistical, unconventional, continually astounding his baffled but faithful companion Dr. Watson, Sherlock Holmes is an unforgettable character and one who still provides inspiration for plays, television dramas and films.

Holmes also contributes this insight: Never overlook *any* character in the story, even the most incidental. He or she may be the one whodunit.

If you were asked to name the five most important characters in the Bible, I doubt you would include the name of Melchizedek. He's one of those incidental characters—kind of a mystery person. He appeared once in Genesis 14:17-24; he was referred to once more in Psalm 110:4. Why then does this clandestine figure appear so prominently in Hebrews? It's not so "elementary, my dear Mr. Watson." Grab your magnifying glass and pay close attention as we work our way through the chapter.

In Hebrews 7, we witness the continued development of the central truth of this letter: the superiority of Jesus Christ. In Him alone is suitable power and capacity to handle life. There is not satisfactory power in the law, in animal sacrifices, in angels or in the priestly system of Moses. Hard work or human striving alone cannot satisfy. Only in Christ

Jesus, our Great High Priest, can we find a better hope, a better promise and a better covenant.[1]

The writer of this letter to the Hebrews strives to persuade his readers that Christ is completely unique and unconventional in His priestly role. Unlike Aaron and the Levitical priesthood of the Old Testament, Christ follows the distinctive pattern of a renegade priest who once ministered to Abraham. His name was Melchizedek.

The writer has mentioned Melchizedek before and has spoken of Jesus as a priest in the order of Melchizedek, but here he develops the idea more fully. As Leon Morris points out, "This is an understanding of Christ's work that is peculiar to this epistle,"[2] but very effective in the hands of the author.

His contemporaries would have assumed that there was no priesthood other than Aaron's. Yet the law itself verifies that there is a more prominent priesthood than that. We need to become acquainted with this mysterious man named Melchizedek.

Before we look at Melchizedek himself, let's revisit the dominant theme and the prevailing problem. The pivotal theme of Hebrews is the superiority, the preeminence of Christ. Among the intended recipients of this letter were those who had chosen not to follow Christ or walk in His ways. Apostates.

They rejected His values and goals and refused to bow their knees to Him. They were doing their own thing in their own time in their own way, and it was affecting the fellowship of believers in a detrimental manner. This was a very pressing, prevailing problem in the mind of the writer as he composed this epistle.

Suffering, heartache, distress and disillusionment drew these people like a magnet back into a life centered around the Mosaic law and the Levitical priesthood. They were returning to the old agreement, and the writer was saying to them, "Hold fast! Stand your ground. Don't go back! Don't do it! Think this through!"

Then he sets out to prove to them that Jesus Christ, not

the priests, is the solution to their problem. In fact, all the tradition and heritage, and all the comfort and consolation of their old religion had been preempted by the Savior.

The Identity of Melchizedek

This Melchizedek was king of Salem and priest of God Most High. He met Abraham returning from the defeat of the kings and blessed him, and Abraham gave him a tenth of everything. First, his name means "king of righteousness"; then also, "king of Salem" means "king of peace." (Hebrews 7:1-2)

In Genesis 14 we have the account of Abram rescuing his nephew Lot from the four kings of Elam, Goiim, Shinar and Ellasar. One who had escaped from the battle scene came to Abram and reported that Lot had been taken captive. When Abram heard that his relative had been taken, he called out 318 trained men born in his household and went in pursuit. He recovered all the goods and brought back Lot and his possessions, together with the women and the other people (Genesis 14:1-16).

This is where we meet Melchizedek for the first time. After Abram returned from defeating Kedorlaomer and the kings allied with him, the king of Sodom came out to meet him in the Valley of Shaveh.

Then Melchizedek king of Salem brought out bread and wine. He was priest of God Most High, and he blessed Abram, saying,

"Blessed be Abram by God Most High,
  Creator of heaven and earth.
And blessed be God Most High,
  who delivered your enemies into your
    hand."

Then Abram gave him a tenth of everything. (Genesis 14:18-20)

This is all the Genesis narrative has to say about Melchizedek, but it is enough for the author of Hebrews. "He finds as much significance in what is not said about Melchizedek as he does in what is said about him."[3] He was king in Salem, reigning over what we know today as Jerusalem ("Salem" is another name for Jerusalem in Psalm 76:2).

He was, at the same time, a priest of the Most High God. It was not uncommon in this time period for one person to fill the dual roles of priest and ruler. However, the dual roles are not as noteworthy as the special characteristics this man possessed. Abraham was one of his contemporaries, but Melchizedek pointed to Christ. He foreshadows the Savior through his name and his title.

The author tells us his name means "king of righteousness" (7:2).[4] Then he goes on to the title "king of Salem," which comes from the Hebrew word *shalom* for "peace." In the New Testament, the Greek word for "peace," *eirene*, possesses the fuller meaning of *shalom* and signifies the presence of positive blessing, the result of Christ's work for men and women like us. "The combination of righteousness and peace is seen in Psalm 85:10. As used here, the two terms point to distinctive aspects of Christ's saving work."[5]

Melchizedek was a priest and so is Christ. Melchizedek was a king and so is Christ. He is righteousness and peace, and so is Christ. The writer is building his argument very carefully by comparing Jesus and Melchizedek. He makes sure he does not miss his mark.

Picture a sloppy woman who lives in a dirty, slovenly house. She leaves her home one afternoon and goes to a movie. For an hour or two she escapes into the glamour and the luxury of the world of film. But she must go back home when it's over. It's an escape but the inevitable return to reality awaits her.

Before I gave my life to Christ at age twenty-one, I used to find escape in a bottle of rum or whiskey. I didn't care what I drank as long as it took me where I thought I wanted to go. It was always possible to find some kind of peace by the route of escape, but it was never a lasting peace. Only the Prince of Peace can offer that. That's where the writer of Hebrews is heading. He's pointing his readers to Jesus, the *Shalom* of God.

The Origin of Melchizedek

> Without father or mother, without genealogy, without beginning of days or end of life, like the Son of God he remains a priest forever. (Hebrews 7:3)

The Bible gives no record of Melchizedek's birth, mother, father, genealogy or death. This person was unique: he came out of nowhere and passed into oblivion. Like an obscure and mysterious character in one of Conan Doyle's stories.

Apparently, the terms "without father" and "without mother" (*apator, ametor*) are used in Greek for orphans and ragamuffins of unknown bloodline, for illegitimate children, for citizens who came from insignificant families and sometimes for deities who were supposed to take their descent from one sex only.[6] In the only record of this man's appearance (Genesis 14:18-20), the Bible says nothing of his ancestry or progeny. Nothing is said of his birth or his death. He appears as a king and priest, and as such, he disappears quickly without a trace.

Bible teachers have wrestled with this passage at length, and some have made Melchizedek into someone other than a historical person. Rabbi Ismael, about 135 B.C., thought him to be Shem, Noah's son. Philo saw in him a figure of the human soul, divine reason functioning in a priestly way as the *logos* that controlled the passions, delighted the soul and honored God with exalted thought.[7]

Many have said he was a christophany ("a preincarnate appearance of Jesus Christ"). But Hebrews 7:3 says he was "like the Son of God," not that he was the Son of God. Taken at face value, the text of Holy Writ says that this king-priest was a real human being. The fact that his mother or father were not named, or that his birth and death dates were not cited, does not mean that he was without any of these. In the silences as well as the statements about him, he is a fitting type of Christ.

One scholar says, "the silences of Scripture were as much due to divine inspiration as were its statements."[8] When nothing is recorded of the parentage of this man, it is not necessarily to be assumed that he had no parents but simply that the absence of the record is significant.

In His eternal being as the Son of God, Christ is really, as Melchizedek was typically, "without beginning of days or end of life." And now, in His risen, exalted, resurrected position at the right hand of God, Jesus "remains a priest forever" (Hebrews 7:3). Melchizedek remains a priest for the duration of his appearance in Scripture. Then he vanishes.

In the antitype, Christ remains a priest continually, forever without qualification or restriction. Furthermore, as F.F. Bruce points out so ably, it is not the type that determines the antitype, but the antitype that determines the type; Jesus is not portrayed after the pattern of Melchizedek, but Melchizedek is "like the Son of God."[9]

Do you see what the writer is doing? The first-century Jews placed great emphasis on the human priest's genealogy. A man couldn't become a priest unless he could certify that he had an unbroken lineage back to Aaron. But was Jesus from Aaron's line? No, he was from the tribe of Judah! So when the author of Hebrews placed emphasis on a far different kind of priesthood, his readers could not miss the point he was making. "Don't do it! Don't go back to a human priesthood. Stay with the priesthood that remains forever!"

Why then was Melchizedek so great?

The Greatness of Melchizedek

> Just think how great he was: Even the patriarch Abraham gave him a tenth of the plunder! (Hebrews 7:4)

The word "plunder" literally means "the top of the heap" and was used of the choicest spoils of war. So Abraham gave a tenth of the very best to this great man Melchizedek. Why was he great? Several reasons are listed in this passage.

First, he took a tithe from Abraham, who was the father of the nation and the most revered patriarch in the land. In the ancient world it was recognized that there was an obligation to pay tithes to important religious figureheads. There is a certain subjection or domination implied as well. The one who pays the tithes is in subjection and vulnerable to the one to whom the tithes are paid.

The author is very interested in the law. He mentions it again in Hebrews 7:5. "Now the law requires the descendants of Levi who become priests to collect a tenth from the people—that is, their brothers—even though their brothers are descended from Abraham."

The law required tithes to be collected by the priests, and there was a sense in which the priests were "brothers" to those from whom the tithes were taken. On the one hand they had no inherent superiority; they were kinfolk. They owed their status to the law and not to any natural superiority. But, on the other hand, things were different with Melchizedek.

"This man, however, did not trace his descent from Levi . . ." (7:6). He was not simply one among brothers, a priest among equals. Like Christ, he does not have his genealogy reckoned among the sons of Levi. He was a solitary figure of splendor and majesty. And he required tithes not simply from his brothers but from Abraham, the patriarch of the nation. His greatness stands out in full measure.

Melchizedek's greatness is further amplified by the fact that he blessed Abraham, the one who had the promises

(7:6). Today's readers often have difficulty appreciating the argument employed here. The act of blessing someone implies superiority. It is different than simply praising someone or extolling his or her virtues.

Rather, it is an official pronouncement of some sort, coming from one who is clearly and properly authorized to make such a statement. It actually bestows something on the person being blessed. "And without doubt the lesser person is blessed by the greater" (Hebrews 7:7). Herveus, in a manner consistent with the implications of the passage, presses the logic one stage further:

> If Melchizedek, who was a sign and shadow, is preferred to Abraham and to all the levitical priests, how much more Christ, who is the truth and the substance! . . . If a type of Christ is greater than he who has the promises, how much more so is Christ himself![10]

Finally, he is "declared to be living," unlike the Levitical priests who die (7:8-10). The writer does not say that Melchizedek lives on but the testimony about him is that he lives. The Bible records nothing about the death of this mysterious priest and king.

"In the one case, the tenth is collected by men who die; but in the other case, by him who is declared to be living" (Hebrews 7:8). Melchizedek stands in strong contrast to the priests of Aaron, and as priest-king, he prefigures Christ. He was a great man, a great leader.

In one of his books, Stuart Briscoe wrote:

> One of my young colleagues was officiating at the funeral of a war veteran. The dead man's military friends wished to have a part in the service at the funeral home, so they requested the pastor to lead them down to the casket, stand with them for a solemn moment of remembrance and then lead them out

through the side door. This he proceeded to do, but unfortunately the effect was somewhat marred when he picked the wrong door. The result was that they marched with military precision into a broom closet, in full view of the mourners, and had to beat a hasty retreat covered with confusion.[11]

This true story illustrates a cardinal rule or two. If you're going to lead, make sure you know where you're going. Second, if you're going to follow make sure that you are following someone who knows where he's going. Melchizedek was a great leader who knew what he had come to do and why. His example is worthy of following.

Yet if Melchizedek, who was a sign and shadow, is preferred to Abraham and to all the Levitical priests, how much more Christ, who is the truth and the substance! It is not Jesus who resembles Melchizedek, but Melchizedek who resembles the Lord Jesus. Melchizedek was the facsimile of which Christ is the reality!

As we come to the end of this section let's review what we've covered. The first half of Hebrews 7 probes the identity of Melchizedek, his origin and the reasons for his "greatness" as seen by the author of this mighty letter. Keep in mind that Melchizedek is simply a type or a sign, a shadow of the reality of Jesus, a pointer that leads the way to Christ, and you can't be satisfied by a silhouette.

The second half of the chapter, 7:11-19, makes it clear to us that the priestly security to which the Levites clung was no security at all. "For it is clear that our Lord descended from Judah, and in regard to that tribe Moses said nothing about priests" (7:14). The priests from Levi did their job, but they were set aside by Jesus Christ when He came with His unique priesthood. No such thing as job security in this line of work!

To be a priest in the Old Testament, one had to be a pure descendant of Aaron. Even then there were 142 physical blemishes which might disqualify him; some of them are detailed in Leviticus 21:16-23. "No man who has any defect may come near: no man who is blind or lame, disfigured or deformed; no man with a crippled foot or hand, or who is hunchbacked or dwarfed, or who has any eye defect, or who has festering or running sores or damaged testicles" (Leviticus 21:18-20).

The ordination ceremony for a priest is outlined in Levit-icus 8. He was bathed in water so that he would be ceremonially clean (8:6). He was clothed in the priestly garments (8:7-9). He was anointed with oil (8:10-12). Then after the priest laid hands on the ram for ordination, some of its blood was placed on the lobe of the right ear, on the thumb of his right hand and on the big toe of his right foot (8:22-23).

Bible scholar William Barclay also points out that every single item in the ceremony affects the priest's body. Once he was ordained to the priesthood he had to observe so many washing with water, so many anointings with oil; he had to cut his hair in a certain way.

> From beginning to end the Jewish priesthood was dependent on physical things. Character, ability, personality had nothing to do with it. But the new priesthood was dependent on a life that was indestructible.[12]

In contrast, Christ's priesthood depended on who He was, His person, what He was in Himself. He is a priest forever, not on the basis of a regulation or law, but on the basis of the power of an indestructible life! Praises!

The point is that only in Christ is there security, strength and sureness. Only in Christ is there purpose and design. Only in Christ is there meaning to life and confidence in death. Only through Christ can we draw near to God.

Len Beadle drove a red Corvette, wore $2,000 suits and was vice president of Canada's largest real estate franchise in the heyday of Toronto's property boom. Now he wears a paper hat, a white jacket and cooks in a hotel kitchen—glad to have a job while thousands are unemployed. "It's a nice, safe feeling," Beadle says.

"Recession has hit white-collar workers especially hard," says Leslie Papp, writing for the *Toronto Star*, "with real estate in a slump, retailers folding and once-stalwart giants like IBM laying off staff. Some unemployed professionals, ready for a career change, are turning to blue-collar jobs traditionally considered beneath them."

Safety. Security. Nice words, but the reality of it all has disappeared in the modern job market. Once again we see that only through Christ and only in Christ can we have any real security and strength. Only in Christ is there purpose and design. Only in Christ is there meaning to life (John 10:10) and confidence in death (John 14:1-4). Only through Christ can we draw near to God (John 14:6).

You may not be a priest forever "in the order of Melchizedek," but as a believer you still have access to the throne of grace, along with its privileges and responsibilities. With that in mind, may I encourage you once again to step inside the holy of holies and, "in view of God's mercy, . . . offer your bodies as living sacrifices, holy and pleasing to God—this is your spiritual act of worship" (Romans 12:1). Surrender your will to the Lord and enjoy the truest communion with the Lord.

The writer of the letter to the Hebrews has explained and confirmed that we don't need a theology that brags about its genealogy. We don't need a priest with a pedigree. What we need is the life that's indestructible and imperishable and a priest who is permanent. We need Jesus Christ! He can do for us what no member of a human priesthood could ever do, so let us draw near while we may.

> Nearer, still nearer, close to Thy heart,
> Draw me, my Saviour, so precious Thou art;
> Fold me, oh, fold me close to Thy breast,
> Shelter me safe in that haven of rest,
> Shelter me safe in that haven of rest.

Nearer, still nearer—nothing I bring,
Naught as an offering to Jesus my King—
Only my sinful, now contrite heart.
Grant me the cleansing Thy blood doth
      impart,
Grant me the cleansing Thy blood doth
      impart.

Nearer, still nearer, while life shall last,
Till safe in glory my anchor is cast,
Through endless ages ever to be
Nearer, my Saviour, still nearer to Thee,
Nearer, my Saviour, still nearer to Thee.[14]

A Superior Priesthood

And it was not without an oath! Others became priests without any oath, but he became a priest with an oath when God said to him:

"The Lord has sworn
   and will not change his mind:
'You are a priest forever.' "

Because of this oath, Jesus has become the guarantee of a better covenant.

Now there have been many of those priests, since death prevented them from continuing in office; but because Jesus lives forever, he has a permanent priesthood. Therefore he is able to save completely those who come to God through him, because he always lives to intercede for them.

Such a high priest meets our need—one who is holy, blameless, pure, set apart from sinners, exalted above the heavens. Unlike the other high priests, he does not need to offer sacrifices day after day, first for his own sins, and then for the sins of the people. He sacrificed for their sins once for all when he offered himself. For the law appoints as high priests men who are weak; but the oath, which came after the law, appointed the Son, who has been made perfect forever. (Hebrews 7:20-28)

Oscar Hammerstein, in his book *Lyrics*, recalls the front cover of a *New York Tribune* Sunday magazine. It featured a picture of the Statue of Liberty taken from a helicopter. It showed the top of the statue's head. The detailing was amazing! The sculptor had done a painstaking job with the lady's coiffure. Yet he must have known that the only eyes that would ever see the detail would be the uncritical eyes of seagulls. And everybody knows what seagulls do on top of statues! Especially in New York!

Anyway, he could not have dreamt that any man would ever fly over this head. But he was an artist, and artists are perfectionists, aren't they? He was artist enough to finish off this part of the statue with as much care as he had devoted to her face and her arms and the torch and everything that people can see as they sail up the bay.[15]

In like manner Jesus Christ goes about His ministry with artistic perfection. He leaves nothing to chance. His work is superlative. His achievement supreme. His priesthood superior. Jesus Christ came onto the scene with a permanent priesthood in the order of Melchizedek. His priesthood was far superior to the one established in the era of the law of Moses.

There's a large amount of material in Hebrews regarding the priesthood of Jesus Christ, and it could sound like a broken record at times. We keep visiting some of the same themes over and over again. Are you understanding the significance of it all?

In verses 20-28 some of the leading ideas of the letter are gathered together and expounded with persuasive and attractive conviction. Do you recall that some of the first readers of this letter had begun to feel nostalgic about the traditional and familiar religious ceremonies of Judaism and were tempted to go back to what was comfortable and convenient rather than pushing ahead toward maturity in Christ? In this section, starting at verse 20, the writer tries to assure them that in Christ they have a better hope, and so do we.

His priesthood is superior to any other priesthood because it embodied a superior oath, a superior guarantee and a superior priest.

A Superior Oath

And it was not without an oath! Others became priests without any oath but [Christ] became a priest with an oath when God said to him:

"The Lord has sworn
   and will not change his mind:
'You are a priest forever.' "
      (Hebrews 7:20-21)

Our Spirit-inspired author continues to examine the text and bleeds from it its last drop of significance for the character of this new priesthood. He now draws our attention to the fact that the acclamation of Messiah as a perpetual priest was validated by a divine oath. What he said about God's oath to Abraham in 6:13-20 is equally true about God's oath here. The bare word of God is enough, but God, who "wanted to make the unchanging nature of his purpose very clear to the heirs of what was promised," confirmed it with an oath (6:17).

I dread the day when my youngest child begins to fully understand that a promise is a promise is a promise. Out of sheer necessity (or sheer neglect), I sometimes change my mind even after I've made a promise to her. She feels disappointed when I do that, and she has every right to feel that way.

When that happens I fumble and stumble in my guilt and shame, and perhaps we all feel the same way when we stumble and fall in this regard. Another broken promise. Another broken heart. In contrast God's oath and mine are as different as day and night. He never breaks a promise.

When the Lord swore, He did not change His mind, and it is impossible for God to lie (Hebrews 6:18). An oath is an oath is an oath, and in this case, God made a personal oath about an eternal priest-king named Jesus.

No priest in the order of Aaron was ever ordained and established on the basis of God's personal oath. Yet three times in Hebrews 7 the writer stresses with conviction that Jesus is a High Priest forever, quoting Psalm 110 as an authority for his confidence. "The Lord has sworn and will not change his mind: 'You are a priest forever.' "

We must remember that in Hebrew thought, when God said something it was done (cf. Genesis 1:3; Luke 7:6-9). They were not mere words, but a resolution to act and *initiate* the event. He made Christ a Priest forever—changeless and permanent. Nothing could be more definitive. The oath declared both the fact and the reliability. Therefore, the invariable, unchanging priesthood of Christ Jesus is far superior to any other because of the personal oath given by Almighty God.

A Superior Guarantee

> Because of this oath, Jesus has become the guarantee of a better covenant. (Hebrews 7:22)

The English word "guarantee" translates a word found only here in the New Testament and it brings before us an unusual idea. Hughes points out that the concept was fairly common in legal and promissory documents of the period.[16] It means a "guarantor" or "one who stands security."

Jesus Himself is our security that there will be no annulment of this new and better covenant. The old covenant was established with a mediator named Moses, but with no one to guarantee that the people would fulfill their obligation. Jesus Christ is the guarantee of a better covenant in two ways.

Jesus guarantees to men that God will fulfill His covenant of forgiveness, and He guarantees to God that those who are in Him are acceptable.[17] Think about it. Jesus is the guarantor, the security, of a better covenant. When the time comes, I'm sure that I will be willing to co-sign for my son's first bank loan to help him secure a good credit rating (provided he uses the money for a worthwhile project).

Yet my reserves are limited, restricted, confined to what little money I've been able to save over the years. By the time the federal and provincial governments are finished with me, there's not much left! In contrast, our heavenly Father has made Jesus the guarantee of an agreement signed in blood. Christ guarantees to men that God will fulfill His covenant of forgiveness, and He guarantees to God that those who are in Him are acceptable.

Missionaries, pastors and elders in our churches, motivated by deep pastoral concern, dread the thought that some of the members of the church might go back to something inferior, temporary, partial, when in Christ there is a better hope, a better covenant, with better promises.

Friends, when we are up against the wall facing opposition, antagonism or adversity, our confidence is not in our material goods or moral efforts or even our spiritual integrity. We rely solely on the blood of Jesus Christ and the guarantee of a better agreement with God.

God ventured His all in Jesus Christ to save us and sanctify us, and now He wants us to invest our all with total abandoned confidence in Him as our only hope and the sure guarantee. There are areas in our lives where authentic faith has not worked in us as yet, places still untouched by the life of God.

There were none of those places in Christ's life, and there should be none in ours. The real meaning of eternal life is a life that can face anything it has to face without defaulting. If we will take this view, life will become a great romance—a glorious opportunity to see wonderful things all the time. God is disciplining us to get us into this central place of power.[18]

In Christ we have security, purification, pardon and access into the grace in which we now stand (Romans 5:1-2). We have hope because of this guarantee! And we rejoice in the hope of the glory of God.

A Superior Priest

Now there have been many of those priests, since death prevented them from continuing in office; but because Jesus lives forever, he has a permanent priesthood. (Hebrews 7:23-24)

Down through the years, for centuries, the Jewish people had been ministered to by hundreds and hundreds of priests. However devoted and faithful a priest might be in the exercise of his special work, death always put an abrupt and permanent end to his service.

But Jesus is the permanent holder of this priestly office because He lives forever. What He accomplished for us affects eternity—a permanent achievement. "Therefore he is able to save completely those who come to God through him . . ." (7:25a). His power knows no limits and His life knows no end. He is able to save His people fully and completely. Nothing is necessary to supplement their salvation.

"For it is by grace you have been saved, through faith—and this not from yourselves, it is the gift of God—not by works, so that no one can boast" (Ephesians 2:8-9). It doesn't matter what your life is like before you come to Christ. Divorced, alcoholic, liar, cheat, murderer, greedy, angry, swindler . . . He is able to save completely those who come to God through Him. He has limitless power.

I grew up in a home that was riddled with alcohol abuse and violence. By the time I started school my family was fragmented and the primary grade years were filled with clandestine, midnight moves while my father was at work. I remember some of the common-law arrangements and my fear.

My mother beat my sister and subjected her to a degree of humiliation and degradation that no teenage girl should ever have to endure. I cannot count the number of times we moved secretly and switched schools as my mother and her boyfriends tried to escape from my father and his toughest allies.

Finally, in the sixth grade, I was sent to another province to live with my grandparents. Stability at last. Twelve months later my grandfather retired, they moved to the west coast and I became excess baggage again. So back to my mother and a different mate several hundred miles away. This time to a mixed farm in northern Alberta which was like the end of the earth to an eleven-year-old city boy. Another venue. A different veneer. But the same old story: drunken brawls, broken promises and verbal abuse that wounded my spirit to its very core.

When I reached high school I joined the coolest crowd I could. I drank booze, smoked dope and did whatever I needed to do to gain acceptance from the people around me. As much as I hated what liquor did to my family, I headed down the same perilous path. It was fun at first. Then it became addictive. Then I didn't know how to find the way out. The shadows grew longer and I was losing my way.

The day after I had a terrible argument with my girlfriend, her mother, Ethel, asked me if we could talk.

"Garth, have you ever heard of the four spiritual laws?" she asked. The "I Found It" campaign sponsored by Campus Crusade for Christ was taking place in the city, but I didn't have the foggiest idea of what Campus Crusade was, nor the four spiritual laws. Ethel defined the plan of salvation for me that afternoon, and instead of going to work like I was supposed to after I left her home, I went back to my apartment to think.

The words to many of the verses Ethel read from the little yellow pamphlet flooded my heart and mind. I could not escape. The holy Hound of Heaven was in hot pursuit! The Spirit of Truth was at work. Later that afternoon I kneeled beside my bed and invited Jesus Christ to take control of my life.

He is able to save *completely* those who come to God through Him. I cling to that promise from the Scriptures. It matters not what you've been through or who you've slept with or how many times. Drug addicts, prostitutes, white-collar embezzlers—Jesus saves completely, entirely, wholly, absolutely, comprehensively, totally and thoroughly those who come to Him in faith.

Then He begins to intercede for us! "He is able to save completely those who come to God through him, because he always lives to intercede for them" (Hebrews 7:25). Day by day and hour by hour Jesus intercedes and intervenes. As our Moderator, Mediator, Messiah, He prays for us *meaning-fully* because He has firsthand experience of our trials and temptations.

Remember: "We do not have a high priest who is unable to sympathize with our weaknesses, but we have one who has been tempted in every way, just as we are—yet was without sin" (4:15). He intercedes for us *compassionately* and charitably, for He knows exactly what we need.

> Jesus went through all the towns and villages, teaching in their synagogues, preaching the good news of the kingdom and healing every disease and sickness. When he saw the crowds, he had compassion on them, because they were harassed and helpless, like sheep without a shepherd. (Matthew 9:35-36)

He prays for us *effectively* and convincingly because He has the power to meet our need. "I pray for them," Jesus said. "I am not praying for the world, but for those you have given me, for they are yours. . . . Holy Father, protect them by the power of your name—the name you gave me—so that they may be one as we are one" (John 17:9, 11).

"Such a high priest meets our need—one who is holy, blameless, pure, set apart from sinners, exalted above the heavens" (Hebrews 7:26). Even the most devout priests who served under the old covenant were transgressors. They were sinners. But Jesus was sinless, holy, blameless, pure, exalted above the heavens.

"Unlike the other high priests, he does not need to offer sacrifices day after day, first for his own sins, and then for the sins of the people. He sacrificed for their sins once for all when he offered himself " (7:27). Jesus was not only the perfect Priest; He was the perfect Sacrifice, the unblemished, flawless Offering.

The Jewish priest offered the blood of bulls and goats both for himself and for the people of Israel. But Christ offered Himself, not the blood of animals, and He did it for others, not for Himself. Moreover, their offerings had to be repeated day after day. But Jesus sacrificed for their sins and ours once for all!

Hebrews 7:20-28 examines the superiority of Christ's priesthood. The preeminence of the oath, the guarantee and the priest come into clear focus. We hear the writer's courteous but convincing voice calling us to a deeper walk of faith; inviting us forward and upward, ever onward. The first readers were being tempted to go back to what was comfortable and convenient rather than moving ahead toward maturity in Christ.

We can also hear the gentle whisper of the Holy Spirit, calling us and wooing us to become like priests in the lives of others. He is the Great High Priest, and no one can compare with Him, but the words of Peter ring softly in our ears: "As you come to him, the living Stone—rejected by men but chosen by God and precious to him—you also, like living stones, are being built into a spiritual house *to be a holy priesthood*, offering spiritual sacrifices acceptable to God through Jesus Christ" (1 Peter 2:4-5, emphasis added).

One of the spiritual sacrifices we can offer is prayer. Let's think about sharing the love of God with one another through prayer. Envision someone you can pray for today.

Become their "priest" and claim the power and authority available to you through Christ to pray for that friend or family member or missionary.

"The Spirit helps us in our weakness. We do not know what we ought to pray for, but the Spirit himself intercedes for us with groans that words cannot express" (Romans 8:26). However, let's use the following prayer, and you can fill in the names of your loved ones at the appropriate time.

Dearest Lord Jesus,

Help me to learn the lessons of faith when life is calm so I may be prepared when the winds of adversity rise up against me.

Help me to understand, as I cling to the security of the seashore, that the hard lessons of faith are only learned on the open sea, where the waves are rough, where the wind is relentless, where the risks are real.

Then when I feel the sting of the wind in my face and the fury of the waves in my soul, may I learn to put my trust in You, not in the strength of my hands or in the smoothness of the circumstances that surround me.

Dearest Lord Jesus, though You may be out of my sight during a storm, I thank You that I am never out of Yours.

I pray now that You would turn Your ever-watching, ever-caring eyes upon some friends (or family) I deeply care for. They are going through some stormy weather, and if You don't intervene, they will certainly end up on the rocks. I pray for _____ and _____. They desperately need You to come near, Lord. They are straining at the oars, struggling to be faithful to the course You've charted for their lives.

But their spirits are drenched with discouragement. Their backs are sore from the pull of responsibilities that fill their hands. Their minds shiver with the fear that this time they might not make it through the storm.

Have mercy on them, Jesus. They are weathered and worn and want so much to find a peaceful harbor where they can find rest for their weary hearts.

Come to them, Lord. Let them see You in the midst of their storm. Let them hear Your voice above the circumstances raging around them. Grant them the grace to fix their eyes on You, Lord, and not on the sting of circumstances whipping around them.

Help them to realize that even in their sinking moments, when life is heavy and their faith has lost its buoyancy, You are there with an outstretched hand to keep them from going under. Calm their troubled hearts, Lord Jesus, because You are the superior Great High Priest, and You know what You're doing. Amen.[19]

Endnotes

1. See the Bible study guide from *Insight for Living* for a good study on this passage of Scripture. The outline they provided is helpful in understanding the text.

2. Leon Morris, *Hebrews, The Expositor's Bible Commentary*, Vol. 12, ed. Frank E. Gaebelein (Grand Rapids, MI: Zondervan, 1981), 62.

3. F.F. Bruce, *The Epistle to the Hebrews* (Grand Rapids, MI: William B. Eerdmans Publishing Company, 1964), 134.

4. Leon Morris points out that this is a translation of the Hebrew name; it might be more accurate to render it "my king is righteous," but NIV gives the sense and brings in the noun "righteousness" that features so largely in the NT vocabulary of salvation.

5 Leon Morris, 63.

6. See Leon Morris' discussion on p. 63.

7. See R.C.H. Lenski, *The Interpretation of the Epistle to the Hebrews and the Epistle of James* (Minneapolis, MN: Augsburg Publishing House, 1966), 207-209.

8. F.F. Bruce, 137.

9. Ibid., 138.

10. As quoted in Philip Edgcumbe Hughes, *A Commentary on the Epistle to the Hebrews* (Grand Rapids, MI: William B. Eerdmans Publishing Company, 1977), 251.

11. *Leadership* (Spring 1989):45. Used by permission.

12. William Barclay, *The Letter to the Hebrews* (Philadelphia, PA: The Westminster Press, 1976), 78.

13. Garth Leno, "Real Security," *Alliance Life* (June 15, 1994): 32.

14. Lelia N. Morris, "Nearer, Still Nearer," *The Hymnal for Worship and Celebration* (Waco, TX: Word Music, 1986), No. 392.

15. *Leadership* (Fall 1984): 46. Used by permission.

16. Philip E. Hughes, 267.

17. Leon Morris, 70.

18. Adapted from *My Utmost for His Highest* by Oswald Chambers, edited by James Reitmann, copyright 1992 by Oswald Chambers Publications Assn., Ltd. Original edition copyright 1935 by Dodd Mead & Co., renewed 1963 by the Oswald Chambers Publications Assn., Ltd., and is used by permission of Discovery House Publishers, Box 3566, Grand Rapids, MI, 49501. All rights reserved.

19. Adapted from Ken Gire, *Incredible Moments with the Savior: Learning to See* (Grand Rapids, MI: Daybreak Books, Zondervan Publishing House, 1990), 70-71.

Discussion Questions for Further Study

1. The author previously used *contrast* to make his points about Jesus. Now he uses *comparison*. Can you list all the ways Jesus is like Melchizedek?

2. Romans 7:12 says the law is holy, righteous and good. Why, then, does Hebrews 7:18 say the regulation regarding the Levitical priesthood "was weak and useless"?

3. What is the "better hope" provided by Christ and His priesthood (7:19)?

4. Jesus is able to save us completely because He always lives to intercede for us (7:25). How are the salvation and the intercession connected? What difference does it make to you that Christ is interceding in heaven on your behalf? How does this affect your perspective on yourself and your present circumstances?

5. How would you summarize this chapter?

7

Hebrews 8:1-13

A Superior Minister

> The point of what we are saying is this: We do have such a high priest, who sat down at the right hand of the throne of the Majesty in heaven, and who serves in the sanctuary, the true tabernacle set up by the Lord, not by man.
>
> Every high priest is appointed to offer both gifts and sacrifices, and so it was necessary for this one also to have something to offer. If he were on earth, he would not be a priest, for there are already men who offer the gifts prescribed by the law. They serve at a sanctuary that is a copy and shadow of what is in heaven. This is why Moses was warned when he was about to build the tabernacle: "See to it that you make everything according to the pattern shown you on the mountain." But the ministry Jesus has received is as superior to theirs as the covenant of which he is mediator is superior to the old one, and it is founded on better promises. (Hebrews 8:1-6)

Charlie Steinmetz was a physically challenged dwarf. But what he lacked physically he made up for mentally. When it came to the subject of electricity, Steinmetz was a wizard, a true genius, an electronic magician. No one in his day knew more about it than he.

Henry Ford realized that when he hired the man to help in the building of those massive generators and turbines that would run his first automobile plant in Detroit. Thanks to Charlie's electrical sagacity, cars began to roll off the line and profit began to pour into Henry's pockets. Things ran along gracefully for months.

Suddenly, without warning, everything ground to a halt. Management panicked. One mechanic after another was unable to locate the problem, much to Ford's frustration and the plant's financial chaos. Finally, he contacted Charlie Steinmetz who showed up and immediately went to work. He fiddled around with some switches and a gauge or two. He tinkered with this motor and that one . . . pushed a few buttons and messed with some wires. He then threw the master switch and wouldn't you know it? Lights blinked on, engines began to whirl and things went back to normal.

Within a few days, Charlie Steinmetz mailed Henry Ford a bill for $10,000. Ford couldn't believe it, so he sent the bill back with a note attached, "Charlie, doesn't it seem a little steep to charge me $10,000 for tinkering around with a few wires and switches?"

Steinmetz rewrote the bill and sent it back. It read: "For tinkering around on the motors, $10. For knowing where to tinker, $9,990."[1]

For several chapters I have been trying to explain and illustrate the book of Hebrews. My personal opinions and ideas have not been that valuable. My sense of humor leaves much to be desired. My tinkering has hardly been worth $10. But hopefully during the process the Spirit of God has been illuminating our minds and challenging our hearts with the truths surrounding the superiority of Christ Jesus . . . and He has this uncanny way of knowing where to tinker, which makes His insights priceless.

As we come to this eighth chapter of Hebrews, the Holy Spirit wants us to focus on yet another aspect of the superiority of our High Priest Jesus Christ. The writer has already written at some length about Christ as High Priest, so we might wonder what is still left to be said. But so far he has not explained how Christ carries out His duties as High Priest.

This forms the theme of the next two-and-a-half chapters of Hebrews. Another important matter, the new covenant, is introduced in the course of the discussion. One of the reasons why this book attracts us and holds our attention is because it frequently addresses and presents the answer to humankind's most basic problem: sin.

The author leads us from his treatment of the priesthood in the order of Melchizedek to emphasize the point that Christ's ministry far surpasses that of the Levitical priests. First-century readers would be familiar with this priesthood. The writer wants to be sure they understand that Jesus has a ministry far excelling it. To bring Him into better focus, we ask ourselves three basic questions about this High Priest: Who is He, what does He do and how does He serve?

Who Is He?

> [Jesus] sat down at the right hand of the throne of the Majesty in heaven . . . . (Hebrews 8:1)

This point, already made in Hebrews 1:3 of the Son, is repeated here with direct application to the high-priest motif. We see again how clearly and carefully the writer has worked out his thesis, constantly tossing out hints that are gems in themselves, but they glisten with new meaning when seen again against a different background.[2]

The phrase, "sat down at the right hand of the throne of the Majesty in heaven" is a Hebrew way of saying that Jesus is now forever with God the Father, in that place of sovereignty and authority. We will see it again in Hebrews 10:12 and 12:2. It signifies a work well and truly done. We have, then, a High Priest who is so great, so magnificent, so distinguished and so transcendent that He took His seat at God's own right hand. He is both King and Priest.

"The Majesty in heaven" is a reverent and respectful way of referring to God. To be at His right hand is to be in the place of highest honor and privilege. *Sitting* points to a completed work.

Let us praise Jesus Christ: the exalted Lord, Emmanuel, eternal God, the everlasting light! "The ascension idea recurs throughout this letter like the main theme of a great symphony; variations are introduced, but only to give further expression to the rich cadences and majestic tones of the most memorable music ever heard."[3]

Jesus is the glorious gift of God, the compassionate, eternal Son of God, the One who invites us to "approach the throne of grace with confidence, so that we may receive mercy and find grace to help us in our time of need" (Hebrews 4:16).

He is the loving Lord of all. So why then do we neglect Him and spurn His camaraderie? Why do we ignore His invitation to fellowship "morning by morning"? Why so prone to wander? Why is it so easy to bypass the devotional hour? I suppose we are not unlike our friend "Sam."

After stopping for gas in Montgomery, Alabama, he drove more than five hours before noticing that he had left his wife at the gas station. So at the next town he asked the police to help him get in touch with her. Then Sam called his wife to tell her he was on his way back. He admitted with great embarrassment that he simply had not noticed her absence. For *five hours*?!

How Sam could forget his wife is beyond my imagination . . . or is it? When I stop and think about the many times I have ignored the wooing voice of my Savior, I can better understand Sam and men like him. Maybe you can too. It is easy to overlook the fact that Jesus is the sovereign yet loving Lord of our lives, that He has all power in heaven and earth, that He can forgive anyone for anything and that He can heal our broken hearts and bind up our wounds.

Hebrews will not let us off the hook easily, however. "The point of what we are saying is this: We do have such a high priest, who sat down at the right hand of the throne of the Majesty in heaven" (Hebrews 8:1). The reminder is there again: In days gone by, men and women would count on blood that came from goats and heifers. However, the effect was never final, but fleeting.

In contrast, the timeless message of Hebrews reminds us that we have a permanent solution in Christ. The priests of old continually offered blood. Christ shed His blood once for all, for all time impacting man's sin problem.

"Day after day every priest stands and performs his religious duties; again and again he offers the same sacrifices, which can never take away sins. But when this priest (meaning Jesus) had offered for all time one sacrifice for sins, he sat down at the right hand of God" (10:11-12). Aha! There it is again! Jesus sat down. Finished His work. Concluded with victory. Ended in triumph.

What Does He Do?

The Bible says Jesus "serves in the sanctuary, the true tabernacle set up by the Lord, not by man" (Hebrews 8:2).

Of course the tabernacle takes us back to the wilderness days of Israel. The tabernacle was the tent of worship during the wilderness wanderings (e.g., Exodus 27:21), and that earthly tent corresponds to a heavenly reality. It is in the heavenly reality that Christ's ministry is discharged. So in addition to being the exalted, glorious Son of God, He is also the humble, submissive Servant. Here, in the heavenly sanctuary, Jesus ministers to us faithfully day after day after day after day.

Who is He? The High Priest who sat down at the right hand of the throne of the Majesty in heaven. What does He do? He *serves* in the heavenly sanctuary. Our blessed Redeemer, in His exalted glory, still stoops to minister to His beloved bride, the Church. It was Arthur Pink who stated so succinctly:

It is required that our faith should not only appre-
hend what Christ did for us while He was here on
earth, but also appropriate what He is now doing for
His people in heaven. Indeed, the very life and efficacy of the whole of His mediation depends upon His
present work on our behalf."[4]

Nowhere does the marvelous grace of our matchless Lord
more wonderfully appear than in the ministry in which He
is now constantly and presently engaged. The shame, suffering, pain and humiliation did not deter Him one iota from
making full atonement for His Church.

All the honor, glory, blessing, power and dominion divert
Him not one second of the day from interceding on our behalf and pleading our case in the courtroom of heaven. He
serves in the heavenly sanctuary.

> Every high priest is appointed to offer both gifts
> and sacrifices, and so it was necessary for this one also
> to have something to offer. If he were on earth, he
> would not be a priest, for there are already men who
> offer the gifts prescribed by the law. They serve at a
> sanctuary that is a copy and shadow of what is in
> heaven. This is why Moses was warned when he was
> about to build the tabernacle: "See to it that you
> make everything according to the pattern shown you
> on the mountain." (Hebrews 8:3-5)

The author has already said, "Every high priest is selected
from among men and is appointed to represent them in matters related to God, to offer gifts and sacrifices for sins" (Hebrews 5:1). So the writer finds it "necessary" that Christ also
have something to offer as high priest. That's what a priest
does.

Using passages such as this one, many Roman Catholic
writers have suggested that the continuous priesthood of
Christ is given distinctive expression in every celebration

of the Mass. They suggest that in heaven Jesus presents His five wounds and pleads the efficacy of the work He accomplished on Calvary, while on earth He continues and applies His sacrifice in the holy Mass, thus remaining a Priest forever.[5]

Yet there is no evidence here that Christ's sacrifice can be continued or repeated. On the contrary, the teaching of this powerful epistle is that the sacrificial work of Christ is unrepeatable, and once for all. A unique sacrifice. Unrivaled. Unequaled. Unmatched.

When Jeffrey Ebert was five years old, before factory-installed seat belts and air bags, his family was involved in a head-on collision with a drunk driver. After a visit to his grandparents' farm, the family had been driving home at night on a two-lane country road. Jeff was sitting on his mother's lap when the other car swerved into their lane. He doesn't have any memory of the collision, but he recalls the fear and confusion he felt as he saw himself literally covered with blood from head to toe.

Later he learned that the blood wasn't his at all, but his mother's. In that split second when the two headlights glared into her eyes, she instinctively pulled him closer to her chest and curled her body around his smaller frame. It was her body that slammed against the dashboard, her head that shattered the windshield. She took the impact of the collision so that Jeffrey wouldn't have to, and his life was spared (and after extensive surgery his mother eventually recovered from her injuries).

In a similar, but infinitely more significant way, Jesus Christ took the impact for our sin upon the cross; His blood, shed once for all, now permanently covers our lives.

That Christ's offering is limited to a single sacrifice is indicated by the singular pronoun *something*: There is no suggestion that He offers a plurality of "gifts and sacrifices," for to do so would be incompatible with the unique and total sufficiency of the one sacrifice He offered on the cross.[6]

How Does He Serve?

> But the ministry Jesus has received is as superior to
> theirs as the covenant of which he is mediator is su-
> perior to the old one, and it is founded on better
> promises. (Hebrews 8:6)

So what is the ministry of Jesus? If the earthly priests
serve at a sanctuary that is only a copy of the real one, and if
Jesus serves in the real sanctuary, the true tabernacle set up
by the Lord, not by man, what does He do there? *How* does
He serve and *why* is His ministry superior?

The present ministry of the Lord Jesus in the heavenly
sanctuary is one of intercession. He prays for His people
meaningfully, compassionately and effectively. Hebrews
7:25 tells us that "He is able to save completely those who
come to God through him, because he always lives to intercede for them." He also serves as our Advocate (1 John 2:1).

He serves as the Fortress of our salvation (Psalm 28:8). He
serves as the Good Shepherd of the sheep (John 10:11). He
serves as the Head of the Body, which is the Church (Colossians 1:18). He supplies strength for the weak; He's available
for the tempted and the tried; He sympathizes and He saves;
He strengthens and He sustains; He guards and He guides;
He heals the sick; He forgives the sinner; He delivers the
captives; He defends the feeble; He rewards the diligent and
He purifies the meek. He is the Rock of my salvation and
the Keeper of my soul. He knows exactly where to tinker in
my life and yours.

In the book *Making Friends*, Em Griffin writes about three
kinds of London maps: the street map, the map depicting
throughways and the map of the subway. "Each map is accurate and correct," he writes, "but each map does not give
the complete picture. To see the whole, the three maps must
be printed one on top of each other. However, that is often
confusing, so I use only one 'layer' at a time."

It is the same with words and phrases used to describe the life and ministry of our Lord Jesus Christ. Each word, like redemption, reconciliation or justification, is accurate and correct, but each word does not give the complete picture. The author of Hebrews has recorded over a million bytes on his computer in order to explain the superiority of Christ, and that's just one "layer."

To see the whole we need to place one layer on top of the other, but that is sometimes confusing. We cannot see the trees for the forest! So we separate each splendid concept and discover that the whole is more than the sum of its parts.

The author took us from his treatment of the priesthood in the order of Melchizedek in Hebrews 7 to underscore the idea that Christ's ministry far surpasses that of the Levitical priests in Hebrews 8:1-6. First century readers would have been accustomed to the priesthood.

The writer wants to be sure they realize that Jesus has a ministry far excelling it. To bring Jesus into better focus, the writer answered three basic questions about the superior minister Jesus Christ, thus providing another "layer" to add to our collection. Who is He, what does He do and how does He serve?

A television program preceding the 1988 Winter Olympics featured blind skiers being trained for slalom skiing, impossible as that sounds. Paired with sighted skiers, the blind skiers were taught on the flats how to make right and left turns.

When that was mastered, they were taken to the slalom slope, where their sighted partners skied beside them shouting, "Left!" and "Right!" As they obeyed the commands, they were able to negotiate the course and cross the finish line, depending solely on the sighted skiers' word. It was either complete trust or catastrophe.[7]

What a beautiful illustration of the Christian life! In this world, we are in reality blind about what course to take. We must rely solely on the word of the only One who is truly sighted—God Himself. We must trust the One who ministers to us from the right hand of the throne of the Majesty in heaven. From His vantage point He sees all the twists, turns and mounds that lie ahead of us. He knows the danger zones and the avalanche areas. His word gives us the direction we need to finish the course. "Right!" "Wrong!" "Pray now!" "Trust and obey!" It is either complete trust or catastrophe. The choice is yours.

A Superior Covenant

For if there had been nothing wrong with that first covenant, no place would have been sought for another. But God found fault with the people and said:

"The time is coming, declares the Lord,
when I will make a new covenant
with the house of Israel
and with the house of Judah.
It will not be like the covenant
I made with their forefathers
when I took them by the hand
to lead them out of Egypt,
because they did not remain faithful to my
covenant,
and I turned away from them,
declares the Lord
This is the covenant I will make with
the house of Israel
after that time, declares the Lord.
I will put my laws in their minds
and write them on their hearts.
I will be their God,
and they will be my people.
No longer will a man teach his neighbor,
or a man his brother, saying, 'Know the Lord,'
because they will all know me,
from the least of them to the greatest.

> *For I will forgive their wickedness*
> *and will remember their sins no more."*

By calling this covenant "new," he has made the first covenant obsolete; and what is obsolete and aging will soon disappear. (Hebrews 8:7-13)

Not long ago my insurance rates increased again. I'm accident-free. I don't smoke, drink, dance or chew. My eyesight is nearly perfect. I'm over forty and I've been driving since I was sixteen. "Tell me why my rates keep going up!" I muttered under my breath as my blood pressure rose.

"I need more bang for my buck," I concluded. "I need a new agent and a new policy." So I looked for another broker.

God instituted a new policy with the best premiums when He created the superior covenant through Jesus Christ. Hebrews brings out the superiority of this new covenant by referring to the suppression of the old one. If there had been "nothing wrong with that first covenant, no place would have been sought for another" (Hebrews 8:7).

That a new covenant had been established proved that the old one was inadequate. It could not bring men to God. "God found fault with the people." It powerfully revealed the sinfulness of humankind, but it was impotent for reconciliation. However, the Lord did not leave matters in their hands. He established a *new* agreement.

This long quotation from Jeremiah 31:31-34 indicates that the old covenant under which Israel functioned is now overturned, upended by a new covenant. Of great interest to the writer, and to us, is the fact that under the new agreement forgiveness of sins is brought about.

As soon as he comes to the words about forgiveness in the Jeremiah passage (Hebrews 8:12), he breaks off his quotation. Amnesty amplified! Pardon pronounced! Grace granted! Here then are the benefits of the new policy with the best Broker the world has ever known: Internal assurance, a deeper relationship with the Agent and a better benefits package.

Benefit #1: Internal Assurance

> This is the covenant I will make with the house
> of Israel
>   after that time, declares the Lord.
> I will put my laws in their minds
>   and write them on their hearts.
>   (Hebrews 8:10)

Why is this new covenant superior to the old one? *New* is not better simply because it is *new*. (At least that's what I keep telling my children who always want something new when we go to the shopping mall.) It is better because it offers exhilarating internal motivation and power instead of external lists of dos and don'ts. Interior as opposed to exterior.

With the old policies the arrangements were written on tablets of stone (Exodus 24:12). Under the new agreement the law would be written on the mind and the heart. "This is the covenant I will make with the house of Israel after that time, declares the Lord. I will put my laws in their minds and write them on their hearts" (Hebrews 8:10). Internal vis-à-vis external.

The apostle Paul also wanted to give his readers internal assurance of their participation in the new covenant, a confidence that right relations exist between them and God. He wrote, "You show that you are a letter from Christ, the result of our ministry, written not with ink but with the Spirit of the living God, not on tablets of stone but on tablets of human hearts" (2 Corinthians 3:3).

Jewish opponents armed with a letter of recommendation (cf. Acts 9:2; 18:27; Romans 16:1) had gone to Corinth to discredit Paul. But the Corinthians themselves were authentic testimony to the power of the gospel, for their astounding transformation (1 Corinthians 6:9-11) was known everywhere, and Paul wanted to encourage them with that news. Our hearts—that's where God wants us to hear and know *His* approval.

In September 1993, with the Major League Baseball season nearing its end, the first-place Philadelphia Phillies visited the second-place Montreal Expos. In the first game of the series, the home team Expos came to bat one inning trailing 7-4. Their first two batters reached base. The manager sent a pinch hitter to the plate, rookie Curtis Pride, who had never gotten a hit in the major leagues. *Could this be the right choice?*

Pride took his warm-up swings, walked to the plate and on the first pitch punched a double, bringing home two runners. The stadium shook as 45,757 fans jumped to their feet and screamed their approval. The Expos' third-base coach called time, walked calmly toward Pride and told him to take off his batting helmet.

What's wrong with my helmet? wondered the rookie. Then, realizing what his coach meant, Pride tipped his cap to the appreciative fans. After the game, someone asked Pride if he could hear the cheering. This person wasn't giving the rookie a hard time. Curtis Pride is ninety-five percent deaf.

"Here," Pride said, pointing to his heart. "I could hear it here."[8]

Our hearts. That's where God wants us to hear and know His approval by responding with an inner, grace-directed motivation. That's why He said, "I will put my laws in their minds and write them on their hearts." It's based on internal impulsion as opposed to external rituals and requisites. I serve God because I want to, not because I have to. His law is no longer written only on tablets of stone. It's in my heart. That's one of the benefits of the new policy.

Benefit #2: A Deeper Relationship with the Agent

> I will be their God,
>   and they will be my people.

No longer will a man teach his neighbor,
> or a man his brother, saying, "Know the Lord,"
because they will all know me,
> from the least of them to the greatest.
>> (Hebrews 8:10-11)

The new covenant is also based on a close, individual and intimate relationship with the One who wrote it instead of One who is frightening or detached. Remember when God gave the Ten Commandments to Moses?

When the people saw the thunder and lightning, heard the trumpet and saw the mountain in smoke, *they trembled with fear*. They stayed at a distance and said to Moses, "Speak to us yourself and we will listen. But do not have God speak to us or we will die" (Exodus 20:19).

They kept their distance because they were afraid. They didn't have a close, intimate relationship with their heavenly Father.

When Moses came down from Mount Sinai with the two tablets of the Testimony in his hands, he was not aware that his face was radiant because he had spoken with the Lord. When Aaron and all the Israelites saw Moses, his face was radiant, and *they were afraid* to come near him (Exodus 34:29-30).

Fear paralyzed the people of God on one of the most significant days of their journey.

In 1992, Kerrin-Lee Gartner of Calgary, Alberta, became the first Canadian in history to win Olympic gold in the women's downhill. In Canada she was an immediate sensation. Shortly after her victory, an announcer interviewing her commented that this must surely be the most significant day of her life.

"No," she replied. "The most significant day was the day of my marriage—but this ranks pretty high." Even the greatest of achievements cannot compare with the greatest of relationships, and through the new covenant we are related to God Himself!

The people were afraid to approach God because they had no close encounters of a personal kind with Him. They were frightened. But under the new covenant God said, "I will be their God, and they will be my people." There is nothing to be afraid of then, not when you're related to the Creator of the universe and the King of the ages!

I have been impressed recently by the Spirit of God as I read the book of Jeremiah in my devotional time each morning. Even after their immeasurable unfaithfulness and godlessness, God still yearns for His people.

> I will bring them back to this place and let them live in safety. They will be my people, and I will be their God. I will give them singleness of heart and action, so that they will always fear me for their own good and the good of their children after them. I will make an everlasting covenant with them: I will never stop doing good to them, and I will inspire them to fear me, so that they will never turn away from me. I will rejoice in doing them good and will assuredly plant them in this land with all my heart and soul. (Jeremiah 32:37-41)

The new covenant is based on a closer, deeper, more intimate relationship with God. Not one that is fearful, distant, apprehensive, alarmed. I'm so happy that God fully commits Himself to me!

When my original insurance policy was in force I never saw the agent who "wrote me up." He never called. No birthday cards. No Christmas greeting. All I received from him were the notices that my rates were increasing "effective January 1." However, when I was shopping for a new agent and offering my business to someone else, I had no end of personal service. He was falling all over us. The good news is that the Lord's service to us, His ministry to us, never ends. He's the best internal assurance Agent ever.

Benefit #3: A Better Benefits Package

> No longer will a man teach his neighbor,
>   or a man his brother, saying, "Know the Lord,"
> because they will all know me,
>   from the least of them to the greatest.
>   (Hebrews 8:11)

The new arrangement is better also because it offers much better benefits than the old one. It provides purpose and promise instead of instability and uncertainty.

All who enter this new covenant will have knowledge of God. There will be no need for one neighbor to teach another. This does not mean that we have no demand for pastors, missionaries or Bible teachers now that the new covenant has been established. Rather, the meaning is that knowledge of God is no longer confined to a privileged or a particular few.

The power brokers do not control the sources any longer. "Stand aside, my friend, I *know* the Boss, and He knows me too! I don't have an appointment, but I *know* He'll see me anytime I come to Him."

Participation in the new covenant also means that pardon, forgiveness and mercy replace the inevitable slide into moral and ethical deficiency, default, degeneration, decay and deterioration. In Jeremiah's oracle the new covenant is to be made "with the house of Israel and with the house of Judah" (Jeremiah 31:31).

In the New Testament fulfillment is not restricted to them, but reaches to all believers of every nation. "For I will forgive their wickedness and will remember their sins no more" (Hebrews 8:12). Yours and mine. Everyone who calls on the name of the Lord will be forgiven (Romans 10:13).

Early in 1993 British police charged two ten-year-old boys with the inhuman murder of two-year-old James Bulger. The two boys pleaded innocence. The young defendants responded to the police questioning with naiveté and not a little inconsistency. The turning point came when the parents of one of the boys assured him that they would always love him. Confronted with irrefutable and conclusive evidence linking him with the crime and the assurance of his parents' love, the boy finally confessed in a soft voice, "I killed James."

The absolute miracle of God's love is that He knows how evil we are, yet He loves us. "The heart is deceitful above all things and beyond cure. Who can understand it?" (Jeremiah 17:9). We can confess our worst sins to God because of the new agreement initiated by Christ's sacrifice: "For I will forgive their wickedness and will remember their sins no more" (Hebrews 8:12). Under the new covenant God promised to forgive our wickedness and corruption and remember our sins no more.

> If we claim to be without sin, we deceive ourselves and the truth is not in us. If we confess our sins, he is faithful and just and will forgive us our sins and purify us from all unrighteousness. (1 John 1:8-9)

Years ago a thunderstorm swept through southern Kentucky on the farm where the Claypool family had lived for six generations. In the orchard, the wind blew over an old pear tree that had been there as long as anyone could remember. Grandfather Claypool was grieved to lose the tree on which he had climbed as a boy and whose fruit he had eaten all his life.

A neighbor came by and said, "Doc, I'm really sorry to see your pear tree blown down."

"I'm sorry too," said Claypool. "It was a real part of my past."

"What are you going to do?" the neighbor asked.

Old Mr. Claypool paused for a moment, then said, "I'm going to pick the fruit and burn what's left."

That's a wise way to deal with many things in our past. We need to learn their lessons, enjoy their pleasures, confess our sins and then go on with the present and the future. Pardon, forgiveness and mercy are all part of the new policy written for you by God.

The new policy that God made with us was signed, sealed and delivered in blood. The old arrangement was limited, temporary, partial. But the new one? Unrestricted in its power, eternal in its duration, complete in its effects. And it's all free (Romans 6:23). God made some definite commitments to His people, and we are the benefactors of His faithfulness and His sure word:

- I *will* make a new covenant.
- I *will* write My laws on their hearts.
- I *will* be their God.
- I *will* reveal Myself to them all.
- I *will* make Myself known to the least as
        well as the greatest.
- I *will* be merciful.
- I *will* forgive them.
- I *will* remember their sins no more.

The hesitancy and tentativeness of the earlier days have gone. We can now be sure. We have better promises!

One last word. With this I'll end the chapter. Warren Bennis, in *Why Leaders Can't Lead*, writes:

The flying Wallendas are perhaps the world's greatest family of aerialists and tightrope walkers. . . . I was struck with [Karl Wallenda's] capacity for concentration on the intention, the task, the decision. I was even more intrigued when, several months later, Wallenda fell to his death while walking a tightrope without a safety net between two high-rise buildings in San Juan, Puerto Rico. . . . Later, Wallenda's wife said that before her husband had fallen, for the first time since she had known him, he had been concentrating on falling, instead of on walking the tightrope.

He had personally supervised the attachment of the guide wires, which he had never done before.[9]

Often the difference between success and failure in the Christian life is the direction we're looking. Keep your eyes fixed on Jesus, not your problems. Focus on the better promises, not the bitter past. Keep looking ahead, not behind, and God will bless you abundantly.

Endnotes

1. David A. Seamands, *Healing for Damaged Emotions* (Wheaton, IL: Victor Books, 1981), 23, as quoted in Charles Swindoll, *Growing Wise in Family Life* (Portland, OR: Multnomah Press, 1988), 251-252.

2. Donald Guthrie, *Hebrews* (Grand Rapids, MI: William B. Eerdmans Publishing Company, 1983), 170.

3. Raymond Brown, *The Message of Hebrews* (Downers Grove, IL: InterVarsity Press, 1982), 142.

4. Arthur W. Pink, *An Exposition of Hebrews* (Grand Rapids, MI: Baker Book House, 1954), 430.

5. See the discussion in Raymond Brown, 145-46.

6. Philip Edgcumbe Hughes, *A Commentary on the Epistle to the Hebrews* (Grand Rapids, MI: William B. Eerdmans Publishing Company, 1977), 291.

7. *Leadership* (Fall 1988): 45. Used by permission.

8. *Leadership* (Spring 1994): 48.

9. *Leadership* (Fall 1992): 47.

Discussion Questions for Further Study

1. The author mentions Christ sitting down at the right hand of God five times (1:3, 13; 8:1; 10:12; 12:2). Why? How does this show that Jesus' ministry is superior to that of the Levitical priests (10:11-12)?

2. Jesus has sat down, but He still serves as High Priest before the Father (8:2). What is His ongoing priestly service?

3. What do the terms "copy," "shadow" and "pattern" indicate to you about the Levitical priesthood (8:5)?

4. How should the fact that your relationship to God is based on Jesus' sacrifice, not on working to please God, affect your feelings and actions?

5. God set the terms of both the old and new covenants. Why did He choose to initiate a new one (8:7-9)?

6. Can you summarize 8:1-13 in your own words?

8

Hebrews 9:1-10:18

Worship in the Earthly Tabernacle

Now the first covenant had regulations for worship and also an earthly sanctuary. A tabernacle was set up. In its first room were the lampstand, the table and the conse-crated bread; this was called the Holy Place. Behind the second curtain was a room called the Most Holy Place, which had the golden altar of incense and the gold-covered ark of the covenant. This ark contained the gold jar of manna, Aaron's staff that had budded, and the stone tab-lets of the covenant. Above the ark were the cherubim of the Glory, overshadowing the atonement cover. But we cannot discuss these things in detail now.

When everything had been arranged like this, the priests entered regularly into the outer room to carry on their ministry. But only the high priest entered the inner room, and that only once a year, and never without blood, which he offered for himself and for the sins the people committed in ignorance. The Holy Spirit was showing by this that the way into the Most Holy Place had not yet been dis-closed as long as the first tabernacle was still standing. This is an illustration for the present time, indicating that the gifts and sacrifices being offered were not able to clear the conscience of the worshiper. They are only a matter of food and drink and various ceremonial washings—exter-

nal regulations applying until the time of the new order.
(Hebrews 9:1-10)

On the Canadian national holiday every year, July 1, hundreds of immigrants say "Yes" to Canada, receiving their citizenship in ceremonies around the country. The immigrants come here for family, for economic opportunity, to flee war, for freedom.

"I am so excited and so full of life. Elated! It's a great country," beamed sixty-nine-year-old Estrella Abella who came with her husband, Vicante, from the Philippines to be closer to their children.

After one of the ceremonies, a man from Lebanon recalled the sixteen years of war he left behind when he came to Canada with his wife and children. "In Canada we have peace," the thirty-nine-year-old father said, clutching his citizenship certificate. "Now I'm Canadian. . . . I have my rights and my responsibilities."

Christians are a citizens of two worlds, the earthly and the heavenly. They must obey the government whenever that is possible, and they must always obey God. Because they are citizens of two worlds, they must learn how to walk by faith in a world governed by sight.

Like Moses, we must see the invisible if we are to surmount the allure of the world. The natural person, the one living without the indwelling, illuminating Spirit of God, says, "Seeing is believing!" The Spirit-filled person says, "Believing is seeing!" and so walks by faith and not by sight.

This faith principle also applies to our relationship to the heavenly sanctuary. We have never seen it. Yet we know it's there. Even though we call the place where we meet for worship the "house of God," God does not live there. The building may carry a cornerstone that reads "Dedicated to the Glory of God," but He dwells not there. The Church of Christ is much more than a construction of mortar and brick.

Chapter 9 of Hebrews presents a dramatic contrast between the old covenant earthly sanctuary and the new covenant heavenly sanctuary where Jesus Christ ministers to the Church. One commentator points out that the entire chapter is a matter of contrasts.[1]

Staying with the Old Testament scene of the tabernacle, rather than the temple, the writer of Hebrews indirectly moves us toward the superiority of Christ and the superior worship in the heavenly sanctuary. He concentrates his attention on the order of the furniture in the tabernacle (9:1-5), and the responsibilities of the priests (9:6-10).

The Order of the Furniture

Now the first covenant had regulations for worship and also an earthly sanctuary. A tabernacle was set up. In its first room were the lampstand, the table and the consecrated bread; this was called the Holy Place. Behind the second curtain was a room called the Most Holy Place, which had the golden altar of incense and the gold-covered ark of the covenant. This ark contained the gold jar of manna, Aaron's staff that had budded, and the stone tablets of the covenant. Above the ark were the cherubim of the Glory, overshadowing the atonement cover. But we cannot discuss these things in detail now. (Hebrews 9:1-5)

The writer of Hebrews has been thinking and writing about Jesus as the One who leads us into reality (see Hebrews 8:3-6). He has been using the idea that in this world we have only copies and shadows of what is truly real in heaven (Hebrews 8:5). The worship that men can offer is only a ghostlike silhouette of the real worship which Jesus, the real High Priest, alone can offer.

Yet even as he thinks of that, his mind wanders back to the tabernacle (Exodus 25-30). In case any of the readers should think that the writer was underestimating the old, he now outlines some of the glories of the old tabernacle. The temple was accessible only to those in Jerusalem; but wherever Jews were, their Scriptures told them all about the tabernacle. Lovingly he remembers its beauty; warmly he ponders its priceless possessions.

He is thrilled by the orderliness of the arrangements in the Levitical worship and strives to present this in order to illustrate the greater glory of the new. The thought in his mind may be this: If earthly worship was as attractive as this, what must the true worship be like?

Perhaps he recalls the words of Jesus: "Yet a time is coming and has now come when the true worshipers will worship the Father in spirit and truth, for they are the kind of worshipers the Father seeks. God is spirit, and his worshipers must worship in spirit and in truth" (John 4:23-24). If all the enchantment of the tabernacle was only a shadow of reality, how surpassingly captivating, fascinating and delightful the reality must be!

Yet the temptation to go back to the comfortable, well-known pattern of Old Testament worship must have been very strong for some of the early New Testament believers. Does he suspect that some of his readers, who have been brought up in the milieu of glorying in the past, are toying with the idea that Christianity is not an adequate substitute for the dignity of the old pattern of worship? While he himself is not unaware of the resplendence of the past, he wants to lead his readers to a truer appreciation of the superior glories of the Christian faith, to prevent them from moving in reverse.[2]

He does not tell us about the tabernacle in detail. He only alludes to some of its treasures. Would he like to have given more enriching typological interpretation of these historical details? We can only guess, and perhaps we should only guess, what he might have said. Yet some writers have used up a lot of ink speculating what the author of Hebrews *might* have introduced at this point. Calvin issues a warning about this:

Since nothing is enough for inquisitive men the apostle cuts out any opportunity for subtleties that are not in keeping with his present purpose in case too much discussion of these things might break the thread of his argument. If anyone disregards the apostle's warning and dwells more minutely on this matter he will do so inopportunely.[3]

Someday we'll know. For now we'll have to settle for restrained speculation and be happy with that.

The Duties of the Priests

When everything had been arranged like this, the priests entered regularly into the outer room to carry on their ministry. But only the high priest entered the inner room, and that only once a year, and never without blood, which he offered for himself and for the sins the people had committed in ignorance. The Holy Spirit was showing by this that the way into the Most Holy Place had not yet been disclosed as long as the first tabernacle was still standing. This is an illustration for the present time, indicating that the gifts and sacrifices being offered were not able to clear the conscience of the worshiper. They are only a matter of food and drink and various ceremonial washings—external regulations applying until the time of the new order. (Hebrews 9:6-10)

In spite of all the splendor of the tabernacle furniture, worship under the Levitical order was severely limited. The people could not approach directly; they had to come through their representatives, the priests. Only the priests entered regularly into the outer room to carry on their ministry. The tabernacle was not accessible to the general public.

Furthermore, only one could enter annually into the Most Holy Place. When he did, he had to offer a sacrifice for his own sins as well as for the sins of the people. "By this," the writer explains, "the Holy Spirit was showing that the way into the Most Holy Place had not yet been disclosed" (9:8). Earthly tabernacle: restricted access. Heavenly tabernacle: open to all the people of God from every tribe and nation and language, 24 hours a day, 365 days a year!

Do you see what he's doing? Under the Spirit's guidance, the writer of Hebrews points us to Christ again and again. "Therefore, brothers, since we have confidence to enter the Most Holy Place by the blood of Jesus, by a new and living way opened for us through the curtain, that is, his body. . . . Let us draw near to God . . ." (Hebrews 10:19-22). He uses the placement of the furniture and the duties of the priests to magnify the Person and ministry of Jesus, the greatest High Priest of all time.

Many of the people who originally received this letter were likely thinking, *If I could just get back to the tabernacle and become involved in that type of ritual and worship, somehow I could cope. I could live with myself again if only I could return to the way things used to be.*

And while we may not be tempted to go back to the tabernacle known to the Israelites, we may very well get caught up in the external shadows of the real thing. We want something to hold. A statue, a chalice, relics from the crusades, a shroud? Anything would do, but please, give us something more!

As humans, we love the tangibles, the concrete, the manifest, the symbols. However, God is eager for us to turn our attention to the interior, the abstract within. To do so is to follow His example. Get rid of the ritual religion onto which you've hung. Cease the empty motions. Give up the status quo.

Put aside the symbols and idols you've come to worship and for which you've fought. Spotlight the internals. Go beneath the veneer and get to the significant. Place far more worth on what's inside. Rest in what Christ has done for you personally; don't rely on traditions.

William Potett wrote in *The Pentecostal Minister* how in 1903 the Russian Czar noticed a sentry posted for no apparent reason on the Kremlin grounds. Upon inquiry, he discovered that in 1776, approximately 127 years earlier, Catherine the Great found there the first flower of spring. "Post a sentry here," she commanded, "so that no one tramples that flower under foot!"

Some traditions die hard, but die they must if they keep us from Christ.

Most immigrants come to a new country with their hearts set on acquiring citizenship in that country. The Christian, on the other hand, is a citizen of two worlds, the earthly and the heavenly. Therefore, we must learn how to walk by faith in a world that is governed by sight.

Again, "Seeing is believing" is the philosophy of the world that focuses mostly on externals. But the spiritual man says, "Believing is seeing!" and so looks beyond the earthly, the natural and the temporal. He goes beneath the surface and turns his attention to the internals. He allows nothing to keep him from Christ. Neither should you because you are citizens of heaven.

> Since, then, you have been raised with Christ, set your hearts on things above, where Christ is seated at the right hand of God. Set your minds on things above, not on earthly things. For you died, and your life is now hidden with Christ in God. When Christ, who is your life, appears, then you also will appear with him in glory. (Colossians 3:1-4)

What glory that will be!

There's Power in the Blood

> *When Christ came as high priest of the good things that are already here, he went through the greater and more perfect tabernacle that is not man-made, that is to say, not a part of this creation. He did not enter by means of the blood of goats and calves; but he entered the Most Holy*

Place once for all by his own blood, having obtained eternal redemption. The blood of goats and bulls and the ashes of a heifer sprinkled on those who are ceremonially unclean sanctify them so that they are outwardly clean. How much more, then, will the blood of Christ, who through the eternal Spirit offered himself unblemished to God, cleanse our consciences from acts that lead to death, so that we may serve the living God!

For this reason Christ is the mediator of a new covenant, that those who are called may receive the promised eternal inheritance—now that he has died as a ransom to set them free from the sins committed under the first covenant.

In the case of a will, it is necessary to prove the death of the one who made it, because a will is in force only when somebody has died; it never takes effect while the one who made it is living. This is why even the first covenant was not put into effect without blood. When Moses had proclaimed every commandment of the law to all the people, he took the blood of calves, together with water, scarlet wool and branches of hyssop, and sprinkled the scroll and all the people. He said, "This is the blood of the covenant, which God has commanded you to keep." In the same way, he sprinkled with the blood both the tabernacle and everything used in its ceremonies. In fact, the law requires that nearly everything be cleansed with blood, and without the shedding of blood there is no forgiveness. (Hebrews 9:11-22)

Lillie Baltrip is a good bus driver. In fact, according to the Fort Worth *Star-Telegram* of June 17, 1988, the Houston school district nominated her for a safe-driving award. Her colleagues even trusted her to drive a busload of them to an awards ceremony for safe drivers. Unfortunately, on the way to the ceremony, Lillie turned a corner too sharply and flipped the bus over, sending herself and sixteen others to the hospital for minor emergency treatment.[4]

Did Lillie, accident-free for the whole year, get her award anyway? No. Award committees rarely operate on the principle of grace. How fortunate we are as believers that, even when we don't maintain a spotless life-record, our final reward depends on God's grace through the shed blood of Jesus Christ, not on our performance!

The book of Hebrews is for people who are weary and hungry—weary of law and hungry for grace—weary of legalism and hungry for spiritual freedom—weary of working for their own salvation and hungry for the free gift of eternal life.[5]

More than any other Scripture, it repeatedly affirms and underscores the superiority of Christ. It continually brings us back to the solid meat of Christianity, refusing to let us stay in the shadows looking for fulfillment in externals, offering grace upon grace for people like Lillie.

The law of Moses and all the covenants of God established in the Old Testament, as important as they are, do not represent God's major message to humanity. The law brings to us the awareness of our need, but it does nothing to solve our deepest and most dreaded disease: sin. That takes blood—the blood of Jesus, Son of God, Savior of the world.

And, along with the blood comes an entirely new covenant between God and humanity. This passage sets forth three reasons why the blood of Jesus Christ is so important to believers. The precious blood of Jesus obtains their eternal redemption, cleanses their consciences and sets them free from sin.

His Blood Obtained Eternal Redemption

When Christ came as high priest of the good things that are already here, he went through the greater and more perfect tabernacle that is not man-made, that is to say, not a part of this creation. He did not enter by means of the blood of goats and calves; but he entered the Most Holy Place once for all by his own blood, having obtained eternal redemption. (Hebrews 9:11-12)

In contrast to the symbolic operations under the first covenant, Christ has now come as High Priest and has instituted the good things of the new covenant discussed in Hebrews 8:10-12. Jesus secured them as High Priest in a superior sanctuary, the actual presence of God, and believers can enjoy them.

Not only is the place of Christ's activities a great improvement over the Old Testament priests', but so is the offering. Goats and calves were the animals whose blood was utilized in the Day of Atonement ritual which was repeated year after year after year. Christ, however, "entered the Most Holy Place once for all by his own blood." This action obtained eternal redemption for its beneficiaries, in contrast to the annual atonement required in the former system (Hebrews 9:12).

Humankind was under the dominion of sin; and just as the purchase price had to be paid in order to free a man from slavery, so the purchase price had to be paid in order to free us from sin. Jesus explained that everyone who sins is a slave to sin (John 8:34). Sinners are slaves. Sinners are doomed to death. Sin is a one-way ticket to nowhere.

Failing redemption, the slavery would continue and the sentence of death would be carried out. The blood of Jesus Christ is seen against this background. It is the price paid to release the slaves, to let the condemned go free.

This discussion reminds me of a story. In the marketplace of Rotterdam, the Netherlands, stood for many years an old corner house known as "The House of a Thousand Terrors." During the sixteenth century, the Dutch people rose in revolt against the cruel King Philip II of Spain. Philip sent a great army under the Duke of Alva to suppress the rebellion. Rotterdam held out for a time but finally capitulated.

From house to house the victors went searching out citizens and then killing them in their houses. A group of men, women and children were hiding in a corner house when they heard soldiers approaching. A thousand terrors gripped their hearts. Then a young man had an idea. He took a goat in the house, killed it and with a broom swept the blood under the doorway out to the street.

The soldiers reached the house and began to batter down the door. Noticing the blood coming out from under the door, one soldier said, "Come away, the work is already done here. Look at the blood beneath the door." The people inside the house escaped because of the blood.

Through His own blood Christ purchased our eternal redemption and released us from bondage of the enemy and the terrors that grip our hearts.

His Blood Cleanses Our Consciences

How much more, then, will the blood of Christ, who through the eternal Spirit offered himself unblemished to God, cleanse our consciences from acts that lead to death, so that we may serve the living God! (Hebrews 9:14)

It is no mere ceremonial cleansing that is effected by the sacrifice of Christ. Here the author presents us with one of the most impressive instances of a favorite New Testament "how much more" argument. (See also Matthew 7:11, 10:25; Luke 11:13, 12:24, 28; Romans 11:12, 24; 1 Corinthians 6:3; Philemon 16.) Is there really any doubt that we need cleansing from time to time?

"Have mercy on me, O God, according to your unfailing love; according to your great compassion blot out my transgressions. Wash away all my iniquity and cleanse me from my sin" (Psalm 51:1-2). "When we were overwhelmed by sins, you forgave our transgressions" (Psalm 65:3).

"I will cleanse them from all the sin they have committed against me and will forgive all their sins of rebellion against me" (Jeremiah 33:8). Ah, the promise of restoration! "On that day a fountain will be opened to the house of David and the inhabitants of Jerusalem, to cleanse them from sin and impurity" (Zechariah 13:1). Jesus Christ "gave Himself for us to redeem us from all wickedness and to purify for himself a people that are his very own, eager to do what is good" (Titus 2:14). Yes, Lord! Yes!

Those earlier rituals might effect external purification, but the blood of Christ, His offering up of Himself to God, cleanses the conscience. It does the very thing they could not do.

In the White House collection is a letter from a child to President Cleveland, written in September, 1895:

> To His Majesty, President Cleveland:
> Dear President, I'm in a dreadful state of mind; and I thought I would write and tell you all. About two years ago—as near as I can remember, it is two years—I used two postage stamps that had been used before on letters, perhaps more than twice. I did not realize what I had done until lately. My mind is constantly turning on that subject, and I think of it night and day. Now, dear President, will you please forgive me? and I promise I will never do it again. Enclosed find cost of three stamps, and please forgive me, for I was then but thirteen years old, for I am heartily sorry for what I have done. From one of your subjects. . . . [6]

Sounds ridiculous, doesn't it? A bit extreme, perhaps? Oversensitive heart strings? Yet stranger things have occurred when people need rescuing from a guilty conscience. Every believer in Jesus may enjoy "decontaminated consciences" thanks to His blood! It doesn't matter what kind of life you've lived or the mistakes you've made along the way. God says you can be clean. You can hold your head high as you serve the King of kings in whatever type of ministry He calls you to.

His Blood Set Us Free from Our Sins

> For this reason Christ is the mediator of a new covenant, that those who are called may receive the promised eternal inheritance—now that he has died as a ransom to set them free from the sins committed under the first covenant. (Hebrews 9:15)

That Jesus is the mediator of a new covenant foretold by Jeremiah has already been stated in Hebrews 8:6. Now the basis of His mediatorship is made plain: His sacrificial death. By virtue of His death redemption has been provided for those who had broken the law of God. The life of Christ was the costly price paid to liberate us from our sins.

"This is my blood of the covenant, which is poured out for many," Jesus said (Mark 14:24). And now that this redemptive death has taken place, "the promised eternal inheritance" has been made good to those "who are called" (Hebrews 9:15). He died as a ransom to set us free from the past and all of its sin.

By the end of his life, musician Giusepppe Verdi was recognized as a master of dramatic composition. His works astonished the world of music with a power and brilliance that marked the ultimate in Italian grand opera. But he didn't begin his career with such success. As a youth, he was denied entrance to the Milan Conservatory because he lacked the necessary training. He was only an innkeeper's son, and he did not possess the formal education and background required.

Yet time does strange things. After Verdi's fame had spread worldwide, the Milan Conservatory, the same one which had denied him entrance, was renamed the "Verdi Conservatory of Music."

This is a good reminder that endings are not always like their beginnings. We are all born sinners. We are lost. We are like sheep who have gone astray (Isaiah 53:6). But "if anyone is in Christ, he is a new creation; the old is gone and the new has come!" (2 Corinthians 5:17).

When we come to Christ in faith, His blood sets us free from our sin, and our sin is removed from us "as far as the east is from the west" (Psalm 103:12). There's *power* in the blood. No blood, no forgiveness! There's no way to get around it. We are set free from sins through the blood of Christ, and every time we sin the blood is efficacious for cleansing. The blood of Jesus keeps on purifying us from all sin (1 John 1:7). You can never exhaust the inventory of His forgiving grace.

The question is: Will you receive His grace and walk in freedom?

Pitch Lake is on the island of Trinidad. It is a mineral deposit that is filled with asphalt. Workers dig great chunks from the tarlike lake and load train cars full of it to pave the roads of the world. For over seventy years Trinidadians have been taking asphalt out of this crater, yet it never runs empty. It is said that no matter how large a hole is made in this great crater, no cavity will remain after seventy-two hours. It immediately fills up from below. Workers have drilled as far as 285 feet into the lake and have found that the black, gumlike substance is at least that deep. There seems to be an unlimited supply.

An infinite reserve of forgiving love is available for you from Jesus Christ our Savior today. "Come, all you who are thirsty, come to the waters; and you who have no money, come, buy and eat! Come, buy wine and milk without money and without cost" (Isaiah 55:1). It's all free for the asking. Won't you come?

> Would you be free from the burden of sin?
> There's power in the blood, power in the blood;
> Would you o'er evil a victory win?
> There's wonderful power in the blood.
> There is power, power, Wonder-working power
> In the blood of the Lamb;
> There is power, power, Wonder-working power
> In the precious blood of the Lamb.[7]

The Perfect Sacrifice

J ason Tuskes was a seventeen-year-old high school honor
student. He was close to his mother, his wheelchair-
bound father and his younger brother. Jason was an expert
swimmer who loved to scuba dive. One Tuesday morning he left home to explore a spring and underwater cave
near his home in west-central Florida. His plan was to be
home in time to celebrate his mother's birthday by going
out to dinner with his family that night.

However, Jason became lost in the underwater cave.
Then, in his panic, he apparently got wedged into a narrow
passageway. When he realized he was trapped, he shed his
yellow metal air tank and unsheathed his diver's knife. With
the tank as a tablet and the knife as a pen, he wrote one last
message to his family: I LOVE YOU MOM, DAD AND
CHRISTIAN. Then he ran out of air and drowned.[8]

A dying message—something communicated in the last
few seconds of life—is something we can't be indifferent toward. God's final words to us are etched on a Roman cross.
They, too, say, "I love you. I gave the only perfect sacrifice
for you—My Son."

The writer develops a motif which has been introduced
many times in the earlier passages of the letter, that of
Christ's perfect sacrifice. The author turns from the sanctuary and what is needed to purify it to the sacrifice that perfectly purifies, a sacrifice that has been offered once for all.
We are exposed to the heavenly purpose of the sacrifice, as
well as its unique character, its enormous price and its perfect impact.

The Heavenly Purpose

It was necessary, then, for the copies of the heavenly things to be purified with these sacrifices, but
the heavenly things themselves with better sacrifices

than these. For Christ did not enter a man-made
sanctuary that was only a copy of the true one; he entered heaven itself, now to appear for us in God's
presence. (Hebrews 9:23-24)

The phrase "it was necessary" points to something much
more than convenience or expediency. There was no other
way. Blood must be shed, for "without the shedding of
blood there is no forgiveness" (Hebrews 9:22). Calvin wrote
that "since the heavenly pattern does not allow of anything
earthly it requires something other than the blood of beasts
to conform to its excellence."[9] Purification comes only
through the blood of Christ, and where atonement really
matters (in the heavenly sphere) better sacrifices are needed
than were provided under the old covenant.

The present mission of the Anointed One which has been
mentioned before is repeated again: We are not fit to stand
before Almighty God and plead our own case. Christ is
there in our place as the One who died as a better sacrifice
for sins (Hebrews 9:23). This is His intercessory work expressed in different terms. He always lives to intercede for
us (Hebrews 7:25, 1 John 2:1).

One winter's night in 1935, it is told, Fiorello LaGuardia,
the irrepressible mayor of New York, showed up at a night
court in the poorest ward of the city. He dismissed the judge
for the evening and took over the bench. That night a tat-
tered old woman, charged with stealing a loaf of bread, was
brought before him. She defended herself by saying, "My
daughter's husband has deserted her. She is sick, and her
children are starving."

The shopkeeper refused to drop the charges, saying, "It's
a bad neighborhood, your honor, and she's got to be punished to teach other people a lesson."

LaGuardia sighed. He turned to the old woman and said,
"I've got to punish you; the law makes no exceptions. Ten
dollars or ten days in jail." However, even while pronounc-
ing sentence, LaGuardia reached into his pocket, took out a

ten-dollar bill and threw it into his hat with these famous words: "Here's the ten-dollar fine, which I now remit, and furthermore, I'm going to fine everyone in the courtroom fifty cents for living in a town where a person has to steal bread so that her grandchildren can eat. Mr. Bailiff, collect the fines and give them to the defendant."

The following day, a New York newspaper reported: "Forty-seven dollars and fifty cents was turned over to a bewildered old grandmother who had stolen a loaf of bread to feed her starving grandchildren. Making forced donations were a red-faced storekeeper, seventy petty criminals and a few New York policemen."[10]

We've all been charged. The law makes no exceptions. The wages of sin is death. But the free gift of God is eternal life in Jesus Christ (Romans 6:23)! He paid the price of atonement and set us free, and now He sits at the right hand of the Judge making intercession for us.

"Therefore he is able to save completely those who come to God through him, because he always lives to intercede for them" (Hebrews 7:25). Christ appears for us in God's presence. There are no other intermediaries between Christ and God. Our High Priest has direct access. This is much superior to the Aaronic high priests who were allowed only once into the Most Holy Place.

The word used here for *presence* (literally "face") is highly suggestive, for the idea of "the face" to express God's presence is very personal and contains the suggestion of communication. It's good to know the Lord is praying for us, face to face with God the Father, because He does for us what we could not do for ourselves. He knows how to effectively intercede for each and every one.

The Unique Character

> Nor did he enter heaven to offer himself again and again, the way the high priest enters the Most Holy Place every year with blood that is not his own. Then

Christ would have had to suffer many times since the creation of the world. But now he has appeared once for all at the end of the ages to do away with sin by the sacrifice of himself. Just as man is destined to die once, and after that to face judgment, so Christ was sacrificed once to take away the sins of many people; and he will appear a second time, not to bear sin, but to bring salvation to those who are waiting for him.

The law is only a shadow of the good things that are coming—not the realities themselves. For this reason it can never, by the same sacrifices repeated endlessly year after year, make perfect those who draw near to worship. If it could, would they not have stopped being offered? For the worshipers would have been cleansed once for all, and would no longer have felt guilty for their sins. But those sacrifices are an annual reminder of sins, because it is impossible for the blood of bulls and goats to take away sins. (Hebrews 9:25-10:4)

When Hebrews describes the work of Christ, it insists, again and again, that it is one for all, once for all and all for free (Hebrews 9:26). The perfect sacrifice also had a unique character: It cannot be repeated, and it cannot be purchased for any price. The preceding sections have brought out the power of the blood of Jesus as a prevailing sacrifice, and now stress is laid on the once-for-all character of that sacrifice.

One of the essential features of the Old Testament sacrificial system was its unfinished nature. Such sacrifices were offered day after day and year after year (see Exodus 29:36-42). They served as a necessary reminder of man's sin, but the ancient system that meant so much to the Jews was no more than an insubstantial, shadowy affair. The real thing is Christ Jesus. To leave Christ in favor of Judaism would be to forsake the substance for the shadow, because Christ has appeared once for all at the end of the ages to do away with sin by the sacrifice of Himself.[11]

That is the unrepeatable nature of Christ's sacrifice when He offered His own body on the tree. It annuls the power of sin. It removes the penalty of sin—something the law and the sacrificial system could never do.

When we amplify the unique character of the death of Christ, I am fearful that we lose something of the dreadful responsibility of our sin that we all carry around in our bodies. On this matter Tozer wrote: "There is a strange conspiracy of silence in the world today—even in religious circles—about man's responsibility for sin, the reality of judgment, and about an outraged God and the necessity for a crucified Saviour. . . . A great shadow lies upon every man and every woman—the fact that our Lord was bruised and wounded and crucified for the entire human race. This is the basic human responsibility that men are trying to push off and evade."[12]

Let us not evade our responsibility or push it off on others. All have sinned. All are guilty. But thanks be to God for the once-for-all death of His Son. Balance between those two perspectives is critical to right thinking and right living.

The Enormous Price

Therefore, when Christ came into the world, he said:

"Sacrifice and offering you did not desire,
    but a body you prepared for me;
with burnt offerings and sin offerings
    you were not pleased.
Then I said, 'Here I am—it is written
    about me in the scroll—
I have come to do your will, O God.' "

First he said, "Sacrifices and offerings, burnt offerings and sin offerings you did not desire, nor were you pleased with them" (although the law required

them to be made). Then he said, "Here I am, I have
come to do your will." He sets aside the first to establish the second. And by that will, we have been made
holy through the sacrifice of the body of Jesus Christ
once for all. (Hebrews 10:5-10)

The human author of Hebrews often clinches his argument by appealing to Scripture. In the foregoing sections,
however, he has been arguing without such appeals. Now he
masterfully develops the theme by showing that the Bible
confirms the accuracy of the position he has advocated.

Animal sacrifices just won't do, yet sin must be atoned
for. Christ's perfect sacrifice of Himself fulfills God's will as
animal sacrifices could never do, as seen prophetically in
Psalm 40 and Jeremiah 31.

Christ's obedient sacrifice, which established the new
covenant, was sufficient. It really put sin in its place. But it
carried a very heavy price, "the sacrifice of the body of Jesus
Christ once for all" (Hebrews 10:10). Nothing but obedience
could open the way to God. Jesus was the perfect sacrifice
because He perfectly obeyed God's will.

In a Japanese seashore village many years ago, an earthquake
startled the villagers one evening during the rice harvest. But,
being accustomed to earthquakes, they soon went back to their
activities. Above the village on a high plain, an old farmer was
watching from his house. He looked at the sea, and the water
appeared dark and acted strangely. It moved against the wind,
running away from the land. The old man knew what it meant.
His one thought was to warn the people in the village.

He called to his grandson, "Bring me a torch! Hurry,
hurry!" In the fields behind him lay his great crop of rice.
Piled in stacks ready for the market, it was worth a fortune.
The old man hurried out with his torch. In a moment the
dry stalks were blazing. Then the big bell pealed from the
temple below: *Fire!*

Back from the beach, away from that strange sea, up the
steep side of the cliff, came the people of the village. They

were coming to try to save the crops of their rich neighbor. "He's mad!" they said.

As they reached the plain, the old man shouted back at the top of his voice, "Look!" They looked, and at the edge of the horizon they saw a long, lean, dim line—a line that thickened as they watched. That line was the sea, rising like a high wall and coming toward the shore faster than a kite flies. Then came a shock, heavier than thunder. The great swell struck the shore with a weight that sent a shudder through the hills. It tore their homes into matchsticks. It drew back, roaring. Then it struck again and again and again.

On the plain, no word was spoken. Then the voice of the old man was heard, saying gently, "That is why I set fire to the rice." He stood among them almost as poor as the poorest, for his wealth was gone—but he had saved 400 lives by the sacrifice.[13]

What sacrifice could be greater than the life of the perfectly obedient Son of God? The will of the Father was the consuming concern of Jesus Christ the Son. And the sacrifice He made was costly.

"For you know the grace of our Lord Jesus Christ, that though he was rich, yet for your sakes he became poor, so that you through his poverty might become rich" (2 Corinthians 8:9).

The Perfect Impact

Day after day every priest stands and performs his religious duties; again and again he offers the same sacrifices, which can never take away sins. But when this priest had offered for all time one sacrifice for sins, he sat down at the right hand of God. Since that time he waits for his enemies to be made his footstool, because by one sacrifice he has made perfect forever those who are being made holy.

The Holy Spirit also testifies to us about this. First he says:

"This is the covenant I will make with them
    after that time, says the Lord.
I will put my laws in their hearts,
    and I will write them on their minds."

Then he adds:

"Their sins and lawless acts
    I will remember no more."

And where these have been forgiven, there is no
longer any sacrifice for sin.
                    (Hebrews 10:11-18)

The death of Jesus Christ put an end to the sacrificial system
of the Old Testament; it spelled the eternal defeat of all the
enemies of God; and it "made perfect forever those who are being made holy" (Hebrews 10:14). The author gives emphasis to
the completeness of Jesus' sacrifice from another angle as he
considers once more the enduring activity of the priests.

"Day after day every priest stands and performs his religious duties; again and again he offers the same sacrifices,
which can never take away sins" (10:11). Jesus, on the other
hand "offered for all time one sacrifice for sins" and then sat
down, signaling the fulfillment of the sacrifice. It was no accident, as Max Lucado makes clear:

Jesus' death was not the result of a panicking, cos-
mological engineer. The cross wasn't a tragic surprise. Calvary was not a knee-jerk response to a world
plummeting towards destruction. It wasn't a patch-
job or a stop-gap measure. The death of the Son of
God was anything but an unexpected peril. . . .

No, it was part of a plan. It was a calculated choice.
"It was the Lord's will to crush him." The cross was
drawn into the original blueprint. It was written into
the script. The moment the forbidden fruit touched

the lips of Eve, the shadow of a cross appeared on the horizon.

And between that moment and the moment the man with the mallet placed the spike against the wrist of God, a master plan was fulfilled. . . . So call it what you wish: An act of grace. A plan of redemption. A martyr's sacrifice. But whatever you call it, don't call it an accident. It was anything but that.[14]

Hebrews 9:23-10:18 explained the heavenly purpose of the sacrifice, as well as its unique character, its enormous price and its perfect impact. And it takes us right back to Calvary, to the cross, to the place where Jesus died.

Is it possible that a new cross has made its way into evangelical circles? It's like the old cross, says Tozer, but different: the likenesses are superficial; the differences fundamental.

From this new cross has sprung a new philosophy of the Christian life, and from that new philosophy has come a new evangelical technique—a new type of meeting and a new kind of preaching. . . .

The new cross is not opposed to the human race; rather, it is a friendly pal and, if understood correctly, it is the source of oceans of good clean fun and innocent enjoyment. It lets Adam live without interference. . . .

The new cross encourages a new and entirely different evangelistic approach. The evangelist does not demand abnegation of the old life before a new life can be received. He preaches not contrasts but similarities. He seeks to key into public interest by showing that Christianity makes no unpleasant demands; rather, it offers the same thing the world does, only on a higher level. . . .

The new cross does not slay the sinner, it redirects him. It gears him into a cleaner and jollier way of living and saves his self-respect. . . . The old cross is a

symbol of death. It stands for the abrupt, violent end
of a human being. . . . The cross made no compromise, modified nothing, spared nothing; it slew all of
the man, completely and for good. It did not try to
keep on good terms with its victim. It struck cruel
and hard, and when it had finished its work, the man
was no more. . . .

God offers life, but not an improved old life. The
life He offers is life out of death. It stands always on
the far side of the cross. Whoever would possess it
must pass under the rod. He must repudiate himself
and concur in God's just sentence against him.[15]

Brothers and sisters in Christ, we are not public relations
agents who have been sent primarily to establish good will
between Christ and the world, or the church and society!
We cannot imagine ourselves commissioned to make Christ
acceptable. We preach Christ crucified (1 Corinthians 1:23,
2:2; Galatians 2:20, 3:1, 6:14).

Talk of the blood may turn some away, "for the message
of the cross is foolishness to those who are perishing" (1
Corinthians 1:18). But we are prophets not diplomats. Our
message is not a compromise but an ultimatum.

I will never hold a candle to Dr. Tozer and his prophetic
ministry, but I want to reissue the call to preach the cross of
Christ and the perfect sacrifice of Jesus in such a way that
we do not jeopardize the integrity of the gospel for any reason for any one.

As preachers, teachers, Sunday school teachers and dedicated laypeople in our churches, we can make a profound
impact if we speak boldly and speak often about the perfect
sacrifice of Jesus and its specific purpose, unique character,
enormous price and its perfect impact.

Jesus, keep me near the cross,
There a precious fountain,
Free to all—a healing stream,

Flows from Calvary's mountain.
In the cross, in the cross,
Be my glory ever,
Till my raptured soul shall find,
Rest beyond the river.[16]

Endnotes

1. William R. Newell, *Hebrews Verse by Verse* (Chicago: Moody Press, 1947), 275-276. The two tabernacles: (a) one earthly, way to God *veiled*; the other in heaven itself—*no veil* there; (b) the one made by hands; the other, not of this creation. The two priesthoods: (a) Levitical priests and (b) Christ, our one Great High Priest. Their offerings: (a) the Levitical priests' continued sacrifices and Day of Atonement every year; (b) Christ's one sacrifice of Himself at the Cross. The results: (a) their sacrifices of animals, goats and bulls could not atone for sin or relieve the conscience of the sinner; (b) Christ offered up Himself, through the Eternal Spirit, which cleansed the conscience to serve the Living God: Christ's one offering obtaining eternal redemption and an eternal inheritance. The sacrifices: (a) the earthly sacrifices, mere copies of things in the heavens; (b) Christ's sacrifice, which brought Him not into a holy place made with hands, but into heaven itself, now to appear before the face of God for us not once a year, but constantly! The frequency: (a) the sacrifices of the Levitical priests constantly repeated; (b) Christ's once for all. Their death: (a) the universal appointment unto men once to die, and after this judgment; (b) Christ, having been once offered to bear the sins of many shall appear a second time, apart from sin, to them that wait for Him, unto salvation.

2. Donald Guthrie, *Hebrews* (Grand Rapids, MI: William B. Eerdmans Publishing Company, 1983). See pages 178ff. for a very good discussion of this passage.

3. John Calvin, *Calvin's New Testament Commentaries: Hebrews and I and II Peter*, trans. W.B. Johnston (Grand Rapids, MI: William B. Eerdmans Publishing Company, 1963), 116.

4. *Leadership* (Winter 1990): 51. Used by permission.

5. From a sermon on Hebrews by Charles Swindoll.

6. Paul Lee Tan, *Encyclopedia of 7700 Illustrations* (Chicago, IL: Assurance Publishers, 1979), 268.

7. Text and music by Lewis E. Jones, "There Is Power in the Blood."

8. *Leadership*, (Summer 1990, Vol. XI, No. 3): 49. Used by permission.

9. John Calvin, 127.

10. *Leadership* (Spring 1990): 48. Used by permission.

11. See Leon Morris, *Hebrews, The Expositor's Bible Commentary*, Vol. 12, ed. Frank E. Gaebelein (Grand Rapids, MI: Zondervan Publishing House, 1981), 92-96.

12. A.W. Tozer, *Who Put Jesus on the Cross?* (Harrisburg, PA: Christian Publications, 1975), 9.

13. Adapted from an article in *Leadership* (Spring 1989, Volume X, Number 2): 44, which was originally adapted from *Christian Living*. Used by permission.

14. Max Lucado, *God Came Near: Chronicles of the Christ* (Portland, OR: Multnomah Press, 1987), 79, 81.

15. A.W. Tozer, *The Best of A.W. Tozer* (Harrisburg: PA: Christian Publications Inc., 1978), 175-178. This article, titled "The Old Cross and the New," first appeared in *The Alliance Witness* in 1946. It has been printed in virtually every English-speaking country in the world and has been put into tract form by various publishers, including Christian Publications, Inc. It still appears now and then in the religious press.

16. "Near the Cross," by Fanny J. Crosby.

Discussion Questions for Further Study

1. How does the conscience of the worshiper (9:9) relate to his ability to draw near to God (7:19)? How is this affecting your life?

2. How would you summarize the author's main point in 9:1-10?

3. Why do you think the author keeps emphasizing that Christ's sacrifice was "once for all" (9:12, 26, 28)?

4. Why do you think the author looks ahead to Christ's return, bringing judgment and ultimate salvation? How is this relevant to the discussion at hand?

5. How is Christ an example for all Christians in his affirmation to the Father: "Here I am, I have come to do your will" (10:9)?

6. What does it mean that we *have been* "made perfect forever," yet *"are being* made holy" (10:14, emphasis added)?

7. What is your personal response to the fact that God has completely and irrevocably forgiven all of your sins?

Hebrews 10:19-39

Holding Fast

> *Therefore, brothers, since we have confidence to enter the Most Holy Place by the blood of Jesus, by a new and living way opened for us through the curtain, that is, his body, and since we have a great priest over the house of God, let us draw near to God with a sincere heart in full assurance of faith, having our hearts sprinkled to cleanse us from a guilty conscience and having our bodies washed with pure water. Let us hold unswervingly to the hope we profess, for he who promised is faithful. And let us consider how we may spur one another on toward love and good deeds. Let us not give up meeting together, as some are in the habit of doing, but let us encourage one another—and all the more as you see the Day approaching. (Hebrews 10:19-25)*

One issue of *Sports Illustrated* magazine featured a lengthy article on Tom Landry, then coach of the Dallas Cowboys football team. When Landry was first introduced as the coach of the Cowboys all he had to work with was a rag-tag bag of unknown athletes.

The first few years were bleak. The crowds were sparse. Instead of cheers there were groans. One losing season led to another, and as you can imagine, the public soon made Landry the target of their savage verbal assaults. But Landry plugged on. Maligned and plagued with misunderstanding, he hung in there with bulldog determination.

He refused to give in to public pressure. The word "quit" wasn't in Landry's vocabulary. His disciplined determination paid off again and again as his Dallas Cowboys became a pro football legend. Tom Landry stood his ground, and that's exactly what Hebrews 10:23-25 encourages us to do. Persevere and not quit. Endure. Hang on until the end of the game.

At this point the author of Hebrews begins a new section of his letter that consists of a series of exhortations based upon the great doctrinal truths that precede it. The superiority of Jesus Christ as the unique sacrifice and perfect priest should be fully apparent to every reader.

Yet these truths must not remain abstract ideas. They must produce appropriate conduct. Faith must be practiced, not only professed. Truth must be lived. Beginning with Hebrews 10:19, the writer urges his readers to hold fast to their faith by looking up, looking back, looking around and finally by looking ahead.

Hold Fast by Looking Up

> Therefore, brothers, since we have confidence to enter the Most Holy Place by the blood of Jesus, by a new and living way opened for us through the curtain, that is, his body. . . . (Hebrews 10:19-20)

We hold fast in the midst of trials by drawing near to God. He invites us to enter His presence with confidence.

The way to God is "new" because what Jesus has done has created a completely new situation. In the Old Testament when Aaron's sons Nadab and Abihu took their censers, put fire in them and added incense, thus offering unauthorized fire before the Lord, contrary to His command, fire came out from the presence of the Lord and con-

sumed them (Leviticus 10:1-2). In contrast, Christians have
an open invitation to come into God's presence, which is no
longer reserved only for the priesthood.

Ransomed men and women need no longer pause in fear
to enter the Most Holy Place. As Tozer once said, "God
wills that we should push on into His Presence and live our
whole life there." We can know this in our present experience with God. It is more than a doctrine to be taught; it is a
life to be enjoyed every moment of every day.

This is glory on earth: Christ in us, the hope of glory (Colossians 1:27). The flame of the presence of God. The greatest fact
of the tabernacle was that Jehovah God was there, a Presence
waiting within the veil. Similarly, the presence of God is the
central fact of our message. God Himself is waiting for us to
push into a conscious awareness of His presence.

This new way is also "living" because it is indispensably
bound up with the Lord Jesus Himself. It is not the way of
dead heifers, goats and turtledoves in the old agreement or
covenant. The writer does not say Jesus is the way, as John
did (John 14:6), but this is close to what he means. The
"way" is the living Lord Himself, and through His precious
blood we can enter God's presence with confidence.

The writer is fond of this word "confidence." He uses it
several times in his letter to encourage and exhort the Jewish
believers (Hebrews 3:14, 4:16, 10:35, 13:6). Perseverance is
never easy, but when we consistently come before God and
enter His presence with conviction, hope and confidence because of the blood of Jesus Christ, we're on the right track.
Confidence in the Lord makes perseverance possible. "Some
trust in chariots and some in horses, but we trust in the
name of the LORD our God" (Psalm 20:7).

A group of botanists went on an expedition into a hard-to-
reach location in the Swiss Alps, searching for new varieties
of flowers. One day a scientist looked through his binocu-
lars, and he saw a beautiful, rare species growing at the bottom of a deep ravine. In order to reach it someone would
have to be lowered into the gorge.

Noticing a local youngster standing nearby, the man asked him if he would help them get the flower. The boy was told that a rope would be tied around his waist and the men would lower him to the floor of the canyon. Excited, yet apprehensive about the adventure, the youngster peered thoughtfully into the deep chasm. "Wait," he said, "I'll be right back," and off he ran.

When he returned, he was accompanied by a man in his mid-forties. Approaching the head scientist, the boy said, "I'll go over the cliff now and get the flower for you, but this man must hold the rope. He's my dad!" That's confidence. You can face any trial or circumstance or step off any cliff if you know the Man who holds the rope.

As we respond to God's call to persevere, to stick it out by the grace of God, we look up and fix our eyes upon Jesus, "the author and perfecter of our faith" (Hebrews 12:2). We push into His presence on the merits of the cross, lay down our rights before the throne, bow in worship, confident that if we ask anything according to His will, He hears us.

But we should also express our gratitude to the Father for everything He's done. The cost of "entering" has been repeatedly emphasized in the earlier chapters of Hebrews, and it is not overlooked here. Jesus inaugurated the new and living way through His flesh by shedding His blood and giving His life on the cross. Sometimes the attitude of gratitude is difficult to resurrect after a long, strenuous day at the office. Yet the sacrifice God made to send His Son never fails to spark gratitude in my heart, and it primes the pump for prayer and praise.

One way to add a spark to your prayer life is to enter the Holy Place with gratitude. Have a look at a sample of verses that remind us to give thanks to His Majesty:

"We give thanks to you, O God, we give thanks, for your Name is near" (Psalm 75:1).

"Enter his gates with thanksgiving and his courts with praise; give thanks to him and praise his name" (100:4).

"Give thanks to the LORD, call on his name; make known among the nations what he has done" (105:1).

"Give thanks to the LORD, for he is good; his love endures forever" (106:1).

"Open for me the gates of righteousness; I will enter and give thanks to the LORD" (118:19).

"Give thanks to the God of gods" (136:2).

"Give thanks to the Lord of lords" (136:3).

"But thanks be to God! He gives us the victory through our Lord Jesus Christ" (1 Corinthians 15:57).

"Thanks be to God for his indescribable gift!" (2 Corinthians 9:15).

Enter with confidence. Enter with gratitude. Hebrews 10:22 also suggests that we enter with sincerity: "Let us draw near to God with a sincere heart in full assurance of faith, having our hearts sprinkled to cleanse us from a guilty conscience and having our bodies washed with pure water."

The water spoken of here does not refer to literal water any more than the text refers to a literal heart. Therefore, this cannot be a reference to baptism. He is speaking of the work of the Holy Spirit as he takes the Word of God and washes us clean, making us pure in His sight.

This is the first of three exhortations: "Let us draw near," "Let us hold unswervingly" (10:23), and "Let us consider" (10:24). The contemplation of what Jesus has done should stir us into action, drawing near to God with a sincere heart. The "heart" stands for the whole of the inner life of humankind, and it's important that when God's people approach Him, they be right inwardly. It is the pure in heart who will see God, according to the beatitude in Matthew 5:8 and the words of David in Psalm 51:7-10, 17.

When two wolves fight over a territorial boundary, the conflict ends in an unusual way. When one animal realizes it can't win, it surrenders by exposing its jugular vein to the teeth of its adversary. For some unexplainable reason, the victor does not kill. Instead, it allows the conquered to go free.

Coming to God with a sincere heart means that we expose the jugular. We surrender. We submit completely, totally and absolutely. Surrender is the secret to the deeper life. We should remember that this is holy business. No careless or casual dealings will suffice. The way to deeper knowledge of God is through the lonely valleys of soul poverty and spiritual honesty. Sincerity before God is the secret to prayer most profound.

So, we enter the Holy Place with confidence, gratitude and sincerity. There we hold on for dear life. The "full assurance of faith" stresses that it is only by trusting in Christ, who has performed for us the high priestly work that gives access to God, that we can look up into His face, draw near to His grace and rest in His love. Hold fast!

Hold Fast by Looking Back

> Let us hold unswervingly to the hope we profess, for he who promised is faithful. (Hebrews 10:23)

It seems that the first readers of this letter were being tempted to forsake their devotion to the Lord. They wanted to go back to the old covenant worship. So the human author urges them to hold unswervingly to the "hope" they profess. He has already expressed the desire that his readers should show diligence to the very end, in order to make their "hope" sure (6:11).

Hope has also been described as an anchor for the soul, firm and secure (6:19). Like an anchor holding a ship safely in position, our hope in Christ guarantees our safety. We can hold fast to our hope because behind it is a God in whom we can have full confidence. Since He is the one who took the initiative in making the promise, He will also fulfill His purposes in keeping it.

And at times when the storms of life are blowing the fiercest, we may also be tempted to retreat. Often when that happens we blame others for our predicament, as the following stories illustrate.

In 1980 a Boston court acquitted Michael Tindall of flying illegal drugs into the United States. Tindall's attorneys argued that he was a victim of "action addict syndrome," an emotional disorder that makes a person crave dangerous, thrilling situations. Tindall was not a drug dealer, merely a thrill seeker. It wasn't his fault.

An Oregon man who tried to kill his ex-wife was acquitted on the grounds that he suffered from "depression-suicide syndrome." Apparently the victims of this syndrome deliberately commit poorly planned crimes with the unconscious goal of being caught or killed. He didn't really want to shoot his wife; he wanted the police to shoot him.

Then there's the famous "Twinkie syndrome." Attorneys for Dan White, who murdered San Francisco Mayor George Moscone, blamed the crime on emotional stress linked to White's junk food binges. White was acquitted of murder and convicted on a lesser charge of manslaughter.

Nowadays, nobody's at fault for anything. No one wants to take responsibility for his own actions. We are a nation of *victims*, experts at playing the blame game. But there's a better way. Christ interrupts the victimization through conversion to create a family of victors. He gives new life to all who ask. Creates somebodies out of nobodies. Makes all things new. "Thanks be to God! He gives us the victory through our Lord Jesus Christ" (1 Corinthians 15:57).

By looking back to the cross we're able to deal with the difficulties, hold fast and maintain the course of our faith. But Calvin is right: "We must take careful note of the condition which follows that God is faithful that promised. This tells us first of all that our faith rests on the foundation that God is true."[1]

This faithfulness theme is often repeated in Scripture, and it has never disappointed anyone who truly trusts the Lord.[2] The emphasis on the divine character is the foundation of everything in our life. Because God is faithful, we can have faith and hope.

Upon God's faithfulness rests our whole hope of future blessedness. Only as He is faithful will His cove-

nants stand and His promises be honored. Only as
we have complete assurance that He is faithful may
we live in peace and look forward with assurance to
the life to come.[3]

Keep pressing into God's presence. Refrain from blaming
others. Glance back at the cross to recalibrate your soul.
Grip your faith with clenched fists of determination. Hold
fast by looking back and remember what Jesus Christ has
done for you.

Hold Fast by Looking Around

And let us consider how we may spur one another on
toward love and good deeds. Let us not give up meeting together, as some are in the habit of doing, but let
us encourage one another.... (Hebrews 10:24-25)

Earlier, our author has entreated his readers to consider,
that is, to pay thoughtful attention to Jesus, "the apostle and
high priest whom we confess" (Hebrews 3:1). Now he urges
them to give similar consideration to their brothers and sisters in the faith. Since Christians are considered brothers in
the same family (Hebrews 3:1, 13:1, 22), partners in the
same enterprise (3:14) and members of the same household
(3:6, 10:21; 1 Timothy 3:15; 1 Peter 2:5), they have a responsibility not only to hold fast themselves, but also to encourage others, spurring them on toward love and action.[4]

The implication is that there are some signs of a weaken-
ing fellowship. That can happen when the heat in the furnace of affliction or persecution gets turned up. Love was
not as evident as it had been. Perhaps the good deeds were
dropping off too. Selfish individualism quickly leads to the
neglect of meeting together for worship and mutual edifica-
tion. The author's point is that we need each other. We cannot hold fast to our faith all by ourselves. We are
interdependent.

John Fawcett pastored a little Baptist church in Wainsgate, England. It was a congregation of plain and simple people, some of whom could not read or write. For his services, Pastor Fawcett was paid the handsome salary of $100 a year.

But a call came from a larger church in London, and Fawcett accepted the invitation to Carter's Lane Church. It would mean a larger congregation, a more sophisticated people and of course a larger salary. The mover arrived at the two-room parsonage in Wainsgate and began loading the personal possessions of the young pastor. However, others gathered at the parsonage that day as well, members and friends of the church.

The pastor began to say goodbye to those he had ministered to, those he had won to Christ, those he had baptized. But the people pleaded with him to stay. Many wept. At every turn he heard the same thing, "You can't leave us." The utter sincerity and love of this faithful congregation was too much for John Fawcett. He said he would stay. The mover was dismissed and Fawcett settled down to pastor the church for fifty-four years!

Though he did not move to the big church in London, his ministry was known by thousands—even King George III, who was so impressed by the man that he offered him "any benefit a king could confer."

As for John Fawcett, he said that he "needed nothing a king could supply" as long as he had the opportunity to live with the people he loved and continue his ministry. As he "looked around" at the genuine devotion of his congregation he was inspired to write this lovely song of fellowship:

> Blest be the tie that binds
> Our hearts in Christian love;
> The fellowship of kindred minds
> Is like to that above.[5]

John Wesley was fond of reminding the early Methodist people of the words of a friend: "The Bible knows nothing of a solitary religion." We really do need each other, and we should be able to find spiritual encouragement as we look around at the lives of other believers. When people observe your life, what do they see? Are they "spurred on" or "turned off"?

Hold Fast by Looking Ahead

> . . . but let us encourage one another—and all the more as you see the Day approaching. (Hebrews 10:25)

This ministry of mutual encouragement should be "all the more" frequent, the first recipients of this letter are advised, as they see "the Day approaching." When spoken of in this absolute manner, "the Day" can mean only the last day, that ultimate eschatological day, which is the day of reckoning and judgment—the Day of the Lord.

If first-century readers, who were so much closer to the time of Christ, needed that exhortation, how much more do we? Two millennia have now passed and the Day has not come. Just as the pledge of the first coming of Christ, though apparently long delayed in its fulfillment, was proved true and trustworthy by the manger in Bethlehem, so it will be with the promise concerning the day of His second coming.[6]

When 15,000 anxious soldiers were evacuated from Clark Air Base in the Philippines in June 1991, they didn't know what to think. Were they in real danger or the victims of a false alarm? Within forty-eight hours, they got their answer. Nearby Mount Pinatubo, after sleeping quietly for more than 600 years, suddenly erupted in a series of explosions that shot plumes of steam and ash as much as thirty kilometers into the sky. Debris rained down on surrounding villages, and a giant mushroom cloud was visible 100 kilometers away in Manila.

Mount Pinatubo's blasts came just one week after Japan's Mount Unzen blew its top, with more deadly results. The red-hot avalanches hurtling down the mountain's slopes killed at least thirty-five people. But the toll could have been much higher if scientists had not sounded the alarm that an eruption was imminent.

In 1980 Mount Saint Helens belched gray steam plumes hundreds of feet into the blue Oregon sky as the boiling gases beneath the mountain's surface bulged and buckled the landscape to its final limits. Some chose to ignore the warning that blared from loud-speakers on patrol cars and helicopters. They paid for it with their lives.

In each it was the kind of disruption that was unexpected. The people near the mountains had lived in complacency, never anticipating such drastic changes. The Bible also speaks about a "day of disruption" that will be unexpected for many complacent people.

"The day of the Lord will come like a thief in the night. While people are saying, 'Peace and safety,' destruction will come on them suddenly, as labor pains on a pregnant woman, and they will not escape" (1 Thessalonians 5:2-3).

When the second coming of Jesus finally occurs, it will be personal in nature, physical, visible, triumphant and glorious. But it will also be unexpected by many. It will happen so quickly that there will be no time to prepare. So now is the time to make ready.

Now is the time to "get your house in order." Today is the day to encourage your brothers and sisters in Christ. We're on the winning team, but we must remind each other of the blessed hope, provoking one another to love and good deeds, boosting perseverance and determination.

As we come to a close, let's review. The author of Hebrews began a new section of his letter with Hebrews 10:19-25 that consists of a series of exhortations based upon the great doctrinal truths that precede it. By now the superiority of Jesus Christ as the unique sacrifice and perfect priest should be fully apparent to every reader.

Yet these truths must not remain abstract ideas. They must produce faith-filled behavior. Faith must be experienced and lived in the workplace, not only professed. Truth must be lived. So the writer urges his readers to hold fast to their faith by looking up, looking back, looking around and finally by looking ahead.

When Mario Cuomo was in law school, teachers apparently told him to change his vowel-laden last name if he wanted to succeed in life. But Cuomo refused. He was fiercely proud of his Italian heritage. When he ran for governor of New York in 1982, his opponent, Lewis Lehrman, spent $13.9 million—$9.6 million from his own personal fortune—compared to Cuomo's $4.8 million.

At times, Cuomo was convinced that he would lose. Writing in his diary one night late in the campaign, he was tired and depressed. Looking for a pencil, he ruffled through some papers in the back of his desk drawer and turned up one of his father's old business cards.

He read, "Andrea Cuomo, Italian-American Groceries— Fine Imported Products," and began to think about his father. When Andrea Cuomo arrived in America, he could not speak English and took a job digging sewer trenches. Eventually they acquired a tiny 24-hour grocery store, behind which the struggling family lived for many years.

After staring at the card, Cuomo wrote in his diary that night:

> I couldn't help wondering what Poppa would have said if I had told him I was tired or—God forbid— that I was discouraged. . . .
>
> One scene in particular came sharply into view. We had just moved into Holliswood from behind the store. We had our own house for the first time; it even had some land around it, even trees. One in particular was a great blue spruce that must have been forty feet high.
>
> Less than a week after we moved in there was a terrible storm. We came home from the store that night to find the great blue spruce pulled almost totally out of the ground and flung forward, its mighty nose

bent in the asphalt of the street. When we saw our spruce defeated, its cheek on the canvas, our hearts sank. But not Poppa's.

Maybe he was 5 feet, 6 inches if his heels were not worn. Maybe he weighed 155 lbs. if he had had a good meal. . . . But he was stronger than Frankie and me and Marie and Momma all together.

We stood in the street looking down at the tree. The rain was falling. We waited a couple of minutes figuring things out and then he announced, "O.K., we gonna push 'im up!"

"What are you talking about Poppa? The roots are out of the ground!"

"Shut up, we gonna push 'im up, he's gonna grow again."

We didn't know what to say to him. You couldn't say "no" to him; not just because you were his son, but because he was so sure.

So we followed him into the house and we got what rope there was and we tied the rope around the tip of the tree that lay in the asphalt, and he stood up by the house, with me pulling on the rope and Frankie in the street in the rain, helping to push up the great blue spruce. In no time at all we had it standing up straight again!

With the rain still falling, Poppa dug away at the place where the roots were, making a muddy hole wider and wider as the tree sank lower and lower toward security. Then we shoveled mud over the roots and moved boulders to the base of the tree to keep it in place. Poppa drove stakes in the ground, tied rope from the trunk to the stakes, and maybe two hours later looked at the spruce—the crippled spruce made straight by ropes—and said, "Don't worry, he's gonna grow again."

I looked at Poppa's card from the desk and wanted to cry. If you were to drive past the house today you

would see the great, straight blue spruce, maybe
sixty-five feet tall, pointing straight up to the heavens,
pretending it never had its nose in the asphalt.

I put Poppa's card back in the drawer, closed it
with a vengeance. I couldn't wait to get back into the
campaign.[7]

Cuomo went on to win the 1982 election by 180,386
votes, in large part because of his dogged determination in
the face of what appeared to be insurmountable obstacles.
You may be feeling discouraged, brokenhearted and troubled yourself. You've got to keep looking ahead. The last
vote hasn't been cast. Jesus is on the way! Hang on. Keep
looking up, looking back, looking around and looking
ahead.

Two Kinds of Christians

*If we deliberately keep on sinning after we have re-
ceived the knowledge of the truth, no sacrifice for sins is
left, but only a fearful expectation of judgment and of raging fire that will consume the enemies of God. Anyone who
rejected the law of Moses died without mercy on the testimony of two or three witnesses. How much more severely
do you think a man deserves to be punished who has trampled the Son of God under foot, who has treated as an un-
holy thing the blood of the covenant that sanctified him,
and who has insulted the Spirit of grace? For we know
him who said, "It is mine to avenge; I will repay," and
again, "The Lord will judge his people." It is a dreadful
thing to fall into the hands of the living God.*

*Remember those earlier days after you had received the
light, when you stood your ground in a great contest in the
face of suffering. Sometimes you were publicly exposed to
insult and persecution; at other times you stood side by side
with those who were so treated. You sympathized with
those in prison and joyfully accepted the confiscation of*

*your property, because you knew that you yourselves had
better and lasting possessions.*

*So do not throw away your confidence; it will be richly
rewarded. You need to persevere so that when you have
done the will of God, you will receive what he has promised. For in just a very little while,*

> *"He who is coming will come and will not delay.*
> *But my righteous one will live by faith.*
> *And if he shrinks back,*
> *I will not be pleased with him."*

*But we are not of those who shrink back and are destroyed,
but of those who believe and are saved. (Hebrews 10:26-
39)*

When Jeremiah came on the prophetic scene his God gave him a two-edged tongue. "See, today I appoint you over nations and kingdoms to uproot and tear down, to destroy and overthrow, to build and to plant" (Jeremiah 1:10). Destroy and build, uproot and overthrow.

Bible prophets had at least two things in common: They were faithful to comfort the afflicted and devoted to afflicting the comfortable. As you read the words of Hosea, Amos, Obadiah, Micah, Nahum and others, you quickly come to the conclusion that they were more faithful to afflict the comfortable than they were to comfort the afflicted. However, when they spoke, those who heard received the very message of God.

In the first century there lived a true prophet whose words continue to shape our lives today. He was the writer of this letter to the Hebrews. To get his point across in Hebrews 10:26-39 he uses comparison, placing two divergent groups of people side by side for the purpose of emphasis—those who fell back as opposed to those who stood their ground and followed Jesus.

This passage reaches its turning point in this earnest appeal: *Don't throw away your confidence!* The writer pleaded with them to draw near to God with a sincere heart in full assurance of faith (10:22), but now he fears that some may deliberately keep on sinning (10:26). He employs two means of recalling them to dynamic and steadfast faith. They must remember those who have fallen and those who have endured.[8]

These are Christians in contrast to one another, and most of us could find ourselves on this page of God's Word somewhere.[9]

Those Who Fell

If we deliberately keep on sinning after we have received the knowledge of the truth, no sacrifice for sins is left, but only a fearful expectation of judgment and of raging fire that will consume the enemies of God. (Hebrews 10:26-27)

The real danger of "falling away" and its dire consequences is now stressed once more (cf. 2:1-4, 3:12-15, 4:1-13, 6:4-8). Believers who deliberately keep on sinning after trusting Christ face judgment. The warning is comparable to Hebrews 6:4-8, which says that a believer who defects once he is enlightened cannot be brought back to repentance. Here the warning is directed to the same problem, but the approach is based upon the fact that there is no other sacrifice than Christ's. If that is finally rejected, then only judgment can ensue.

Who are the people described here? The answer depends on which side of the theological coin you find yourself. Some say these people were definitely believers,[10] while a few commentators make it difficult to discern exactly where they stand on the issue.[11] Others aggressively oppose the idea and suggest reasons why these people must be non-Christians.[12]

I believe this warning was written to believers. "If we deliberately keep on sinning . . . " the author says. Who? *Believers*. It follows in a logical sequence with the other exhortations given thus far. The believer who begins to *drift* from the Word (Hebrews 2:1-4) will soon start to *doubt* the Word (3:7-4:13). Soon, he will become *dull* toward the Word (5:11-6:20) and become "lazy" in his spiritual life. This will result in *despising* the Word, which is one of the themes of this passage.[13]

They had received "the knowledge of the truth" where "truth" stands for "the content of Christianity as the absolute truth."[14] The people in question know what God has done. They know who Jesus is. Their acquaintance with the faith is more than superficial. Now some of them are living on the brink of disaster, being tempted to throw it all away; to deny their faith, throw in the towel and turn away.

What happens if they do? If they "deliberately keep on sinning," if they revert to an attitude of rejection, of continual sin or premeditated disobedience, then there remains no sacrifice for sin. Calvin wrote:

> He is not dealing here with this or that kind of sin but he is exposing by name those who withdraw themselves of their own accord from the fellowship of the Church. There is a great difference between individual lapses and a universal desertion of this kind which makes for a total falling away from the grace of Christ.[15]

If a man deliberately keeps on sinning after he has believed in Christ, he has rejected the sacrifice of Christ. If a woman consciously keeps on sinning after she trusts in Christ, she is caught in the whirlpool of carnality and her life is thrown upside-down and ripped inside out. If we determinedly keep on sinning after we believe in Christ, our lives will look just like the unsaved. Outsiders will notice no distinction.

What characterizes the lives of these people who are in danger of total apostasy? Essentially three things: They reject God's truth, they spurn God's Son and they insult God's Spirit. Those who insult the Spirit of God condemn themselves and they deny the only way of forgiveness. They make pardon impossible, laughing in the face of the only One who can woo them back and pardon the error of their ways.

What foolishness! Instead of falling into the arms of a loving God, they choose to fall into the hands of a God who becomes their judge. Absurdity at its best. For we know Him who said, "It is mine to avenge; I will repay," and again, "The Lord will judge his people" (Hebrews 10:30-31; cf. Deuteronomy 32:35-36). "It is a dreadful thing to fall into the hands of the living God."

What do these people need? "If we deliberately keep on sinning after we have received the knowledge of the truth, no sacrifice for sins is left . . ." (Hebrews 10:26). They need *repentance*. They need to stop their sinful behavior before they go any deeper into this wicked, carnal lifestyle. They need to stop what they're doing before it's too late. They need to confess their sins and forsake them. They need to get to the cross and let God deal with the self-life. What is it that draws a man away from God anyway? Is it not self? Self-righteousness? Self-pity? Self-confidence? Self-sufficiency? Self-love and a host of others like them?

Tozer said, "They dwell too deep within us and are too much a part of our natures to come to our attention till the light of God is focused upon them." But once that light comes, my dear brother, follow it all the way to the cross. The righteousness of Christ will deliver us from the power of the self-sins, but "we must invite the cross to do its deadly work within us. We must bring our self-sins to the cross for judgment."[16] The believers to whom the author of Hebrews wrote this letter needed this experience, and I suspect some of the readers of this book need it, too.

Verse 26 begins with the word "if." There is another important "if" that we should look at in this connection. First

John 1:9 says, "If we confess our sins, he is faithful and just and will forgive us our sins and purify us from all unrighteousness." The man who wrote the book of Hebrews has the heart of a pastor. He's a shepherd, a counselor.

In Hebrews 10:26-31 he warns his readers about the dangers of falling away—of shrinking back. There are a number of believers who dance on the borderline of desertion everyday. To these the writer says, "Pay attention!" and in verse 32 he moves from warning to encouragement, from talking about those who shrink back to those who stand fast.

Those Who Stand Their Ground

> Remember those earlier days after you had received the light, when you stood your ground in a great contest in the face of suffering. Sometimes you were publicly exposed to insult and persecution; at other times you stood side by side with those who were so treated. You sympathized with those in prison and joyfully accepted the confiscation of your property, because you knew that you yourselves had better and lasting possessions.
>
> So do not throw away your confidence; it will be richly rewarded. (Hebrews 10:32-35)

After another section containing stern warnings, the author again expresses his confidence in his readers and encourages them to take the right way right away. In the early days of their Christianity they had faced some opposition and came out triumphant, shining as stars in the night sky, holding fast to the hope they professed and standing their ground in a great contest.

If they persevered and won then, they could surely do it again. Their previous experience of privilege and power should also teach them that in Christ they had blessings of a kind they could never have had if they had given way to persecution.

Who are the people described here and how are they living? They are professing Christians who suffer abuse and
persecution. The important thing to notice is that although
they may be unsteady, they endure suffering without flinch-
ing. They still stand in faith. Suffering for the name of
Christ was taken for granted and considered a privilege.

At times their persecution took the form of public disgrace
and taunting; at other times, quiet but personal insult. Accepting Jesus as the Messiah immediately laid them open to
attack from their unconverted countrymen. The writer invites his readers to look not only at the obstinate, unrepent-
ant position of others, but also at their own firm reliance and
perseverance.

The text says they were familiar with hardship and pain.
Sometimes they were publicly exposed to insult and persecution, but they stood firm. Verse 34 tells us they had great
concern for others as they "sympathized with those in prison
and joyfully accepted the confiscation of (their) property."

Sometimes their sufferings were caused by their willingness to identify themselves as companions of their fellow
Christians, even when remaining silent might have meant
escape. They were free from materialism because they knew
they had better and lasting possessions (10:34).

Like Peter they could joyfully praise the God and Father
of our Lord Jesus Christ, for "[i]n his great mercy he has
given us new birth into a living hope through the resurrection of Jesus Christ from the dead, and into an inheritance
that can never perish, spoil or fade . . ." (1 Peter 1:3-4).
Tozer called this "the blessedness of possessing nothing."
He wrote:

> The blessed ones who possess the kingdom are they
> who have repudiated every external thing and have
> rooted from their hearts all sense of possessing. . . .
> These blessed poor are no longer slaves to the tyr-
> anny of *things*. They have broken the yoke of the op-
> pressor; and this they have done not by fighting but

by surrendering. Though free from all sense of possessing, they yet possess all things. Theirs is the kingdom of heaven.[17]

Have you discovered the blessedness of possessing nothing?

What do they need? In contrast to the former group, consisting of people who had a need of repentance, this group needs *endurance*—they need endurance or perseverance.

> So do not throw away your confidence; it will be richly rewarded. You need to persevere so that when you have done the will of God, you will receive what he has promised. For in just a very little while,
>
> "He who is coming will come and will not delay.
> But my righteous one will live by faith.
> And if he shrinks back,
> I will not be pleased with him"
> (Hebrews 10:35-38).

Perhaps the easiness of our times creates the temptation to shrink back. "Ease has ruined far more men than trouble ever did," writes William Barclay, quoting the example of Hannibal's armies.[18] To turn aside now, in the midst of your suffering and pain, would be to lose the great prospect of reward.

Jesus said, "Blessed are you when people insult you, persecute you and falsely say all kinds of evil against you because of me. Rejoice and be glad, because great is your reward in heaven, for in the same way they persecuted the prophets who were before you" (Matthew 5:11-12).

Loss of confidence means loss of conviction about the truth of the gospel and loss of boldness in our witness. When you lose confidence you shrink back, and if you shrink back, God says He will not be pleased (Hebrews 10:38).

In writing the former group the author wrote to afflict the comfortable. In writing to this group, the author wrote to comfort the afflicted. "But we are not of those who shrink back and are destroyed, but of those who believe and are saved" (Hebrews 10:39). Their lives were characterized by faith, perseverance, determination and steadfastness.

Even though the author has spoken rather severely about the importance of unwavering faith and the dire consequences of falling back, he is confident also that true faith will emerge in victory. Faith is the victory that overcomes the world. It spreads its sail to catch the breeze of God's revelation and then responds to His Word and His grace.

We have witnessed the author's use of comparison in Hebrews 10:26-39. He places two opposite groups of people side by side for the purpose of emphasis—those who fall back to follow the world and those who stand their ground to follow the Lord. Did you find yourself in either crowd?

Sometimes at staff meetings I bait the other pastors on my staff to make them think theologically. Maybe I'm a bit demented, but I enjoy arguing the fine points of theology. I have even used this quote by Dr. Tozer to justify my hobby: "We being what we are and all things else being what they are, the most important and profitable study any of us can engage in is without question the study of theology. . . . The secret of life is theological and the key to heaven as well."[19]

However, it would be easy to get sidetracked in this chapter over whether believers can forsake their salvation or not and miss the application of God's truth altogether. Let's not do that.

Perhaps we could compare our situation to riding in the back of a pickup truck. All true believers are on board. Some Christians believe the tailgate is closed and locked; others believe it is open. In either case, the logical thing to do is not to see how daring we can be in leaning out of the truck but to ride as close to the cab as possible.[20]

May I suggest that you take a few minutes right now to answer the following personal questions? Let's focus on application rather than the particulars of a specific theological viewpoint.[21]

Where am I going in my spiritual life? Am I shrinking or standing? Am I backsliding or moving forward in faith? Do I know the conscious presence of God in my life, or am I afraid to enter the Most Holy Place?

What will happen if I don't alter my course? If I only maintain the spiritual status quo, what will happen to me at the end of my life? Will my albums be full of bright memories or shaded regrets?

Is there a better time than right now for either repentance or endurance?

Endnotes

1. John Calvin, *Calvin's New Testament Commentaries: Hebrews and I and II Peter*, trans. W. B. Johnston (Grand Rapids, MI: William B. Eerdmans Publishing Company, 1963), 142.

2. See 1 Corinthians 1:9; 10:13; 1 Thessalonians 5:24; Hebrews 11:11.

3. A.W. Tozer, *The Knowledge of the Holy* (San Francisco, CA: Harper & Row Publishers, 1961), 87.

4. Raymond Brown, *The Message of Hebrews* (Downers Grove, IL: InterVarsity Press, 1982), 186.

5. This particular hymn story was copied out of a book and given to me by a friend. I cannot locate the source or the author.

6. Philip Edgcumbe Hughes, *A Commentary on the Epistle to the Hebrews* (Grand Rapids, MI: William B. Eerdmans Publishing Company, 1977), 416.

7. Quoted by Alan Loy McGinnis in *Bringing Out the Best in People: How to Enjoy Helping Others Excel* (Minneapolis, MN: Augsburg Publishing House, 1985), 59-61.

8. See also Hebrews 10:19-20, and Raymond Brown, *The Message of Hebrews* (Downers Grove, IL: InterVarsity Press, 1982), 188-193.

9. Once again I express my thanks to Charles R. Swindoll for his homiletical and practical advice. While the content of this chapter is my own, I have gleaned much from Dr. Swindoll's sermons and Bible study guides on the book of Hebrews. I cannot commend his work highly enough to aspiring preachers and teachers of the Word. He has an unusual gift of placing rich, biblical truth in practical terms that are easy to apply.

10. Raymond Brown (189); Warren Wiersbe (116); Charles Swindoll; W.H. Griffith Thomas (135-136); Homer A. Kent, Jr. (204): "Just as in the case of the previous warnings, it should be understood that the readers are Christians"; Philip E. Hughes (418).

11. For example, Leon Morris says: "The people in question, then, know what God has done in Christ; their acquaintance with Christian teaching is more than superficial." (106) *Hebrews, The Expositor's Bible Commentary*, Vol. 12, ed. Frank E. Gaebelein (Grand Rapids, MI: Zondervan Publishing House, 1981), 106.

12. "When the gospel of Jesus Christ is presented to an unbeliever, only two responses are possible. After he has heard the basic truths and claims of Jesus Christ, he either believes and is saved or he disbelieves and becomes apostate. Apostasy, as we will see, is the sin of rejecting the gospel for which there is no forgiveness." John MacArthur, *The MacArthur New Testament Commentary: Hebrews* (Chicago, IL: Moody Press, 1983), 270.

13. Adapted from Warren W. Wiersbe, *Be Confident* (Wheaton, IL: Victor Books, 1983), 116.

14. Walter Bauer, *A Greek-English Lexicon of the New Testament and Other Early Christian Literature.* A translation and adaptation of the fourth revised and augmented edition of

Walter Bauer's *Griechisch-Deutsches Worterbuch zu den Schriften des Neuen Testaments und der ubrigen urchristlichen Literatur*. Second edition (Chicago: The University of Chicago, IL Press, 1979), 35.

15. John Calvin, 146.

16. A.W. Tozer, *The Pursuit of God* (Harrisburg, PA: Christian Publications, 1948, Mass Market Edition assigned 1976 to Horizon House Publishers), 46.

17. Ibid., 23.

18. William Barclay, *The Letter to the Hebrews*, rev. ed., (Philadelphia, PA: The Westminster Press, 1976), 126-127.

19. A.W. Tozer, *The Best of A.W. Tozer* (Harrisburg, PA: Christian Publications, 1978), 106, 108.

20. *Leadership* (Fall 1986): 42. Used by permission.

21. The questions were adapted from Charles Swindoll's study guide on Hebrews.

Discussion Questions for Further Study

1. What confidence do believers now have as a result of what Christ accomplished at the cross (10:19)?

2. Where and how does the writer's mood change in 10:19-39?

3. Hebrews 10:22-25 contains five important exhortations. List these. In your own words summarize the exhortations (10:19-25) and the warnings (10:26-31).

4. The triad of faith, hope and love is mentioned over and over in Scripture. How does the author use this triad to address the needs of his readers under persecution (10:22-24)?

5. How are you being tempted to "shrink back" (10:39)? How can you go about resisting this temptation?

6. What one exhortation or promise from this chapter would you like to take to heart this week?

10

Hebrews 11:1-16

Characteristics of Faith

> *Now faith is being sure of what we hope for and certain of what we do not see. This is what the ancients were commended for.*
>
> *By faith we understand that the universe was formed at God's command, so that what is seen was not made out of what was visible. (Hebrews 11:1-3)*

God often tells us to do things that are the opposite of our natural inclination. It takes faith to trust Him and do whatever He says. Authentic faith is the main theme of Hebrews 11. It is well illustrated in the life of Ben Patterson:

> In 1988, three friends and I climbed Mount Lyell, the highest peak in Yosemite National Park. Two of us were experienced mountaineers. I was not one of the experienced two. Our base camp was less than 2,000 feet from the peak, but the climb to the top and back was to take the better part of a day, due in large part to the difficulty of the glacier one must cross to get to the top. The morning of the climb we started out chattering and cracking jokes.
>
> As the hours passed, the two mountaineers opened up a wide gap between me and my less-experienced

companion. Being competitive by nature, I began to look for shortcuts to beat them to the top. I thought I saw one to the right of an outcropping of rock—so I went, deaf to the protests of my companion.

Perhaps it was the effect of the high altitude, but the significance of the two experienced climbers not choosing this path did not register in my consciousness. It should have, for thirty minutes later I was trapped in a cul-de-sac of rock atop the Lyell Glacier, looking down several hundred feet of a sheer slope of ice, pitched at about a forty-five degree angle. . . . I was only about ten feet from the safety of a rock, but one little slip and I wouldn't stop sliding until I landed in the valley floor some fifty miles away! It was nearly noon, and the warm sun had the glacier glistening with slippery ice. I was stuck and I was scared.

It took an hour for my experienced climbing friends to find me. Standing on the rock I wanted to reach, one of them leaned out and used an ice axe to chip two little footsteps in the glacier. Then he gave me the following instructions:

"Ben, you must step out from where you are and put your foot where the first foothold is. When your foot touches it, without a moment's hesitation swing your other foot across and land it on the next step. When you do that, reach out and I will take your hand and pull you to safety."

That sounded real good to me. It was the next thing he said that made me more frightened than ever. "But listen carefully: As you step across, do not lean into the mountain! If anything, lean out a bit. Otherwise, your feet may fly out from under you, and you will start sliding down."

I don't like precipices. When I am on the edge of a cliff, my instincts are to lie down and hug the mountain, to become one with it, not to lean away from it!

But that was what my good friend was telling me to
do. I looked at him real hard. . . . Was there any reason, any reason at all, that I should not trust him? I
certainly hoped not! So for a moment, based solely
on what I believed to be the good will and good sense
of my friend, I decided to say no to what I felt, to stifle my impulse to cling to the security of the mountain, to lean out, step out and traverse the ice to
safety. It took less than two seconds to find out if my
faith was well founded. It was.[1]

Is God loving and faithful? Can we trust Him and live in
faith?

He is. We can.

Faith is the ability to trust what we cannot see. Faith sees
the invisible, believes the incredible, receives the impossible,
does without the indispensable, bears the intolerable. However, any attempt to define faith in epigrammatic fashion
will surely fall short of the mark.

The 11th chapter of this magnificent epistle begins with
some general observations on the nature of faith. They do
not establish a formal definition of faith nor provide an exhaustive interpretation. Instead, the writer is calling our attention to some of the important *characteristics* of faith and
what it does. As we focus on faith through the lens of Hebrews 11:1-3, we shall observe that authentic faith embraces
the Word of God, secures the favor of God and discovers the
power of God.

Faith Embraces the Word of God

> Now faith is being sure of what we hope for and
> certain of what we do not see. (Hebrews 11:1)

In the Greek construction of this verse, the verb "is" (*estin*)
is the first word, which leads to the idea that faith is a present and continuing reality for the believer.[2] Faith *is*. It is not

something that *was* practiced only in ancient civilization. It *is*. Current for our generation. A living entity, a way of life, a force to be reckoned with. Faith is the basis, the substructure of all that the Christian life means and all that the Christian hopes for.[3]

Years ago Dr. Tozer wrote about "what we do not see":

> The world of sense intrudes upon our attention day and night for the whole of our lifetime. It is clamorous, insistent and self-demonstrating. It does not appeal to our faith; it is here, assaulting our five senses, demanding to be accepted as real and final. But sin has so clouded the lenses of our hearts that we cannot see that other reality, the City of God, shining around us.
>
> The world of sense triumphs. The visible becomes the enemy of the invisible; the temporal, of the eternal. That is the curse inherited by every member of Adam's tragic race. At the root of the Christian life lies belief in the invisible. The object of the Christian's faith is unseen reality.[4]

How can faith empower people with such extraordinary ability? Because it embraces the Bible as God's Word. We believe that the Scriptures are inspired by God, for "All Scripture is God-breathed and is useful for teaching, rebuking, correcting and training in righteousness . . ." (2 Timothy 3:16).

By inspiration we mean that supernatural influence of the Holy Spirit upon the writers of Scripture which rendered their writings an accurate record of the revelation of Almighty God. Through inspiration, what they wrote actually was the Word of God.

Genuine faith accepts the Bible as the revealed will of God and responds in loving obedience. It does not merely agree with God's Word, but acts upon it . . . even if it doesn't fully understand every jot and tittle.

Faith Secures the Approval of God

> This is what the ancients were commended for. (He-
> brews 11:2)

"The ancients," more specifically "the elders" (*hoi presby-
teroi*), are synonymous with those described as "our forefathers" in Hebrews 1:1. They were endorsed and accorded a
good report, and the unexpressed agent of this approval is
God Himself.

By exercising genuine faith, the ancients, the men and
women of old, acquired the divine commendation and the
warm smile of God. So can we! For the Christian, living for
God's glory and pleasing God is of the greatest possible importance and the highest calling imaginable.

As Christian workers, clergy or laity, we come to our task
of serving God and His people not with eloquence or superior wisdom. We have resolved to know nothing except Jesus
Christ and Him crucified (1 Corinthians 1:23). Indeed, we
come in weakness and fear most of the time, with much
trembling.

Our message about Jesus and our preaching are not with
wise and persuasive words, but hopefully with a demonstra-
tion of the Spirit's power, so that the faith of our students
and congregations might not rest on men's wisdom, but on
God's power (1 Corinthians 2:1-5).

We want to please God, not people. As the apostle Paul
says in Second Corinthians 5:9, "So we make it our goal to
please him. . . ." "Without faith it is impossible to please
God" (Hebrews 11:6). Genuine faith secures the approval of
God.

When Julius Caesar landed on the shores of Britain with
his Roman legions, he took a bold and decisive step to ensure
the success of his military venture. Ordering his men to
march to the edge of the Cliffs of Dover, he commanded
them to look down at the water below. To their amazement,
they saw every ship in which they had crossed the channel

engulfed in flames. Caesar had deliberately cut off any possibility of retreat. Now that his soldiers were unable to return to the continent, there was nothing left for them to do but advance and conquer!

The commendation of God awaits the faith-filled servants who simply refuse to retreat. I hope you're one of them!

Faith Discovers the Power of God

> By faith we understand that the universe was formed at God's command, so that what is seen was not made out of what was visible. (Hebrews 11:3)

Genesis 1 provides the magnificent background to this majestic verse. "In the beginning God created the heavens and the earth. . . . And God said, 'Let there be light,' and there was light. . . . And God said, 'Let there be an expanse.' . . . And it was so. . . . And God said, 'Let the water under the sky be gathered to one place.' . . . And it was so" (Genesis 1:1, 3, 6-7, 9).

The apostle John picked up the same theme in John 1:3 where he wrote, "Through him all things were made; without him nothing was made that has been made." So from Genesis to Revelation the Bible affirms the creative powers of God. Yet it is only by faith that we can accept the astonishing statement that the *visible* came forth from the *invisible*.

Only by faith can we understand that the cosmos was fashioned with a word from God. God's incomparable power is such that he can call the universe into being from nothing, *ex nihilo*. He simply declared that it was to be, and once He said it, it was done.[5]

Some time ago, *Maclean's* magazine, a Canadian weekly, published a piece titled "The Jehovah Factor." The author, Terence Dickinson, wrote:

> If there is one belief, one incentive shared by scientists through the ages, it is this: Nothing is unknow-

able, nothing can escape clarification by the scientific method. But now, it seems, that resolution is faltering. Some scientists are admitting defeat—at the hands of their own equations. The more astronomers learn about the early history of the universe, the more convinced they become that they will never know how it came into being.

For scientists, that is tantamount to blasphemy. To admit that something that can be observed and measured has an unknowable cause conjures up a realm of faith and magic—precisely what science has tried to banish. "It's like a bad dream," remarks a physicist. "We climb the highest mountain in science and we find the theologians have been sitting there for centuries."[6]

By *faith* we conceive that the universe was designed at God's command. Science won't give us that much yet. By faith we believe that what is seen was not made out of any existing building materials, and thus we discover the power of the mighty God.

This passage has reviewed some of the important *characteristics* of faith and what it does. We focused the lens of Hebrews 11:1-3 and observed some of the characteristics of authentic faith. It embraces the Word of God, secures the favor of God and discovers the power of God. But if we begin to look for shortcuts in the life of faith, like the inexperienced mountaineer, we may find ourselves trapped. The faith-walk must be lived one day at a time.

Right about now you may feel like you're looking down several hundred feet of a sheer slope of ice, pitched at about a forty-five degree angle. One little slip and you won't stop sliding for a long while. God wants to give you some direction today: "Beloved, step out from where you are and plant your feet *where I tell you*. I'll make your feet like the feet of a deer and enable you to stand on the heights." (See Psalm 18:33.)

"I'm going to lift you out of the slimy pit you're in, out of the mud and mire. I will set your feet on a rock and give you a firm place to stand." (See Psalm 40:2.)

"You have planned your course, but I will determine your next step." (See Proverbs 16:9.) When your feet make contact, without a moment's hesitation reach out and I will take your hand and pull you to safety.

But remember, there's risk involved. "As you step across, do not lean into the mountain! If anything, lean out a bit. Otherwise, your feet may fly out from under you, and you will start sliding down." What's that? You don't like precipices? *Join the club!* You'd rather lie down and hug the mountain? *Forget it.* That's not faith; that's fear. And God has not given us a spirit of fear, but a spirit of power, of love and of self-discipline. (See 2 Timothy 1:7.)

Is there any reason, any reason at all, that you should not trust the Lord?

Say "no" to what you feel. Stifle the impulse to cling to the security of the mountain. Lean out. Step out. Walk by faith, not by sight. Embrace the Word of God. Secure His favor, and discover the power of God. All by faith!

The same God who called the universe into being from nothing is the God who can answer your prayers, care for your concerns, heal your broken heart and bind up your wounds (Psalm 147:3), forgive your worst nightmare of sins, refashion your future and grant you the desires of your heart as you delight yourself in Him (Psalm 37:4).

Ordinary Men with Extraordinary Faith

> *By faith Abel offered God a better sacrifice than Cain did. By faith he was commended as a righteous man, when God spoke well of his offerings. And by faith he still speaks, even though he is dead.*
>
> *By faith Enoch was taken from this life, so that he did not experience death; he could not be found, because God had taken him away. For before he was taken, he was*

> *commended as one who pleased God. And without faith it*
> *is impossible to please God, because anyone who comes to*
> *him must believe that he exists and that he rewards those*
> *who earnestly seek him.*
>
> *By faith Noah, when warned about things not yet seen,*
> *in holy fear built an ark to save his family. By his faith he*
> *condemned the world and became heir of the righteousness*
> *that comes by faith. (Hebrews 11:4-7)*

History drips with reports about inspiring people of faith. Their names are household words in Christian circles: Hudson Taylor, George Mueller, William Carey, Billy Graham, A.B. Simpson, Corrie Ten Boom. These are people with whom we may have a hard time identifying because they seem like super-saints who are super-charged with super-faith. Easily overlooked are the masses of simple, plain, ordinary believers who model the "faith-life" away from the limelight. These are the people I resonate with. People like John Akhwari.

At 7 p.m. on October 20, 1968, a few thousand spectators remained in the Mexico City Olympic Stadium. It was cool and dark. The last of the marathon runners, each exhausted, were being carried off to first-aid stations. More than an hour earlier, Mamo Wolde of Ethiopia, looking as fresh as when he started the race, crossed the finish line, the winner of the 26-mile, 385-yard event.

As the remaining spectators prepared to leave, those sitting near the marathon gates suddenly heard the sound of sirens and police whistles. All eyes turned to the gate. A lone figure wearing the colors of Tanzania entered the stadium. His name was John Stephen Akhwari. He was the last man to finish the marathon. His leg bloodied and bandaged, severely injured in a fall, he grimaced with each step. He hobbled around the 400-meter track.

The spectators rose and applauded him as if he were the winner. After crossing the finish line, Akhwari slowly walked off the field without turning to the cheering crowd.

In view of his injury and having no chance of winning a medal, someone asked him why he had not quit. He replied, "My country did not send me 7,000 miles to start the race. They sent me 7,000 miles to finish it."[7]

How shall we run the race set before us? By following the examples of Abel, Enoch and Noah, for starters. Hebrews 11:4-7 mentions three men: Abel, Enoch and Noah. A shepherd, a preacher and a builder. All have now become heroes, but back when they were up against unbeatable odds and forced to trust in God alone, they were nobodies—ordinary men, just like Akhwari and just like you and me.

Yet they possessed an unusual kind of faith. When they were under pressure they believed God. They allowed faith to dethrone doubt. From their example we will learn how to recognize our responsibility before God, how to sustain our walk with God and how to demonstrate our obedience to God.

Abel: By Faith You Recognize Your Responsibility Before God

> By faith Abel offered God a better sacrifice than Cain did. By faith he was commended as a righteous man, when God spoke well of his offerings. And by faith he still speaks, even though he is dead. (Hebrews 11:4)

Why was Abel's offering a "better sacrifice" than Cain's (Genesis 4:1-8)? Dr. F.F. Bruce canvasses a number of opinions as to the reasons for the superiority of Abel's offering: It was living, whereas Cain's was lifeless; it was stronger, Cain's weaker; it grew spontaneously, Cain's by human ingenuity; it involved blood, Cain's did not.

However, Scripture never says there was anything inherently superior in Abel's offering. "There was no precedent to blood sacrifices and there is no evidence to suggest that God had instructed the brothers about what kind of offerings they should make."[8] Contrary to popular opinion,

Abel's offering was a "better sacrifice" not because it contained blood. God's requirements for blood sacrifices came later than Cain and Abel. It was a better sacrifice because it was offered *in faith*.

Genesis 4:5 records that Cain was very angry, and his face was downcast. His whole attitude and approach to God was defective. It lacked the pleasing-God sort of faith. He was bringing a sacrifice to God, but he was doing it with a heart that was not pure, with mixed motives and tarnished faith. He was envious of his brother, and therefore he was sinning against God.

King David learned from Cain's mistake too. "You do not delight in sacrifice, or I would bring it; you do not take pleasure in burnt offerings. The sacrifices of God are a broken spirit; a broken and contrite heart, O God, you will not despise" (Psalm 51:16-17). We have an obligation to come to the Lord in faith, with a broken and contrite heart. We approach Him in faith, seeking His grace, His forgiveness, His mercy. Only by faith do we fully recognize our responsibilities to God.

Enoch: By Faith You Sustain Your Walk with God

> By faith Enoch was taken from this life, so that he did not experience death; he could not be found, because God had taken him away. For before he was taken, he was commended as one who pleased God. And without faith it is impossible to please God, because anyone who comes to him must believe that he exists and that he rewards those who earnestly seek him. (Hebrews 11:5-6)

Apparently Enoch lived for sixty-five years before he started walking with God (Genesis 5:21-24). What happened to bring about the change and keep him going? All we know for certain is that he and his wife had a son named Methuselah. Then after that he altered his life and "walked with God 300 years."

First there was a decision point, a turning point in his life. Perhaps raising his son in those wicked times turned him around. Maybe an illness in the family that drove him to seek after the Creator. Possibly a business deal that went sour. We just don't know. But many people turn to the Lord in the midst of raising children or illness or disappointment.

God is no respecter of persons or situations (Acts 10:34) and He uses *any* set of circumstances to bring people closer to Himself.

Second, Enoch sustained an extraordinary walk with God that was especially pleasing. And he kept it going for 300 years on earth before he was promoted to continue it in heaven. How pleased God must have been with him can only be estimated by the duration and location of his service.

A few years ago a television documentary pointed out that the cheetah survives on the African plains by running down its prey. The big cat can sprint seventy miles per hour. But the cheetah cannot sustain that pace for long. Within its long, sleek body is a disproportionately small heart, which causes the cheetah to tire quickly. Unless the cheetah catches its prey in the first flurry, it must abandon the chase.[9]

Sometimes Christians seem to have the cheetah's approach to life and ministry. We speed into projects with great energy. But lacking the heart for sustained effort, we fizzle before we finish. We vow to start faster and run harder, when what we need may not be more speed but more staying power, stamina that comes only from a bigger heart, endurance that comes from walking with God. On the way, we should discern how to be well-pleasing to God.

Noah: By Faith You Demonstrate Your Obedience to God

By faith Noah, when warned about things not yet seen, in holy fear built an ark to save his family. By

his faith he condemned the world and became heir of
the righteousness that comes by faith. (Hebrews 11:7)

Noah is an excellent example of the believer who is eager
to hear what God says and ready to do what He commands
(Genesis 6:9-9:17). He not only received a warning, he built
an ark. God said it, so Noah did it. But he must have seemed
very strange to his peers. Noah lived a few hundred miles
from the sea, yet he constructed a massive boat that was supposed to save his family and innumerable animals from a
flood that was going to cover the whole earth. Can you
imagine the gossip coming from the neighbors? What a scandal!

Noah brought an audacious, obedient response to God's
word. He was warned about "things not yet seen." He
obeyed God even though he couldn't see the outcome. He
complied with God when he didn't understand the implications of what was about to happen. What seemed foolhardy
to others was treasured by Noah. God exercised His merciful patience. Noah offered his persistent obedience. A beautiful combination! We please God through faith. Faith is the
victory that overcomes the world (1 John 5:4; Matthew 7:24-
27).

In July 1976, Israeli commandos made a daring raid at an
airport in Entebbe, Uganda, in which 103 Jewish hostages
were freed. In less than fifteen minutes, the soldiers had
killed all seven of the kidnappers and set the captives free.

As successful as the rescue was, however, three of the
hostages were killed during the raid. As the commandos
entered the terminal, they shouted in Hebrew, "Get down!
Crawl!" The Jewish hostages understood and lay down on
the floor, while the guerrillas, who did not speak Hebrew,
were left standing. Quickly the rescuers shot the upright
kidnappers.

But two of the hostages hesitated, perhaps to see what was
happening, and were also cut down. One young man was lying down and actually stood up when the commandos en-

tered the airport. He too was shot with the bullets meant for the enemy. Had these three heeded the soldiers' command, they would have been freed with the rest of the captives.[10]

The deeper Christian life is open to every believer, but we must demonstrate our obedience to Christ by faith on a daily basis, heed His commands "when warned about things not yet seen," and make Him Lord of all.

A shepherd, a preacher and a builder. All heroes, but back when they were pushed against the wall and facing terrible odds, forced to trust in God, they were nobodies . . . common men of uncommon faith. They believed God and allowed faith to depose doubt.

Maybe you're walking through a dark tunnel today. Feel like you're the last person in the marathon? Bloodied and bruised along the path of life, you grimace as you think about walking another mile with God. Could it be that God wants to use your present state of affairs to magnetize and attract your attention?

Won't you turn to Him today? He's waiting for you. Surrender your heart. Present yourself again as a living sacrifice, holy and acceptable in His sight (Romans 12:1). Then, when others taunt you with the prospect of quitting in light of your momentary affliction, you can say, "My Father in heaven did not send His Son to earth to merely start me on the race. He sent Jesus to help me finish it victoriously by faith. And by faith, I will do it!"

The Faith of Abraham

> *By faith Abraham, when called to go to a place he would later receive as his inheritance, obeyed and went, even though he did not know where he was going. By faith he made his home in the promised land like a stranger in a foreign country; he lived in tents, as did Isaac and Jacob, who were heirs with him of the same promise. For he was looking forward to the city with foundations, whose architect and builder is God.*

> *By faith Abraham, even though he was past age—and Sarah herself was barren—was enabled to become a father because he considered him faithful who had made the promise. And so from this one man, and he as good as dead, came descendants as numerous as the stars in the sky and as countless as the sand on the seashore. (Hebrews 11:8-12)*

Fraser of Lisuland in northern Burma translated the Scriptures into the Lisu language and then left a young fellow with the task of teaching the people to read. When he returned six months later, he found three students and the teacher seated around a table, with the Scriptures opened in front of the teacher.

When the students each read, they left the Bible where it was. The man on the left read it sideways, the man on the right read it sideways but from the other side, and the man across from the teacher read it upside-down. Since they always occupied the same chairs, that's how each had learned to read, and that's how each thought the language was written.[11]

We're just like that sometimes. When we learn something from only one perspective, we may think it's the only perspective. Occasionally it's good to change seats in order to assume a different perspective on the same truth. That's what we're doing with Hebrews 11:8-12.

We're going to walk in Abraham's shoes, sit in his Lazy-Boy, sleep in his tent and watch him very carefully as he looks for that "city with foundations" with eyes of faith. Maybe we'll pick up some tips on living by faith. His faith is worth duplicating because it illustrates what submissive, sacrificial, fearless, reliant faith can do.

A Submissive Faith

> By faith Abraham, when called to go to a place he would later receive as his inheritance, obeyed. . . .
> (Hebrews 11:8)

Submissive faith is demonstrated by Abraham's willingness to do what the Lord required of him. "The LORD had said to Abram, 'Leave your country, your people and your father's household and go to the land I will show you. . . . So Abram left, as the LORD had told him . . .'" (Genesis 12:1, 4).

In fact, the words "when called" (Hebrews 11:8) translate a Greek present participle that indicates a very prompt obedience. "He obeyed the call while . . . it was still sounding in his ears."[12] As God was calling (Genesis 12:1-5), Abraham was responding in obedience.

"The immediateness of his response is suggested by the coupling of the present participle *kaloumenos* with the aorist of the main verb *hupakousen*: as he was being called he obeyed."[13] His obedience was the outward evidence of his inward faith. He would not have obeyed the call had he not taken God at His word.

In more than one case the writer to the Hebrews is eager to point out that submissive men and women of the Old Testament were prepared to take God at His word. They did so because they knew it was a word of unrivaled authority, of decisive importance, of immense power. It was a word of complete reliability.

Living the Christian life requires submissive faith to the Word of God and the calling of God, not a wait-and-see attitude.

A Sacrificial Faith

By faith Abraham, . . . obeyed and went. (Hebrews 11:8)

When Abraham left Ur he knew nothing about his target destination. He had to entrust himself completely to God's direction. It was only after Abraham had left Ur and then had subsequently left Haran that God revealed that the land of Canaan was to belong to his progeny (Genesis 12:6-7). Hence it was clearly by faith in the bare word of God that the patriarch was compelled to make his momentous departure.

Sacrificial faith is evident in Abraham's willingness to go out from all that was secure, prosperous, peaceful and enjoyable. The Genesis story mentions that Abraham left his extended family and the comfort of his father's house. Have you ever "gone out" in this way? If so, there is no logical answer possible when anyone asks you what you are doing.

You don't even know what you're sacrificing because you do not know the future as God does (Jeremiah 29:11-13). The only thing you know is that God knows what He is doing. All you can say is, "Many, O LORD my God, are the wonders you have done. The things you planned for us no one can recount to you; were I to speak and tell of them, they would be too many to declare" (Psalm 40:5). God knows. That's all you need in the life of faith.

Tim Bowden, in his book *One Crowded Hour* about cameraman Neil Davis, tells about an incident that happened in Borneo during the confrontation between Malaysia and Indonesia in 1964. A group of Gurkhas from Nepal were asked if they would be willing to jump from transport planes into combat against the Indonesians if the need arose. The Gurkhas had the right to turn down the request because they had never been trained as paratroopers. Bowden quotes Davis's account of the story:

> Now the Gurkhas usually agreed to anything, but on this occasion they provisionally rejected the plan. But the next day one of their NCO's sought out the British officer who made the request and said they had discussed the matter further and would be prepared to jump under certain conditions.
>
> "What are they?" asked the British officer.
>
> The Gurkhas told him they would jump if the land was marshy or reasonably soft with no rocky outcrops, because they were inexperienced in falling. The British officer considered this, and said that the

dropping area would almost certainly be over jungle, and there would not be rocky outcrops, so that seemed all right. Was there anything else?

Yes, said the Gurkhas. They wanted the plane to fly as slowly as possible and no more than 100 feet high. The British officer pointed out the planes always did fly as slowly as possible when dropping troops, but to jump from 100 feet was impossible, because the parachutes would not open in time from that height.

"Oh," said the Gurkhas, "that's all right, then. We'll jump with parachutes anywhere. You didn't mention parachutes before!"[14]

That kind of sacrifice is what God called Abraham to make. *Are you willing to jump, Abraham, even if you don't have a 'chute?* He was. And he did. Are you?

A Fearless Faith

. . . [Abraham] obeyed and went, even though he did not know where he was going. By faith he made his home in the promised land like a stranger in a foreign country; he lived in tents, as did Isaac and Jacob, who were heirs with him of the same promise. For he was looking forward to the city with foundations, whose architect and builder is God. (Hebrews 11:8-10)

The author has already referred to Abraham's faith in the promise of God and his patient waiting for its fulfillment. Here he enlarges on the same theme. Even when he seized the promise of the inheritance, it was only the promise he received, not the visible possession of the land. But to Abraham the promise of God was as good as gold. He lived after that in the integrity and honor of that promise. Year after year he pitched his moving tent amid the settled inhabitants of Palestine.[15]

He owned not a single square foot of real estate until he bought the field of Machpelah near Hebron as a family burial plot. The people around him lived in cities while he and his family lived in tents. Yet he did not grow impatient and demanding. Some visible signs of the word of God he did receive in Isaac and Jacob.[16]

Bishop Newbigin tells of the negotiations which led to the formation of the United Church of South India. Things were frequently held up by cautious people who wished to know just where each step was taking them, until in the end the chairman reminded them that a Christian has no right to ask where he is going.

Most of us are comfortable with a safe and cautious life on the principle of safety first but to live the Christian life and to be effective in ministry, a certain reckless abandon to adventure is necessary. If faith can see every step of the way, it's not real faith. There are times we must be like Abraham and go in fearless faith without knowing what the final destination will be.[17]

We need the courage to believe that what God promised, He will do.

A Reliant Faith

> By faith Abraham, even though he was past age—and Sarah herself was barren—was enabled to become a father because he considered him faithful who had made the promise. And so from this one man, and he as good as dead, came descendants as numerous as the stars in the sky and as countless as the sand on the seashore. (Hebrews 11:11-12)

Abraham was past age for producing children. He was as good as dead. Sarah was barren. Yet they relied on God because they "believed that the one who had given the promise was utterly trustworthy" (Phillips translation, 11:11). Because Abraham believed God and held fast to His promise, what started out with a very small beginning (one man) turned into a blessing that was beyond human calculation. One plus God is *always* a winning majority!

The three-year-old felt secure in his father's arms as Dad stood in the middle of the pool. But Dad, for fun, began walking slowly toward the deep end, gently chanting, "Deeper and deeper and deeper," as the water rose higher and higher and higher on the child. The boy's face registered increasing degrees of panic, and he held all the more tightly to his father, who, of course, easily touched the bottom of the pool.

Had the little boy been able to analyze his situation, he'd have realized there was no reason for increased anxiety. The water's depth in any part of the pool was over his head. Even in the shallowest part, had he not been held up, he'd have drowned. His safety anywhere in that pool depended on Dad.[18]

Our Father in heaven is never out of His depth, and we can trust Him to hold us up. That reliant, dependent faith is what He's looking for from us.

When we learn something from only one perspective, we may think it's the only viewpoint. Sometimes it's good to change seats to assume a different perspective on the same truth. That is what we have done with Hebrews 11:8-12. Since Abraham is the supreme example of faith, the first established man of faith and the pattern of faith for people of all ages, we looked at his faith from his perspective and found that his faith was submissive, sacrificial, fearless and reliant. It merits duplication in our lives.

Living the Christian life requires submissive, responsive, obedient faith to the Word of God and the calling of God, not a wait-and-see attitude. Are you responding to God even as the call is ringing in your ears?

The Power of Faith

> All these people were still living by faith when they
> died. They did not receive the things promised; they only

saw them and welcomed them from a distance. And they admitted that they were aliens and strangers on earth. People who say such things show that they are looking for a country of their own. If they had been thinking of the country they had left, they would have had opportunity to return. Instead, they were longing for a better country—a heavenly one. Therefore God is not ashamed to be called their God, for he has prepared a city for them. (Hebrews 11:13-16)

Some night you should take a walk down your street and observe the homes. They all draw electricity from the same source, but some houses may be brilliantly lit up and delightfully warm, while others are dim and cold. The same power is available to all, but some of your neighbors have not made full use of that power. The homes that are beaming are using lamps of sufficient wattage and a furnace of adequate strength. The others may have light bulbs of smaller capacity and a heating unit of limited output.

In much the same way, divine energy to live the Christian life and to show forth the Savior's power is available to all believers. Nevertheless, if we want to know and experience His power, if we want to see results for the glory of God, we must exercise true faith. When we consistently do so, we shall see that faith generates abounding confidence, an effective testimony, clear insight and ample security to sustain us in the storms of life.

Faith Generates Abounding Confidence

All these people were still living by faith when they died. They did not receive the things promised; they only saw them and welcomed them from a distance. (Hebrews 11:13)

The writer of Hebrews breaks off his discussion of Abraham until 11:17 in order to make some general remarks about "all these people," meaning those he has dealt with in the preceding verses. They lived out their faith and died in faith without receiving or possessing what was promised to them. What is said applies to every one of them. They died *in faith*, under the rule of faith, with the promises of God deeply engraved on their hearts and minds. They did not have the joy of seeing God's promises fulfilled in their lifetime.

Verse 13 says they *saw* the things that were promised and "welcomed them from a distance." Moses prayed that God would let him enter the land (Deuteronomy 3:23-25), but the most God would permit was for him only to "see" it (Deuteronomy 3:26-28; 34:1-4). The forefathers had excellent spiritual vision. They had an inner awareness of what the promises meant. Even though they did not receive the things promised, they "saw."

Our assurance does not rest on our ability to *see* God, it depends on our willingness to *believe* God. Our certainty depends on the sharpness of our spiritual vision, what we can see with our spiritual eyes.

Faith Generates an Effective Testimony

> And they admitted that they were aliens and strangers on earth. (Hebrews 11:13)

The patriarchs showed in their disposition and speech that they knew themselves to be nothing more than "aliens and strangers on earth." It was not simply an attitude of mind; they gave expression to it in their conversation with other people. They spoke of their conviction regarding life on this earth as aliens and strangers. They spoke of a better life in heaven. Faith refuses to be silent. It must share its testimony with others.[19]

When Peter was brought before the Sanhedrin to be questioned by the high priest because he did not obey their strict orders not to teach in the name of Jesus, he and the other apostles replied: "We must obey God rather than men! . . . We are witnesses of these things" (Acts 5:29, 32). Bona fide faith refuses to be silent.

Later, at Cornelius' house, the blinders dropped from Peter's eyes, and he realized that God does not show favoritism. He recounted what happened throughout Judea, how God anointed Jesus with the Holy Spirit and power and how He went around doing good and healing all who were under the power of the devil. Then Peter said, "We are witnesses of everything he did in the country of the Jews and in Jerusalem" (Acts 10:39).

His clear testimony had amazing results. "While Peter was still speaking these words, the Holy Spirit came on all who heard the message" (Acts 10:44). No telling what God will do when His people give testimony to His powerful deeds!

Faith Generates Clear Insight

> People who say such things show that they are looking for a country of their own. If they had been thinking of the country they had left, they would have had opportunity to return. Instead, they were longing for a better country—a heavenly one. (Hebrews 11:14-16)

Had the ancients been earthly minded, they may have gone back to where they came from. There was nothing physical to stop them from doing so. But their hearts were set on the heavenly home, the new Jerusalem; and they did not go back. For example, when Abraham wanted a wife for Isaac he wanted her to be from his homeland; but he did not go back there himself. Instead, he sent a servant (Genesis 24:1-6).

After Jacob spent twenty years in Mesopotamia, he still regarded Canaan as "my own homeland" (Genesis 30:25). Abraham buried Sarah in Canaan, not Mesopotamia, and in due course he was buried there himself (Genesis 23:19, 25:9-10). If these men had their hearts set on this world, if they had been earthly-minded men, they could have gone back to Mesopotamia. But their hearts were set on things above.

They walked the path of faith. They not only admitted that they were aliens and strangers on earth, they also demonstrated keen insight into the mind and heart of God. They quickly discerned that all the marks of transience, impermanence and perishability were upon the things of earth, looking away from such material gains to something which was better, the heavenly home of the people of God.

The man or woman who possesses genuine faith has the ability to distinguish between good and evil, eternal and temporal, permanent and perishable. They have spiritual insight and understanding (Colossians 1:9) and know how to make the best of both worlds. Genuine faith produces the kind of insight that enables one to look longingly into heaven, maintaining a heavenly perspective, and at the same time to look at life on earth and live it realistically.

Faith Generates Ample Security

> Instead, they were longing for a better country—a heavenly one. Therefore God is not ashamed to be called their God, for he has prepared a city for them. (Hebrews 11:16)

Exiles were not viewed with preference in the ancient world, and these people testified openly to being "aliens and strangers on the earth." To reside in a country other than one's own country carried a stigma in ancient times. But these pilgrims of heaven were marching toward home. So firm was their commitment to their heavenly calling that God "is not ashamed to be called their God, for he has prepared a city for them." That is security!

One commentator makes a fascinating observation about this idea of the city of God. Three concepts of the city were prevalent in the first-century world: Jewish, Greek and Stoic. The Jew thought the city was the home of *divine sovereignty* (Psalm 48:2). The Greek thought the city was the place of *special privilege*. It was not meant for all people, only for a select company. The Stoic thought the city was the focus of *universal hope*.[20]

Perhaps the New Testament idea of "the city of God" makes use of all three of these ideas. By divine sovereignty, it is God's city. He dwells among His people. By special privilege, it is the city inhabited by believers, a special company through faith. By universal hope, and by His mercy, God calls into this city all who will believe in Jesus.[21]

The city of God provides our security. It is the home we are waiting for.

In some American cities an astonishing fifty percent of the youngsters wear keys around their necks. But there's no such thing as a latchkey child in God's family because the Father is always at home. The Christian never has to sigh, "Oh, I'm on my own, what can I do?"

The Scriptures assure us, "The LORD is near to all those who call on Him, to all who call on him in truth" (Psalm 145:18). "Let the beloved of the LORD rest secure in him" (Deuteronomy 33:12). Our "lot" is secure in Him, (See Psalm 16:5.) and so is our "heart." (See Psalm 112:8.) "He who fears the LORD has a secure fortress, and for his children it will be a refuge" (Proverbs 14:26). In Jesus Christ you are always safe and secure from all alarm!

I'm asking you in this chapter to break the mold, to think about risking like Abraham and his family risked. Move out in faith and trust God.

David Seamands, in his book *Healing for Damaged Emotions*, tells this story that helps me illustrate what I'm saying.

I remember some years ago talking with a salesman in a used car lot. As we looked out the showroom win-

dow, we saw a man who was going around kicking
tires on the cars. He was also raising the hood and
banging the fenders. The salesman said disgustedly,
"Look at that guy out there. He's a wheel-kicker.
They are the bane of our existence. They come in
here all the time, but never buy cars because they
can't make up their minds. Now watch him out there.
He's kicking the tires. He'll say the wheels are out of
line. He'll listen to the motor and say, 'Hear that
knock?' Nobody else can hear the knock, but he can
hear it. Something is always wrong. He is afraid to
choose; he can never make up his mind, so he always
finds an excuse."[22]

Life is full of tire-kickers, and so is the church. People
who are afraid of failure because they're afraid of trying
something new. Afraid of making the wrong choices; afraid
of dreaming big. Afraid of risk; afraid of launching out in the
Holy Spirit and really surrendering to the Lord. Are you
one of those fearful believers? I hope not. Not after all this
ink on faith. Risky faith. Real faith. Not after reading about
Abel, Enoch and Noah again. Not after Abraham, Isaac and
Jacob. Not *now*! Please!

However, if you want to know the power of the sanctified
life, the deeper life, you must employ genuine faith and re-
sign as the official tire-kicker in your church. Authentic
faith, in turn, will generate abounding confidence, an effective testimony, clear insight and ample security to sustain
you in the storms of life.

Endnotes

1. *Leadership* (Winter 1994): 46. Used by permission.
2. Leon Morris, *Hebrews, The Expositor's Bible Commentary*,
   Vol. 12, ed. Frank E. Gaebelein (Grand Rapids, MI:
   Zondervan Publishing House, 1981), 113.
3. See Leon Morris, 113, for a more detailed discussion.

4. A.W. Tozer, *The Pursuit of God* (Harrisburg, PA: Christian Publications, Inc., Mass Market Edition assigned 1976 to Horizon Books), 56.

5. Philip Edgcumbe Hughes has written an extensive excursus on the doctrine of creation in Hebrews 11:3. It is contained in his helpful commentary on *Hebrews* (Grand Rapids, MI: William B. Eerdmans Publishing Company, 1977), 443-452.

6. Taken from an article that was clipped from *Maclean's*. Bibliography unknown.

7. *Leadership* (Spring 1992): 49. Used by permission.

8. Donald Guthrie, *Tyndale New Testament Commentaries: Hebrews* (Grand Rapids, MI: William B. Eerdmans Publishing Company, 1983), 228.

9. *Leadership* (Summer 1986): 39. Used by permission.

10. *Leadership* (Winter 1990): 50. Used by permission.

11. *Leadership* (Fall 1990): 49. Used by permission.

12. Quoted by Leon Morris, 118.

13. Philip Edgcumbe Hughes, *A Commentary on the Epistle to the Hebrews* (Grand Rapids, MI: William B. Eerdmans Publishing Company, 1977), 466, footnote 28.

14. *Leadership* (Spring 1990): 48. Used by permission.

15. F.F. Bruce tells us in a footnote that "Abraham the Hebrew" in Genesis 14:13 is rendered in the LXX "Abram the Migrant," 296.

16. See F.F. Bruce for an excellent treatment of these two verses, *The Epistle to the Hebrews* (Grand Rapids, MI: William B. Eerdmans, 1964), 295-297.

17. William Barclay, 144.

18. *Leadership* (Winter 1988): 37. Used by permission.

19. Raymond Brown, *The Message of Hebrews* (Downers Grove, IL: InterVarsity Press, 1982), 206-207.

20. Ibid., 208.

21. Ibid.

22. David Seamands, *Healing for Damaged Emotions* (Wheaton, IL: Victor Books, 1981), 23.

Discussion Questions for Further Study

1. What are the key elements of faith?

2. Compare Hebrews 11:1-2 to Second Corinthians 4:16-18. What additional insights do you gain about living by faith?

3. How can believers please God? See Hebrews 11:5; Matthew 3:17; John 8:29; Hebrews 13:16.

4. How can you show this kind of holy fear (11:7) that leads to active faith? See also Nehemiah 5:15-16; Job 1:1-5, 21-22; Acts 5:1-11; 10:2.

5. Do you consider yourself a pilgrim and an alien on the earth? How does this affect your priorities and actions? How should it affect them in deeper ways?

11

Hebrews 11:17-40

Faith at Work in the Family

> *By faith Abraham, when God tested him, offered Isaac as a sacrifice. He who had received the promises was about to sacrifice his one and only son, even though God had said to him, "It is through Isaac that your offspring will be reckoned." Abraham reasoned that God could raise the dead, and figuratively speaking, he did receive Isaac back from death.*
>
> *By faith Isaac blessed Jacob and Esau in regard to their future.*
>
> *By faith Jacob, when he was dying, blessed each of Joseph's sons, and worshiped as he leaned on the top of his staff.*
>
> *By faith Joseph, when his end was near, spoke about the exodus of the Israelites from Egypt and gave instructions about his bones.*
>
> *By faith Moses' parents hid him for three months after he was born, because they saw he was no ordinary child, and they were not afraid of the king's edict. (Hebrews 11:17-23)*

Jonathan Edwards' father was a minister and his mother as a pastor's daughter. Among their descendants were fourteen college presidents, more than 100 college professors, more than 100 lawyers, 30 judges, 60 physicians, more than 100 clergymen, missionaries and theology professors and about 60 authors. There is scarcely any great American industry that has not had one of his family among its chief promoters. Such is the outcome of one Christian family, reared in faith.

The contrast is presented in the Jukes family. They would not study and they would not work. They had cost the state of New York a million dollars. Their entire record is one of indigence and crime, insanity and imbecility. Among their 1,200 known descendants, 310 were professional beggars, 440 were physically wrecked by their own wickedness, 60 were habitual thieves, 130 were convicted criminals, only 20 learned a trade (and ten of these learned it in a state prison), and this notorious family produced seven murderers. Such is the outcome of another family, reared without faith, without any Christian role model.

Hebrews 11:17-23 is not about family per se, but it reveals how genuine faith influences the family for the future. It also provides several models of faith for us to emulate to one degree or another. The patriarchs had a faith that looked beyond the grave. They were utterly convinced that death cannot frustrate the purposes and plans God has for His people. These verses give us some personal portraits through which we can watch faith in progress.

Abraham's Faith

> By faith Abraham, when God tested him, offered Isaac as a sacrifice. He who had received the promises was about to sacrifice his one and only son, even though God had said to him, "It is through Isaac that your offspring will be reckoned." Abraham reasoned that God could raise the dead, and figuratively speaking, he did receive Isaac back from death. (Hebrews 11:17-19)

God "tested" Abraham. Sometimes this word is used in the sense of tempted, but the term itself denotes only a testing. It becomes associated with temptation only when the person is enticed to do evil, and of course "God cannot be tempted by evil, nor does he tempt anyone" (James 1:13). God didn't keep testing Abraham with this matter. It happened once with wonderfully abiding results. We may assume that Abraham learned his lesson well.

Faith in God means more than citing a creed divorced from practical application to life. Instances are cited in Hebrews 11 which show the heights to which faith can attain. As we look at these verses we really must pull away from our world long enough to enter into Abraham's. That's not easy for modern-day people like us to do, but let's try. The ultimate test appears on the pages of Genesis 22.

Here we find a man who has been told to take his son's life, the son who was called the "one and only son." A precious young life full of potential. Abraham had other sons, but none who were born in the way Isaac was. And none bearing the kind of promises that were made about Isaac. In this way Isaac was unique and irreplaceable, thus the phrase "one and only son." God promised him a nation through Isaac; yet now He called on him to offer Isaac as a sacrifice.

Though he did not understand, Abraham knew how to obey. His faith told him that God would work out His purpose, even if he himself could not see how that could be. So he offered Isaac as a sacrifice. He complied without resistance. The perfect tense of the Greek verb *prosphero* ("offered") indicates that as far as Abraham was concerned the sacrifice was complete.

In will and purpose he did offer his son. He held nothing back. He gave everything. But immediately the same verb is used (in the latter half of v. 17) in the imperfect tense which means that the action was not in fact completed.[1]

Abraham was chosen as an example of faith because his response was not branded with revolt, outrage or disillusionment. Instead, he trusted God. Thus he faced the test. Would he pass, though?

"Abraham reasoned that God could raise the dead, and figuratively speaking, he did receive Isaac back from death" (Hebrews 11:19).

Genesis 22 makes it clear that God was the one who sent this ultimate test into Abraham's life. The same God who told Abraham to leave Ur, who gave Abraham the promise of a nation and opened Sarah's womb in her old age, is the God who told Abraham to take the son of promise and offer him as a sacrifice.

This text also explains that Abraham's faith was without delay (Genesis 22:3), and it was characterized by confidence (22:4-5). Abraham said to his servants who had accompanied him to the mountain, "Stay here with the donkey while I and the boy go over there. We will worship and then we will come back to you" (22:5).

We will worship and then we will come back? How could he be so sure? Why was Abraham so confident? God told him to *sacrifice* Isaac. *Go to the region of Moriah and sacrifice him there. Plunge that butcher's knife into his heart. Yes, Isaac. There's no mistake. Isaac. Your one and only son.*

So where did his assurance, certainty and boldness come from? Hebrews 11:19 says, "Abraham reasoned that God could raise the dead. . . ." Abraham brought the Lord into the midst of this supreme test; and he reasoned, he calculated, on the basis of the character of God, that God could raise the dead. Just like that. Simple, straightforward faith. Abraham faced the test of his life and passed because he believed God and did not trust in natural wisdom, nor his own instinct nor the council of the ungodly. In the midst of all that pressure he did what pleased God. And God honored him for it.

What sort of tests are you facing? Whatever they are, you can be sure that God's will always requires obedience. "The reason I wrote you was to see if you would stand the test and be obedient in everything" (2 Corinthians 2:9). Obedience to the Word of God and the will of God is critical during a time of testing. Stand firm and do what is right in the sight of God.

Isaac's Faith

> By faith Isaac blessed Jacob and Esau in regard to
> their future. (Hebrews 11:20)

Just as Abraham acted in view of things to come, so did
Isaac. He blessed his two sons in terms that looked into the
distant future.

Moving to Isaac himself, the author of Hebrews refers to
Genesis 27:1-28:5. But we have a problem here. Isaac's pronouncement of the blessing upon Jacob was the result of
some trickery by Jacob and his mother Rebecca. How can
Isaac bless this deceptive son "by faith"?

The answer lies in the content of the blessing. It dealt
with the future, with things to come (Genesis 27:28, 29, 39,
40; 28:3-4); consequently it looks like Isaac did believe the
promises made to Abraham (Genesis 28:4) and wanted
them inherited by his sons. When the deception was discovered, Isaac did not veto the blessing upon Jacob on the
grounds that it had been fraudulently obtained. Instead he
confirmed it with these words, "and indeed he will be
blessed" (Genesis 27:33). Therefore, even Isaac was firm in
faith regarding the reality of God's promises to the Abra-
hamic family.[2]

The faith relationship spoken of in this verse is father to son.
Isaac was the father of Jacob and Esau, and in Genesis 27 he
blessed them both before he died. In that culture the oldest son
was supposed to receive the lion's share of the inheritance and
the blessing, but that was not the case in this situation.

Old and nearly blind, Isaac had been deceived by his wife
and his youngest son. He had to employ his senses of taste
and smell to distinguish between his sons. In the end, he
freely gave the blessing of the firstborn to Jacob, the
younger son. However, the writer of Hebrews is not as concerned with the details surrounding the craftiness of Jacob as
he is with the faith that undergirded Isaac's blessing and the
fact that both blessings concerned "their future."

Let's not miss the point: On each occasion Isaac spoke out of a firm conviction that a blessing given in accordance with God's purposes could not possibly fail. By faith Isaac believed that God would oversee the sequence of events and control the outcome of the blessing. The Father is always reliable. "Unless the LORD builds the house, its builders labor in vain" (Psalm 127:1).

Promises for raising a family. For sustaining health. For maturing holiness. For everything *in* the future, we trust His promise *for* the future.

Jacob's Faith

> By faith Jacob, when he was dying, blessed each of Joseph's sons, and worshiped as he leaned on the top of his staff. (Hebrews 11:21)

Jacob had come to the same point in his life that his father, Isaac, had come with him. His eyesight had dimmed. Death was a nearing reality. Joseph, the faithful and favorite son of Jacob, visited his dad, bringing along his own sons Manasseh and Ephraim. So the relationship in this verse is grandfather to grandsons.

In Genesis 48 we witness how the blessing was again given to the younger son, Ephraim, going against the natural order of birth,

> And Joseph took both of them, Ephraim on his right toward Israel's left hand and Manasseh on his left toward Israel's right hand, and brought them close to him. But Israel reached out his right hand and put it on Ephraim's head, though he was the younger and crossing his arms, he put his left hand on Manasseh's head, even though Manasseh was the firstborn. (Genesis 48:13-14)

Joseph attempted to correct what seemed to him to be a

serious error, but Jacob refused to change the blessing. He blessed them both, but he blessed the youngest grandson first, and that wasn't supposed to happen. Once again the overarching principle is the sovereignty of God.

Nothing can frustrate God's purpose. God will have His way with us. He fulfills His purposes as He chooses. That's the principle that Jacob was transmitting to his grandsons that day when he said, "In your name will Israel pronounce this blessing: 'May God make you like Ephraim and Manasseh' " (Genesis 48:20). Yet fulfillment could be known only by faith.

This concept of blessing your children or grandchildren (Jacob blessed his *grandchildren* in this particular case) is not reserved for patriarchs in Bible times. It's a marvelous ministry that can be fulfilled in our families today. I was so touched when I read *The Blessing* by Gary Smalley and John Trent. It came at just the right point in my pilgrimage as a father of three children.

They tell us that "a family blessing begins with meaningful touching. It continues with a spoken message of high value, a message that pictures a special future for the individual being blessed, and one that is based on an active commitment to see the blessing come to pass."[3] I started blessing my three children the same day I read that, and my wife and I have seen some awesome results in terms of improved attitudes and respect for others.

Don't withhold the blessing. Bless your children—be an Isaac. Bless your grandchildren—be a Jacob. Let them know that you love them and that you love Jesus, while you still have the opportunity. That's family-style faith in action.

Joseph's Faith

> By faith Joseph, when his end was near, spoke about the exodus of the Israelites from Egypt and gave instructions about his bones. (Hebrews 11:22)

Though his words referred to nothing more than his burial arrangements, the commission to carry his bones to Canaan gives testimony of his deep conviction that in due time God would send the people back to that land. Joseph arrived in Egypt as a slave when he was seventeen years old, sold into slavery by his own brothers. They despised him and they were jealous of him (Genesis 37:12-36). Joseph became securely established in the Egyptian lifestyle; yet amid the influence and authority granted him in time, he never forgot his roots.

Many years later, when his brothers discovered that the one who had saved their lives from starvation was the same brother they had sold into slavery, they were terrified.

> But Joseph said to them, "Don't be afraid. Am I in the place of God? You intended to harm me, but God intended it for good to accomplish what is now being done, the saving of many lives. So then, don't be afraid. I will provide for you and your children." And he reassured them and spoke kindly to them. (Genesis 50:19-21)

When Joseph had the chance to get even he passed. On his word his brothers would have been flogged or tortured or killed. He could have reciprocated the cruel treatment, but the grace of God welled up in his heart. By faith he chose to forgive. Throughout his life Joseph's relationship to his brothers was characterized by faith. He had been abused and harassed by his own family, just as some of you have been mistreated. Yet he moved beyond the hurt and the rejection by faith. He forgave those in his family who sinned against him. He took the risk of loving again. Do you need to step into the path of forgiveness also?

Moses' Parents' Faith

> By faith Moses' parents hid him for three months after he was born, because they saw he was no ordi-

nary child, and they were not afraid of the king's
edict. (Hebrews 11:23)

Moses is mentioned eleven times in the book of Hebrews.
He lived by faith. But here the reference to him begins with
the faith exercised by his mother and father.[4] The Greek
term *pateron* is usually translated "fathers." Sometimes it was
used to represent both parents (Ephesians 6:4; Colossians
3:21). This would seem to be the case here since it was his
mother's role which was emphasized in the Exodus account.
Although the father was not even mentioned, likely both
parents were involved in the plan.

The Pharaoh of Egypt launched a program of devastation.
One decree followed another until finally Pharaoh ordered
that the Hebrew sons be cast into the Nile River and
drowned at birth (Exodus 1:22). Presumably, anyone who
disobeyed would be severely punished. But within the tribe
of Levi was a family that believed they had to overrule these
orders.

They obeyed God rather than Pharaoh. By faith they
placed their infant son, Moses, into hiding. They were people of faith. They believed God had a special plan for their
beautiful baby boy, "a fine child" (Exodus 2:2). So they hid
him, trusting God rather than fearing Pharaoh. He was no
ordinary child. And in the years to come, as the story of his
"salvation" was replayed again and again for Moses, he also
came to believe that God had a special plan for him.

From the vantage point of Hebrews 11:17-23, we have
watched faith at work in several different homes. Now how
about where you live? What does faith look like at your
house when the doors are closed, when the shades are drawn
and nobody else can see inside? Do the people in your family see faith in action? Do your children have a positive
model of faith in the home? A faith that believes God can
overrule any circumstances?

Carle Zimmerman, in *Family and Civilization*, recorded his
poignant observations as he compared the disintegration of

various cultures with the parallel decline of family life in those cultures. Eight specific patterns of domestic behavior typified the downward spiral of each culture Zimmerman studied.

- Marriage loses its sacredness . . . is frequently broken by divorce.
- Traditional meaning of the marriage ceremony is lost.
- Feminist movements abound.
- Increased public disrespect for parents and authority in general.
- Acceleration of juvenile delinquency, promiscuity and rebellion.
- Refusal of people with traditional marriages to accept family responsibilities.
- Growing desire for and acceptance of adultery.
- Increasing interest in and spread of sexual perversions and sex-related crimes.[5]

The right message about faith begins right at home. Faith was never meant to remain a theoretical study. Faith is best learned at home in the context of family relationships. Therefore, we should use our Christian homes as teaching centers, not merely maintenance shops (Deuteronomy 6:4-9). Home is a teaching center for making disciples, not a repair shop for periodic tune-ups.

In addition, we have an obligation and an opportunity in our homes to develop a contagious confidence in God, not a demoralizing determination to endure. Let's put the fullest measure of trust and confidence in the Lord and model the faith for our children and grandchildren. Let's follow the example of Isaac and Jacob and bless our kids with meaningful touching, speak messages of high value to them, messages that picture a special future for them based on the sovereignty of Almighty God and on an active commitment to see the blessing come to pass.

Faith Limits Your Choices

> By faith Moses, when he had grown up, refused to be known as the son of Pharaoh's daughter. He chose to be mistreated along with the people of God rather than to enjoy the pleasures of sin for a short time. He regarded disgrace for the sake of Christ as of greater value than the treasures of Egypt, because he was looking ahead to his reward. By faith he left Egypt, not fearing the king's anger; he persevered because he saw him who is invisible. By faith he kept the Passover and the sprinkling of blood, so that the destroyer of the firstborn would not touch the firstborn of Israel. (Hebrews 11:24-28)

I'd like to express my appreciation for my father-in-law. Bud is the senior pastor of a church in Toronto, Canada—been there for over twenty years. Faithful, dependable, diligent, godly, resourceful, supportive, giving and encouraging.

Not long ago, after I had read Exodus 18 in my devotions one morning, I called him on the telephone to tell him he was like a Jethro to me. He gives good advice but he never meddles. Interested in what I do, but never interfering. Encouraging, not encroaching. Like Jethro and Moses, we have an abiding friendship and camaraderie that has a strong, healthy spiritual foundation. Bud Downey consistently models the life of faith for his family and his congregation.

Some of my models, like Bud, are alive and well and still growing in the Lord. Others have long since died, but their names are recorded in the Hall of Faith in Hebrews 11: Abel, Enoch, Noah, Abraham, Isaac, Jacob and Joseph. And Moses. That man made choices that were anything but simple and easy, choices that serve as models for us to follow.

Refuse the Pleasures of Sin

> By faith Moses, when he had grown up, refused to
> be known as the son of Pharaoh's daughter. He chose
> to be mistreated along with the people of God rather
> than to enjoy the pleasures of sin for a short time. He
> regarded disgrace for the sake of Christ as of greater
> value than the treasures of Egypt, because he was
> looking ahead to his reward. (Hebrews 11:24-26)

The author passes over the baby in the reeds, the discovery of the child by Pharaoh's daughter and the upbringing in the palace. He comes quickly to Moses' faith as an adult. Stephen tells us that Moses was about forty years old at the time (Acts 7:23). "The author appears to be saying that the decision Moses reached was that of a mature man—not the decision of a child or rebellious adolescent."[6] With full knowledge Moses refused to be known as the Pharaoh's grandson.

He made a choice to be mistreated along with God's people rather than to enjoy the riches of the Egyptian royal residence when he renounced the status which he enjoyed as a member of the royal household. His decision was not made in haste by a man who dreamed of being great. Neither was it made in ignorance or on the crest of emotion after singing twenty-four stanzas of "Just As I Am."

He was human, so you can be sure that he had wrestled with the continuing tension caused by the penchant to embrace the temporal at the expense of the spiritual. God's Word openly admits that sin can be fun, pleasurable, enjoyable. Yet to have the insight it takes to reject the sinful, faith must eclipse my feelings. If Moses had made his decision based on how he felt, he would have chosen the wrong road.

But when faith overshadows your feelings, it becomes much easier to look ahead to your eternal reward and away from everything else, setting your heart on things above, where Christ is seated at the right hand of God (Colossians 3:1-4), confident that "he who began a good work in you will carry it on to completion until the day of Christ Jesus" (Philippians 1:6).

Leave the "Comfort Zone"

> By faith he left Egypt, not fearing the king's anger; he persevered because he saw him who is invisible. (Hebrews 11:27)

When Moses *left* Egypt, he did this too *by faith*. Moses actually left Egypt on two different occasions. He fled to Midian after he had slain the Egyptian tyrant (Exodus 2:11-15), and he went out with the rest of the Israelites at the time of the Exodus. On the whole it seems best to take the words in Hebrews 11:27 as referring to the flight to Midian, but readers may want to investigate this more fully.[7]

Moses had grown up in the lap of luxury. He was raised as the son of Pharaoh's daughter. All of the benefits of royalty were his to enjoy. The palace had been his home since he was a baby. Egypt was all he knew. Yet that which Jehovah God offered Moses surpassed everything in Egypt.

"By faith he left Egypt. . . ." He was willing to take the risk of faith and leave the familiar behind. For you and me to have the resolve it takes to leave the familiar, faith must be our security.

Every time one of our young people makes a commitment to pursue overseas missions as a vocation, he or she determines to leave the familiar behind. Faith must become a shield in countries like Zambia where every day 400 to 500 Zambians are infected with the AIDS virus. There will be one million people infected with HIV by 1997, 2 million by 2000, with 100,000 dead. Nearly 78,000 children have been orphaned so far. In 1997, the figure may be 600,000. [8]

As I write this chapter missionaries in India are facing a setback. Only a month after India's government lifted its ban on the World Hindu Federation (VHP) in 1995 for its complicity in the Hindu-Muslim rioting in 1993 that claimed 1,200 lives, the group announced plans to clamp down on Christian missionaries. A VHP leader promised to raise up 10,000 Hindu missionaries, oppose economic liberalization and support the supremacy of Hinduism in India.[9]

Friends of ours have left Indonesia after many years of fruitful ministry there. The government will not renew their visas. Such is the opposition and circumstances our missionaries face every day.

God may not be calling *you* to leave your city or your country to follow Him, but He may be asking you to step outside of your comfort zone. Leaving the familiar is an act of faith. God may ask you to step out of your customary ministry and get into a brand new area of service. If God whispered your name and asked you to leave the familiar behind, would you follow?

Proceed with the Peculiar

> By faith he kept the Passover and the sprinkling of blood, so that the destroyer of the firstborn would not touch the firstborn of Israel. (Hebrews 11:28)

Pharaoh would not permit the Jews to leave Egypt to worship God. In spite of repeated judgments on the land and untold suffering to his people, Pharaoh hardened his heart. He refused to submit to the authority of Jehovah God. But the Lord had one more plague—the visitation of the angel of death (Exodus 12:12-13). Only those found in houses marked by the blood of a lamb would be delivered from death (12:7).

It required faith for Moses and his people to obey the instructions for Passover. They could not go by past history because there had never been such an event as this before. They certainly could not go by their personal feelings. No doubt many of them sat in their houses trembling and afraid. No doubt many of them were critical of Moses' leadership and his ideas. And yet when God gave the unusual orders, they obeyed. Moses did not shy back. In faith he was willing to do the peculiar. He had no tradition to fall back upon, yet he obeyed. And the critics were silenced.

To this very day, the life of Moses declares a strong message that cannot be ignored. He teaches us how to make tough decisions that please the Lord. So how does your faith compare to Moses'? Are you making the right choices? If we love God, we must love His Word and act upon it. Take a holy, radical stand. Surrender the illusion of power and find it replaced by the power of the Spirit of God. That was certainly one of Alexander Solzhenitsyn's greatest discoveries in the Soviet gulag.

Like other prisoners, Solzhenitsyn worked in the fields. His days were filled with backbreaking labor and slow starvation. One day the hopelessness became too much to bear. He felt no purpose for his suffering. His determination died. His expectations expired. Laying down his shovel, he walked slowly to a bench. He knew at any moment a guard would order him back to work. When he failed to respond, he would be beaten to death. He had seen it happen many times. Now it was his turn.

As he sat waiting, head down, he felt a presence. Slowly he lifted his eyes. Next to him sat an old man with a wrinkled, utterly expressionless face. Hunched over, the man drew a stick through the sand at Solzhenitsyn's feet, quickly and deliberately tracing out the sign of the cross.

As Solzhenitsyn stared at that rough outline, his entire perspective shifted. He knew he was merely one man against the all-powerful Soviet empire. Yet in that moment, the hope of the gospel flooded his soul like the waves that break over the reef near the beach. He knew that the desire of all mankind was represented by that simple cross. Through its power anything was possible. Solzhenitsyn slowly got up, picked up his shovel and went back to work. Years later his writings on truth and freedom would enflame the whole world.[10]

Such is the power God's truth affords one man willing to stand against seemingly hopeless odds. Such is the power of the cross. "For the message of the cross is foolishness to those who are perishing, but to us who are being saved it is the power of God" (1 Corinthians 1:18). Have you discovered the power of the cross in your daily life? Have you surrendered your will to the Father? For devoted followers of Jesus, true faith limits your choices. It involves refusing the pleasures of sin, leaving the comfort-zone called "familiar" and proceeding with the peculiar.

Decisions made in response to the work of Christ on the cross can change the face of eternity, my friend! It's not what we do that matters so much, but what a sovereign God chooses to do through the Spirit-directed choices we make. God doesn't want our success; He wants us.

Don't "give Him your problems." Give Him you. He doesn't demand our achievements; He demands our obedience. The kingdom of God is a kingdom of paradox, where through the scandal of the cross, a holy God is utterly glorified. Victory comes through defeat; healing through brokenness; success through failure; finding self through losing self; expanding possibilities by limiting choices.

Miracles by Faith

> By faith the people passed through the Red Sea as on dry land; but when the Egyptians tried to do so, they were drowned.
>
> By faith the walls of Jericho fell, after the people had marched around them for seven days.
>
> By faith the prostitute Rahab, because she welcomed the spies, was not killed with those who were disobedient. (Hebrews 11:29-31)

Rob Quan grew up in a Chinese community in Vietnam. Although his native tongue is Cantonese, he learned English as a second language. In 1982, his

parents moved to Canada to start a new life. Rob accepted
Christ as his Lord and Savior not long after they immi-
grated. He worked with a Christian organization and served
the Lord faithfully, but after two years the day-to-day routine wore him out. Personal and ministry demands piled up
and his enthusiasm evaporated. He was burned out emotionally and spiritually.

Thus began an intense internal struggle. Was he in the
will of God? Was he channeling his energies in the right direction? Had he missed what God planned for him? Each
day rolled into the next and his routine became mechanical.
No joy. No devotion. No excitement.

One Sunday he sat in church, lost in his thoughts. Suddenly what the pastor was saying broke through the fog like
a steamship with its horn blaring. He was calling people forward who needed a fresh touch from the Lord. Rob knew it
was for him. Standing before the altar he hesitantly raised
his hands and worshiped the Lord. One of the pastors and
his wife prayed for him, and he continued to worship God
as they prayed. Soon the senior pastor's wife came over and
started to pray for him. Rob said:

> I was completely awed by what she prayed. Not so
> much for the content, but for the vehicle. She was
> praying in perfect Cantonese! This becomes espe-
> cially significant because I had never told anyone that
> my native tongue was Cantonese.
>
> God was telling me to cross the border and to kick
> down the wall. She repeated this several times. *Cross
> the border and kick down the wall.* I tried to catch her
> eye when she stopped praying as I wanted to tell her
> what had happened, but she had moved off before I
> could say anything.
>
> I returned to worshiping, a little distracted by the
> awesomeness of God, but I knew that I needed to
> stay before the Lord longer, to see what else He
> would say. After a while our senior pastor came over

and started to pray for me. He prayed in English, exactly the same way his wife had prayed in Cantonese.
Twice the same message from two people in two lan-
guages, one language unknown by the other. *Cross the
border and kick down the wall.* I knew that only God
could show me the border and the wall.[11]

Was it the gift of tongues or a genuine miracle? If I told
you that it happened in a fundamentalist, ultra-conservative,
exclusively King James Version, short-haired, hymns-only
church, you'd say miracle. *For sure!*

If I said it occurred in one of those churches where they
roll in the aisles and shout "Amen" and dance in the Spirit
and laugh during the service, you'd say tongues. Well, I'm
going to keep you guessing. To know *where* it happened
would spoil the effect.

Regardless of where it happened (and the documentation
confirms it *did* happen), I think it was a supernatural work of
God's providence which is not explicable on the basis of the
usual patterns of nature. And it happened because one
young man dared to believe God still answers prayers of
faith and the cries of His people.

When we come to stories as striking and sensational as the
ones in Hebrews 11:29-31 (parting of the Red Sea, walls of
Jericho crashing down and the redemption of that wicked
prostitute Rahab), the authenticity of the events is difficult
to lay hold of. To some, miracles have been an obstacle
rather than an aid to faith.

That's unfortunate. Genuine miracles glorify God. They
don't happen only in charismatic churches either. In biblical
times they established the supernatural basis of the revelation
which often accompanied them. Many missionaries in primi-
tive areas would affirm that God still authenticates His Word
by miracles. They occur also to meet genuine human needs.

Our Lord was frequently moved with compassion for the
needy, hurting people who came to Him (Matthew 9:36,
14:14, 15:32, 20:34; James 5:11). He healed them to relieve

the suffering caused by such things as blindness, leprosy and bleeding. [12]

As we come to the miracles of the Exodus generation, keep in mind that Jesus is the same yesterday and today and forever (Hebrews 13:8).

The First Miracle

> By faith the people passed through the Red Sea as on dry land; but when the Egyptians tried to do so, they were drowned. (Hebrews 11:29)

The author moves quite naturally from Moses to the people associated with him. Some of the people who left Egypt with Moses were anything but shining examples of biblical faith. But they must have had some faith, and that's what the writer focuses on. Early in their flight from Egypt, the people of Israel come to a dead end—the Red Sea.

Checked to the south by a desert and to the north by a mountain range. Behind them, closing off the only visible escape route, was the approaching Egyptian army. They had nowhere to go. No government official to turn to for professional advice on national security. No special bionic powers. No wings that could fly them away from the danger of the moment.

So they cried out. They were in a desperate and impossible situation (Exodus 14:10). Moses answered the people with some unusual advice: "Do not be afraid. Stand firm and you will see the deliverance the LORD will bring you today. The Egyptians you see today you will never see again. The LORD will fight for you; you need only to be still" (Exodus 14:13-14).

The Lord will fight for us? I thought the Lord helps those who help themselves? *We need only to be still?* What are you? Crazy!? That doesn't fit into our thinking, does it? The twentieth-century, Type-A personality, success-oriented, do-it-all-for-yourself-or-it-won't-get-done Christian can hardly conceive of this scenario. It must be Old Testament. Very old. Very ancient. Very non-contemporary indeed.

But God told Moses to lift up his staff. Stretch out his hand over the sea and divide the water so that the Israelites could go through on dry ground (Exodus 14:16). Not a muddy seabed or wet sand. Only dry ground. God sent a wind that dried out the sea bottom overnight, and the next day as the Israelites passed through on dry ground, they could see into the depths of the water walled up on each side.

When they were all safely on the other shore, the waters of the sea miraculously returned to their original space. The pursuing Egyptian army was drowned and the people of God were free. End of miracle number one.

The Second Miracle

> By faith the walls of Jericho fell, after the people
> had marched around them for seven days. (Hebrews
> 11:30)

The crossing of the Red Sea was followed by forty years of wandering in the wilderness. They crossed on dry ground to dry ground. Doesn't sound very enticing, does it?

Even when the Promised Land was entered at last, under the capable command of General Joshua, there were still daunting obstacles in the path of the Israelites. The first of these, after the Jordan had been crossed, was the walled city of Jericho, which appeared impregnable to Joshua's ill-equipped army. But Joshua was a man of faith. Ringing in his ears were the words from his commissioning service: "Be strong and courageous. Do not be terrified; do not be discouraged, for the LORD your God will be with you wherever you go" (Joshua 1:9).

God told Joshua that He had already delivered Jericho into their hands, along with its kings and its fighting men.

March around the city once with all the armed men.
Do this for six days. Have seven priests carry trumpets of rams' horns in front of the ark. On the seventh
day, march around the city seven times, with the
priests blowing trumpets. When you hear them
sound a long blast on the trumpets, have all the people give a loud shout; then the wall of the city will
collapse and the people will go up, every man straight
in. (Joshua 6:3-5)

Did you see that? Did those words sink in? Nothing
seems more foolish! Grown men marching around a strong
fortress for seven days, led by seven priests blowing rams'
horns? "Apart from the conviction that God would act,
nothing could have been more pointless than the behavior of
those warriors."[13] Who ever heard of a war being won with a
horn? Well, we have. Right here. And all *by faith*. Genuine,
biblical faith was vindicated, for the walls tumbled down.

End of miracle number two.

The Third Miracle

By faith the prostitute Rahab, because she welcomed the spies, was not killed with those who were
disobedient. (Hebrews 11:31)

This particular event seems out of place in this list. In the
first place, Rahab was a woman, and in fact she is the only
woman specifically mentioned by the author of Hebrews in
this chapter, apart from Sarah in verse 11.

Second, Rahab was a lady of the night, a prostitute who
gave lodging to Israeli spies before Jericho was destroyed.

Third, from the viewpoint of the Israelites, Rahab was a
foreigner. She didn't fit the mold. She did not belong to the
chosen people, but through faith she was accepted into their
company. Through faith she enjoyed the privileges and
blessing from which she had been excluded. In this she was

an example of the truth of the covenant promise that in the seed of Abraham all the nations of the earth would be blessed (Genesis 22:18; Galatians 3:8-9).

This is not the only place in the New Testament where she receives honorable mention. In James 2:25 her kind treatment of Joshua's spies is one of two arguments for the idea that faith without works is dead; the other argument being Abraham's offering up of Isaac. Her actions demonstrated her seed-sized faith, a faith for which God rewarded her. Before leaving the city, the two spies promised that she would be unharmed, her life would be spared. So after the walls of Jericho collapsed, Joshua dispatched men to retrieve her.

So where's the miracle? What's the fuss? The miracle was that her home was not destroyed when the wall collapsed. She was saved, salvaged, spared. Furthermore, after Rahab exhibited such faith, the Lord pulled her life together again. She remarried a man named Salmon, and together they had a son named Boaz who is listed in the genealogy of the Lord Jesus Christ (Matthew 1).

A lowdown, filthy, good-for-only-one-thing prostitute becomes part of the genealogy of Jesus! *Another* miracle: Her worth and her dignity were restored by God, and her value was restored in the eyes of others. End of miracle number three, but just the beginning of the faith adventure for you and me.

The waters of the Red Sea. The walls of Jericho. The welcome of a harlot. Now don't think for a minute that the record of these three miracles has been preserved simply to remind us of the great faith of yesteryear's heroes. What Jesus did then, He can do now. He is the same today as He was yesterday. With God all things are possible (Matthew 19:26; Mark 9:23; 10:27).

There are times when we feel as if life and people are loading more and more burdens into our baskets. What do we do then? Look to the Father. He knows exactly how much we can carry. "No temptation has seized you except what is common to man. And God is faithful; he will not let you be tempted beyond what you can bear. But when you are tempted, he will also provide a way out so that you can stand up under it" (1 Corinthians 10:13). God specializes in parting the seas of pressure.

Furthermore, we should wait for Jesus to break down the walls. Perhaps you've been praying that God will break through in the lives of your family, your friends, your spouse? Then keep on praying. Don't give up on anybody. God is God and He specializes in fortresses with thick, double walls.

Finally, trust in Jesus to renew your worth in the eyes of others. Maybe you've had a Rahab-like past. If not immoral, shameful. If not disgusting, dishonorable. If not an active participant externally, maybe you compromised on the inside. People are people, but God is God; and He specializes in redeeming the worthless past of people like us. If God can take a prostitute and turn her into a princess, imagine what He can do for you! He's a God of miracles.

The Incredible Faith of God's Significant Nobodies

> *And what more shall I say? I do not have time to tell about Gideon, Barak, Samson, Jephthah, David, Samuel and the prophets, who through faith conquered kingdoms, administered justice, and gained what was promised; who shut the mouths of lions, quenched the fury of the flames, and escaped the edge of the sword; whose weakness was turned to strength; and who became powerful in battle and routed foreign armies. Women received back their dead, raised to life again. Others were tortured and refused to be released, so that they might gain a better resurrection. Some faced jeers and flogging, while still others were chained and put in prison. They were stoned; they were sawed in two; they were put to death by the sword. They*

went about in sheepskins and goatskins, destitute, perse-
cuted and mistreated—the world was not worthy of them.
They wandered in deserts and mountains, and in caves
and holes in the ground.

These were all commended for their faith, yet none of
them received what had been promised. God had planned
something better for us so that only together with us
would they be made perfect. (Hebrews 11:32-40)

Tony Campolo tells a great story about a kid with cerebral palsy:

I was asked to be a counselor in a junior high camp. Everybody ought to be a counselor in a junior high camp—just once. A junior high kid's concept of a good time is picking on people. And in this particular case, at this particular camp, there was a little boy who was suffering from cerebral palsy. His name was Billy. And they picked on him.

Oh, they picked on him. As he walked across the camp with his uncoordinated body they would line up and imitate his grotesque movements. I watched him one day as he was asking for direction. "Which . . . way is . . . the . . . craft . . . shop?" he stammered, his mouth contorting. And the boys mimicked in that same awful stammer, "It's . . . over . . . there . . . Billy." And then they laughed at him. I was irate.

But furor reached its highest pitch when on Thursday morning it was Billy's cabin's turn to give devotions. I wondered what would happen, because they had appointed Billy to be the speaker. I knew that they just wanted to get him up there to make fun of him. As he dragged his way to the front, you could hear the giggles rolling over the crowd. It took little Billy almost five minutes to say seven words.

"Jesus . . . loves . . . me . . . and . . . I . . . love . . . Jesus."[14]

When Billy finished, there was dead silence. Campolo looked over his shoulder and saw junior high boys bawling all over the place. A revival broke out in that camp after Billy's short testimony. And as Tony travels the world, he says that he finds missionaries and preachers who say, "Remember me? I was converted at that junior high camp."

The camp counselors had tried everything to get those kids interested in Jesus. They even imported baseball players whose batting averages had gone up since they had started praying! But God chose not to use the superstars. He chose a kid with cerebral palsy to break the spirits of the haughty and arrogant and mockers. He's that kind of God. He delights in using nobodies to accomplish His plan.

"God's Significant Nobodies" are the people you seldom hear about, but their courage and faith have always played a very key role in the development of the Christian church. Their faith inspires courage, advances tenacity and creates anticipation for the final perfection that awaits us.

Faith Inspires Courage

> And what more shall I say? I do not have time to tell about Gideon, Barak, Samson, Jephthah, David, Samuel and the prophets, who through faith conquered kingdoms, administered justice, and gained what was promised; who shut the mouths of lions, quenched the fury of the flames, and escaped the edge of the sword; whose weakness was turned to strength; and who became powerful in battle and routed foreign armies. Women received back their dead, raised to life again. (Hebrews 11:32-35)

The author cannot continue mentioning every example of genuine faith in Israel's history. To do so he would have to write a lengthy treatise. He must be content with more general statements and a few representative names. Sufficient examples have been given for the illustration of his theme.

He now breaks off from the more specifically biographical enumeration of the conquest of faith and concludes this section with a great summary of the triumphant faith of God's people in the face of every kind of cruel opposition.

The mere mention of these names should inspire courage in the readers. Barak, for example, was the military leader God used to deliver Israel from the oppression of the northern Canaanites under Jabin of Hazor and his general, Sisera (Judges 4-5).

Samson was God's instrument to defeat Israel's enemies the Philistines on numerous occasions (Judges 13-16). In the closing episode of his life, as a blind and wretched prisoner, while being mocked at a pagan Philistine feast, he cried out to God for strength to accomplish his final victory over Israel's enemy (Judges 16:28).

Jephthah was the judge of Israel who delivered his people from the threat of Ammonite domination (Judges 11-12). David was the founder of the dynasty from which Messiah had been prophesied to come, the man after God's own heart (1 Samuel 13:14; 16:1, 12; Acts 13:22). Samuel was the prophet who anointed David as king (1 Samuel 16:13). His faith glowed brightly in a day of spiritual declension.

The author of Hebrews says he does not have time to tell about Gideon, Barak, Samson, Jephthah, David, Samuel and the prophets, but the mere mention of their names inspires courage in us. If they conquered kingdoms, administered justice and gained what was promised through faith, why can't I? If they shut the mouths of lions, quenched the fury of the flames and escaped the edge of the sword by faith, why can't my faith accomplish great things too? If, by faith, their weakness was turned to strength, and they became powerful in battle and routed foreign armies, what prevents me from exercising the same faith to stand firm in the face of the enemy, Satan and all his cohorts? Nothing, absolutely nothing! That's right. Faith inspires courage.

"More Job Layoffs," the newspaper headline read. The story below said, "Beleaguered steel giant Dofasco Inc. is eliminating another 2,000 jobs, more than one-fifth of its work force, by closing an outdated facility." The Hamilton, Ontario, company made the layoffs because it lost $118 million in the first nine months of the year. The company, which once employed 12,000 people, now would operate with half that number.

Layoffs. Cutbacks. Retrenchment. Red ink. These are the marks of an ailing economy and the cause of much disappointment and despair. It's dangerous for us to build our lives around things that can disappear so quickly. We're not made to put our trust in such temporary security.

But there is Someone in whom we can place our absolute trust. God the Father. "He who dwells in the shelter of the Most High will rest in the shadow of the Almighty" (Psalm 91:1).

Personal faith in a powerful God inspires peculiar courage.

Faith Advances Tenacity

> Others were tortured and refused to be released, so that they might gain a better resurrection. Some faced jeers and flogging, while still others were chained and put in prison. They were stoned; they were sawed in two; they were put to death by the sword. They went about in sheepskins and goatskins, destitute, persecuted and mistreated—the world was not worthy of them. They wandered in deserts and mountains, and in caves and holes in the ground. (Hebrews 11:35-38)

This segment of God's nobody population had just enough faith to cope with fierce hostility and cruel persecution. He gave them sufficient faith to face torture, mockery and suffering.[15] That faith advanced their defiant determination and their obstinate tenacity in the face of overwhelming odds, not unlike the story I heard from fragile Colombia.

After many months of captivity, missionaries Tim Van Dyke and Steve Welsh were killed during a clash between their guerrilla captors and a Colombian military patrol. The pair, missing for five months, was abducted at the New Tribes Mission base at Villavicencio. Only a short while before they were killed they had been spotted alive and well.

Now they were dead. In the jungle. In a pool of blood. Asinine, foolish, senseless, heartless conduct that led to the wasted lives of two fine missionaries. They gained a better resurrection. The world was not worthy of them. Yet, seven fatherless children and two widows were left behind to pick up the shattered pieces of their lives. How does one make good sense out of such bad news?

Only time will tell, but one friend of mine in South America told me that the missionary family there has "solidified its resolve." "We shall not be moved," he said. "We shall go on. We will not quit. The victory is ours by faith." And so it is. So it is. By faith. In a God who is sovereignly working out His plan all around us.

Do we view our faith as an imposing philosophy or a living truth? As an abstract, sometimes academic hypothesis or a living Person for whom we are prepared to lay down our lives? The most destructive and tyrannical movements of the twentieth century, communism and Nazism, have resulted from fanatics single-mindedly applying deceptive, dangerous and unreliable philosophies.

What would happen if we were actually to apply God's holy truth for the glory of His kingdom? Faith advances that kind of tenacity in the inner beings of the fully devoted followers of Jesus. Can we count you in?

Faith Anticipates Perfection

These were all commended for their faith, yet none of them received what had been promised. God had planned something better for us so that only together

> with us would they be made perfect. (Hebrews
> 11:39-40)

The first word in Hebrews 11:39, "these," refers to the preceding heroes of the faith. The word "all" omits none of them. God never forgets any of His faithful servants. Rich as it was, the faith of these Old Testament saints was confined to the limits of the old covenant. None of them received what had been promised. Verse 33 tells us that they "gained what was promised." But here it is not a question of "the promises," but of "the promise."

Leon Morris points out that God made many promises to His people and kept them. So there were many blessings that they had received along the way. But the ultimate blessing (which the author of Hebrews characteristically sees in terms of promise) was not given under the old covenant. God kept that until Jesus came. So their faith strained forward to something better. They anticipated the fulfillment of God's promise in Jesus Christ.

The unavoidable conclusions rest on two extremes. On the one hand, undeserving and sinful Christians like us—God's no-bodies—often rejoice in unexpected triumphs. We may not be conquering kingdoms, shutting the mouths of lions or routing foreign armies, but our weaknesses are being turned into God's strength (2 Corinthians 12:9; Philippians 4:13).

Our minor triumphs along the way are no less significant. Little by little He's changing me to become more and more like His Son. "For those God foreknew he also predestined to be *conformed to the likeness of his Son* . . ." (Romans 8:29, emphasis added). That gives me goosebumps just thinking about it! *Being conformed to the likeness of His Son.* . . . The unexpected triumphs.

On the other hand, godly and great Christians often suffer through unexplained tragedies. Some face jeers and persecution. They are mistreated, maligned and misunderstood. Godly men and women who are living for Jesus often suffer through inexplicable pain: the death of a loved one, the rebellion of a cherished child, the rejection by an unbelieving spouse, cancer, depression, divorce, unexplained suffering.

It's important to understand that tragedy does not happen only to the fractious, the heartless, the hypocritical, the ungodly, the perverted. It happens to the mature, responsible, obedient and tender believers as well. In this generation, a hocus-pocus illusion is spreading: that people of true faith experience only wealth, health and happiness. Scripture does not support such a superficial teaching.

On the one hand, unexpected triumphs. On the other, unexplained tragedies. Both extremes link us with an uninterrupted history: a history we call God's Plan. Hebrews 11:40 says, "God had *planned* something better for us. . . ." Only by faith can we come to accept God's plan for what it is: God's plan. And by faith we wait for the ultimate perfection—the return of Jesus Christ. Until then, may your faith inspire courage in others and encourage indefatigable tenacity in the lives of many.

Even so, come, Lord Jesus!

Endnotes

1. Leon Morris, *Hebrews, The Expositor's Bible Commentary*, Vol. 12, ed. Frank E. Gaebelein (Grand Rapids, MI: Zondervan Publishing House, 1981), 122.

2. Homer A. Kent, Jr., *The Epistle to the Hebrews: A Commentary* (Grand Rapids, MI: Baker Book House, 1972), 232.

3. Gary Smalley and John Trent, *The Blessing* (New York: Pocket Books, 1990), 27.

4. Leon Morris makes a good point. "In the account in Exodus the role of Moses' mother receives all the attention, his father not being mentioned. In the LXX, however, the plural verbs in Exodus 2:2-3 show that both parents were involved, and the author follows his customary practice of depending on LXX. In any case, the

mother could not have hidden the child without the father's agreement. So both parents were necessarily involved" (125).

5. Carle C. Zimmerman, *Family and Civilization* (New York: Harper & Brothers, 1947), 776-777, as quoted in Charles R. Swindoll, *The Quest for Character* (Portland, OR: Multnomah Press, 1987), 90.

6. Leon Moris, 125.

7. Ibid., 127.

8. *Pulse*, Vol. 30, No. 5, March 10, 1995, 7.

9. Ibid., 6.

10. The story of Alexander Solzhenitsyn and the old man who made the sign of the cross was first told by Solzhenitsyn to a small group of Christian leaders and later recounted by Billy Graham in his New Year's telecast, 1977. It has been retold subsequently, most publicly by Senator Jesse Helms (R-NC). I found it again in Charles Colson's, *Loving God* (Grand Rapids, MI: Zondervan Publishing House, 1983), 172.

11. This testimony by Rob Quan was penned by Dan Vanderveer in Huntsville, Ontario, where this incident took place. This testimony has been confirmed by Pastor Randy Cox.

12. See Millard J. Erickson, *Christian Theology* (Grand Rapids, MI: Baker Book House, 1985), 406-410.

13. Leon Morris, 128.

14. Tony Campolo, "Just a Kid with Cerebral Palsy," *Discipleship Journal*, Issue 84, November/December, 1994: 66.

15. Readers would benefit from reading William Barclay's treatment of Hebrews 11:35-40. He says, "In this passage the writer to the Hebrews is intermingling different periods of history. Sometimes he takes his illustrations from the Old Testament period; but still more he takes them from the Maccabaean period which falls between

the Old and the New Testaments" (p. 166). It is the illustrations from the Maccabaean period that Barclay so
clearly elucidates for us. A fascinating read!

Discussion Questions for Further Study

1. How did the actions of Isaac, Jacob and Joseph demonstrate faith (11:20-22)?

2. The Old Testament faithful were all ordinary human beings with failures and shortcomings like anyone else.
   What does this reveal about what faith can accomplish
   even through imperfect people?

3. How does Hebrews 11 contribute to the author's overall
   purpose of convincing his Hebrew readers not to lapse
   away from Christianity when under pressure?

4. How does your current situation call for genuine faith?
   How can you act in faith this week under these circumstances?

5. Is faith limiting your choices when it comes to pleasure,
   entertainment, television shows that you watch and
   magazines that you read? Do you think it should limit
   your choices, and if so, how?

12

Hebrews 12:1-29

Running the Race

> *Therefore, since we are surrounded by such a great cloud of witnesses, let us throw off everything that hinders and the sin that so easily entangles, and let us run with perseverance the race marked out for us. Let us fix our eyes on Jesus, the author and perfecter of our faith, who for the joy set before him endured the cross, scorning its shame, and sat down at the right hand of the throne of God. Consider him who endured such opposition from sinful men, so that you will not grow weary and lose heart. (Hebrews 12:1-3)*

A few years ago, in an NCAA cross-country championship held in Riverside, California, 123 of the 128 runners missed a turn. One competitor, Mike Delcavo, stayed on the 10,000-meter course and began waving for fellow runners to follow him. Delcavo was able to convince only four other runners to go with him.

Asked what his competitors thought of his mid-race decision not to follow the crowd, Delcavo responded, "They thought it was funny that I went the right way."[1]

Delcavo was one who ran correctly. In the same way, our goal is to run right—to finish the race marked out for

us by Jesus Christ. We can rejoice over those who have
courage to follow, ignoring the laughter of the crowd on
the sidelines.

The apostle Paul said to young Timothy,

> I have fought the good fight, I have finished the race,
> I have kept the faith. Now there is in store for me the
> crown of righteousness, which the Lord, the right-
> eous Judge, will award to me on that day—and not
> only to me, but also to all who have longed for his ap-
> pearing (2 Timothy 4:7-8)

Hebrews 12:1-3 calls for that kind of response from the runners of the race. Even when there is no audible applause or tangible trophies. When we became Christians, we entered a new
stadium. It's full of reality. Pain, heartache, sickness, sorrow,
pressure, hardship and even death. To these things we added
our own humanity, wrong habit patterns, personal weaknesses
and conflicts with others. Then there's the world that's bent
against God. Add a host of satanic forces that are committed to
our failure and defeat, and you'll quickly see why we have need
for endurance and encouragement.

Every believer in Jesus Christ is engaged in a spiritual
contest. An endurance marathon. The question is: How do
we handle that race in order to please God?

The Best Preparation for Running

> Therefore, since we are surrounded by such a great
> cloud of witnesses, let us throw off everything that
> hinders and the sin that so easily entangles, and let us
> run with perseverance the race marked out for us.
> (Hebrews 12:1)

The first two verses here are a continuation of the last
chapter. They bring out a more direct way in which the old
order differs from the new. The heroes of the past are now

viewed as spectators, "a great cloud of witnesses," whereas the Christians are on the track running the race. The focus shifts to the present, but the value of the examples of the past is incorporated into the whole picture. As Morris suggests, perhaps we should think of something like a relay race where those who have finished the race and handed off their baton are watching and encouraging their teammates.[2]

However, we cannot run the race well if we don't take the writer's words seriously, and prepare properly for the contest. "Let us throw off everything that hinders and the sin that so easily entangles . . ." (Hebrews 12:1). Another translation says, "Let us also lay aside every encumbrance. . . ." An encumbrance is an excess weight—needless baggage, pointless paraphernalia. Some things may not be wrong in themselves, but they hinder us in putting forth our very best for God.

For eight years Sally had been the Romero family pet. When they got her, she was only one foot long. But Sally grew until eventually she reached eleven-and-a-half feet and weighed eighty pounds. Then on July 20, 1993, Sally, a Burmese python, turned on fifteen-year-old Derek, strangling the teenager until he died of suffocation.

Worldly habits that seem little and harmless will grow. Tolerate or ignore little sins, and they will eventually lead to death. To run a spiritual race with any success, we have to set aside the excess baggage that weighs us down: an indifferent attitude, procrastination, apathy, impatience, anger, greed, gossip. All these things hinder us from running the race. They pile up quickly if we let them.

"Let us throw off everything that hinders and the sin that so easily entangles." That's the best preparation for running the race with endurance. Get rid of the rubble. Dispose of the debris. Travel lightly.

The Finest Technique for Running

> Let us fix our eyes on Jesus, the author and perfecter of our faith, who for the joy set before him endured

the cross, scorning its shame, and sat down at the
right hand of the throne of God. (Hebrews 12:2)

Having set aside the hindrances, we're told how to run:
Run with perseverance the race marked out for us. But what
is the best technique?

As runners, our eyes must be trained and *fixed* on Jesus
Christ alone. The earlier witnesses, Isaac, Jacob, Joseph,
Moses, Gideon, Barak, Samson, David and all the rest, supply incentive in abundance. But in Jesus we have One who
is *par excellence* the faithful witness (Revelation 1:5). He is the
trailblazer of our faith. Therefore we should have no eyes for
anyone or anything but Jesus. We cannot yield to distractions. No divided attention allowed. We stare into His face
in order to gain His perspective, His instruction, His encouragement.

Jesus Christ understands the race in its entirety. As the
Author, He is the origin of this faith-life, and as Perfecter,
He completed it as well. The whole life of Jesus was characterized by an unbroken and unquestioning faith in His Father. "It was sheer faith in God, unsupported by any visible
or tangible evidence, that carried Him through the taunting,
the scourging, the crucifying and the more bitter agony of
rejection, desertion and dereliction."[3]

He endured the cross, scorning its shame and sat down
at the right hand of God (Hebrews 12:2). To die by cruci-
fixion was to plumb the lowest depths of disgrace. It was a
punishment reserved for those who were deemed most unfit to live. A punishment for sub-men. By ancient statute
Roman citizens were exempt from so degrading a death.
The distinction of the Roman name would be polluted by
being brought into association with anything so vile as a
cross.

It was Cicero who wrote, "Let the very mention of the
cross be far removed not only from a Roman citizen's body,
but from his mind, his eyes, his ears."[4] Jesus did not regard
this concern with disgrace worthy of consideration. He was

doing the will of God. That's all that concerned Him. Obedience mattered most. Who cares what the Romans think?

So He brought faith to perfection by His endurance of the cross. Now the place of highest exaltation is His. He has taken His place at the right hand of the throne of God (Hebrews 12:2). And He knows how to get you there, too. The best technique for running the race is to keep your eyes glued on the One who has already been around the track. He knows the way.

The Proper Attitude for Running

> Consider him who endured such opposition from sinful men, so that you will not grow weary and lose heart. (Hebrews 12:3)

Once again there is the call to perseverance in the face of hardship or tribulations. "Consider" means to reckon, compare, to think about or weigh carefully. The Greek word *analogisasthe*, a word used in calculations, is used only here in the New Testament.

Readers are encouraged to take account of Jesus. The idea is that I meditate upon and occupy my mind with the Lord Jesus Christ. The psalm writer put it this way: "My eyes are ever on the LORD, for only he will release my feet from the snare" (Psalm 25:15). A heavenly mindset, the proper attitude for running the race set before me, requires a conscious decision and a continuous effort to keep my primary goal in front of me.

Most runners are very careful about the food they eat. They want to digest certain foods before a big race so the energy is there when they need it most. Similarly, meditating upon Christ and being preoccupied with Him will bring us bursts of encouragement and spiritual energy when we need it most. What He thinks of me and what I think of Him is all that matters. Steve Lyons demonstrated that principle very well.

Steve could be remembered as an outstanding infielder, or the player who played every position for the Chicago White Sox or the guy who always dove into first base. But he won't. He'll be remembered as the player who dropped his drawers on the field on July 16, 1990.

The Sox were playing the Tigers in Detroit. Lyons bunted and raced down to first. He knew it would be tight, so he dove at the bag. *Safe!*

Absorbed in the game and keeping a close eye on the pitching ace, Lyons felt dirt trickling down the inside of his pants. Without missing a beat he dropped his britches, wiped away the dirt and . . . uh oh . . . 20,000 jaws hit the bleachers' floor. Within twenty-four hours of the exposure, he received more exposure than he'd gotten his entire career: seven live television and approximately twenty radio appearances.[5]

I don't know Steve Lyons. I'm not a White Sox fan, because I live near Toronto where the Blue Jays rule. But Steve Lyons deserves a trophy. He paid the price. He dove into first. He got dirty doing it. But he had the right attitude. He was more concerned about getting the job done than saving his own pride.

We need people in the church who are more eager to please God. People who will dive headfirst into service for Jesus Christ. Men and women who don't grow weary and lose heart before the game is over. Young people eager to say "no" to a greedy culture and "yes" to missions. We need people of faith who can run with perseverance the race marked out by Christ.

Faith is not some sort of mystical adventure. It is the daily fiber that keeps us running our race with determination. In order to do that we may need to claim the grace to hang on. And remember, you are never alone. God has said, "Never will I leave you; never will I forsake you" (Hebrews 13:5).

Hebrews 12:1-3 reminds us that every believer in Jesus Christ is engaged in a spiritual contest that takes place in the ugly arena of life. Only when I fully surrender my heart and will to Him, will I run in a way that pleases the Lord.

All to Jesus I surrender;
    All to Him I freely give.
I will ever love and trust Him,
    In His presence daily live.
All to Jesus I surrender;
    Humbly at His feet I bow,
Worldly pleasures all forsaken.
    Take me, Jesus, take me now.[6]

Dealing with Divine Discipline

In your struggle against sin, you have not yet resisted to the point of shedding your blood. And you have forgotten that word of encouragement that addresses you as sons:

*"My son, do not make light of the Lord's
        discipline,
    and do not lose heart when he rebukes you,
because the Lord disciplines those he loves,
    and he punishes everyone he accepts as a son."*

Endure hardship as discipline; God is treating you as sons. For what son is not disciplined by his father? If you are not disciplined (and everyone undergoes discipline), then you are illegitimate children and not true sons. Moreover, we have all had human fathers who disciplined us and we respected them for it. How much more should we submit to the Father of our spirits and live! Our fathers disciplined us for a little while as they thought best; but God disciplines us for our good, that we may share in his holiness. No discipline seems pleasant at the time, but painful. Later on, however, it produces a harvest of righteousness and peace for those who have been trained by it.

Therefore, strengthen your feeble arms and weak knees. "Make level paths for your feet," so that the lame may not be disabled, but rather healed. (Hebrews 12:4-13)

"Science fiction is modern man's new mythic literature," writes Peter Kreeft in *Making Sense Out of Suffering*. "Many of the same images and many of the same themes occur spontaneously in this new mythic form as in the old. Forgotten to consciousness, they are not forgotten to the great collective unconscious, which this genre pulls on more than others."[7]

He goes on to suggest that one of these themes, one of the most popular in all of science fiction, is the "anti-utopian theme." A futuristic society that has abolished suffering by technology, cured disease, abolished war and poverty, controlled accidents, sometimes even conquered death by artificial immortality. But in these stories, such a society is always a counterfeit. Apparently happy, but experiencing deep failure. Apparently humane, but really inhumane. The abolition of suffering turns out to be the abolition of humanity.[8]

A world without suffering appears more like hell than like heaven.[9]

"God whispers to us in our pleasures, speaks in our conscience, but shouts in our pain: It is His megaphone to rouse a deaf world." C.S. Lewis was right. Pain often creates an openness toward God. Suffering is a part of life. Yet if pain or discipline can rouse a deaf world, perhaps it can also be God's megaphone to rouse a sleeping, sluggish, sappy Christian, or even an entire church.

In addition to teaching us much about suffering and discipline, Hebrews 12 serves as a prescription for the troubled heart. The writer points to the importance of discipline and moves on to show that for Christians suffering is properly understood only when we treasure God's Word, His care and His purpose in divine discipline.

Treasure God's Word in Discipline

In your struggle against sin, you have not yet resisted to the point of shedding your blood. And you have forgotten that word of encouragement that addresses you as sons:

"My son, do not make light of the Lord's
    discipline,
  and do not lose heart when he rebukes you,
because the Lord disciplines those he loves,
  and he punishes everyone he accepts as a son."
    (Hebrews 12:4-6)

All Christians struggle against sin. But here the reference is not about inner turmoil but to those who are antagonistic to the Christian faith. Those responsible for such sin are personified as sin itself. Although the struggle has been intense, the resistance has not been "to the point of shedding your blood" (a reference to martyrdom).

The first readers of this letter had endured severe persecution, but they had not been called on to seal their testimony with blood. Jesus Himself had challenged His followers to take up their cross and follow Him (Luke 14:27), and since none of the readers had yet faced as much physical suffering as Jesus had, the challenge was still apropos.

One New Testament scholar says of Hebrews 12:4-6, "These words remind the man who would be truly wise that when hardship is his lot he should accept it as God's method of training and disciplining him, and as a token that he is really a beloved son of God."[10] God is the Master Designer of divine discipline.

Apparently, these first-century Hebrew Christians were in danger of forgetting that fundamental principle from Theology 101. They may have to face fiercer trials than had come their way so far, so this was no time to be discouraged. Buckle up, folks, and get back to the Word. The author then reminds them that Scripture links suffering and sonship, and he quotes from Proverbs 3:11-12. The writer gently rebukes them, and says, "Remember God's word. . . ." He takes them right back to the Word of God. And that's the best place to go.

Many Christians dismiss too quickly the fact that God's hand can work in the midst of pain and suffering. Remember that Christ, God's unique Son, learned through suffering (Hebrews 2:10), and believers should adopt His mind on this matter. In Second Timothy 1:8, Paul boldly invites us to join in suffering for the gospel "by the power of God."

In Matthew 5:11-12 Jesus said, "Blessed are you when people insult you, persecute you and falsely say all kinds of evil against you because of me. Rejoice and be glad, because great is your reward in heaven, for in the same way they persecuted the prophets who were before you." "I have told you these things, so that in me you may have peace. In this world you will have trouble. But take heart! I have overcome the world" (John 16:33). When you're suffering or being persecuted or facing troubles, run to the Book. There you find comfort and relief and contentment.

The editor of a London newspaper sent a letter of inquiry to 100 important peers, members of Parliament, university professors, authors and others. His question was simple: "Suppose you were sent to prison for three years and you could only take three books with you. Which three would you choose? Please state them in order of their importance."

Out of the replies, ninety-eight put one book first on their list. The Bible. Few of those men were keen about the Lord. Many did not attend church. Others were agnostics or atheists. Yet they knew that no other book could give them comfort to help in the dark, difficult days.[11]

Treasure the Word of God. It's a lamp for your feet and a light for your path (Psalm 119:105). When your soul faints you can put your hope in God's Word (Psalm 119:81), but remember: "No life can have any value apart from discipline."[12]

Treasure God's Care in Discipline

Endure hardship as discipline; God is treating you
as sons. For what son is not disciplined by his father?

If you are not disciplined (and everyone undergoes discipline), then you are illegitimate children and not true sons. Moreover, we have all had human fathers who disciplined us and we respected them for it. (Hebrews 12:7-9)

Sonship and fatherly chastisement invariably go together. God disciplines His children because He loves them and cares for their welfare. Yet it's easy to grieve the Spirit of God by despising the discipline of the Lord. Thus we are exhorted to "endure hardship as discipline." Why? Because "God is treating you as sons."

Suffering is not misery, nor is it an accident. It's discipline, and God teaches us important lessons through the misery of our earthbound, sin-infested lives. These are the things the readers have been forgetting entirely. They are emphatically pointed out here, first by the Spirit who inspired the words and then by the human author.

If our experience of being set apart from sin and being made holy through the process of sanctification is still very slight and shallow, we have a tendency to mistake the reality of God for something else. When the Spirit of God gives us a sense of warning or restraint, we are liable to say mistakenly, "Oh, that must be from the devil." But am I fully prepared to allow God to grip me forcefully by His Word and do a work in me that is truly worthy of the Spirit?

Discipline is not my idea of what I want God to do for me. Discipline is God's idea of what He wants to do for me. However, I must be in the right state of mind, heart and spirit whereby I relinquish my "rights" (which are not really mine anyway) and summon Him to sanctify me fully, whatever the cost.

In the process He cares for me and loves me as a father loves his only son—like I'm the only one who matters. His treasured possession and choice servant. If you're not disciplined by the Father, then you're an illegitimate child and not a true descendant.

But we need to understand that discipline is not judgment. The word "discipline" comes from the Greek word *paideia* which means upbringing, training or instruction. It's the same word from which we derive the word *pedagogy*: the art or profession of teaching. Discipline is teaching or training which corrects. Discipline is training that molds us and strengthens us as believers. It's part of God's heavenly program for educating His earthly children.

However, the writer uses the words "discipline" *and* "punish" in verse 6: "The Lord disciplines those he loves, and he punishes everyone he accepts as a son." How are they different? The second term literally refers to the act of flogging with a whip. It's used here figuratively of God's chastening of His children. Unfortunately, this has been misunderstood by some believers and used as a proof-text for beating the tar out of their kids. This clause is an instance of Hebrew poetic parallelism in the quotation of Proverbs 3. It does not promote strict corporal punishment, but it does add the idea of corrective discipline to the more general reference of child training.

I should also draw attention to the fact that "those he loves" comes first in the Greek.[13] This gives it a certain emphasis. God disciplines people He loves, not those He is indifferent to. Readers should see their suffering as a sign of God's love. It is the son that is punished and "every son" (*panta huion*) at that. The point is that proper training must include correction of faulty behavior. Permissiveness is not an option.

We are reminded here that the Father treasures His children. "God is treating you as sons." The very fact that we experience discipline proves that we are God's children. It shows that God is treating us as children. It demonstrates that God cares for us. So remember God's Word and God's care, and cast all your anxiety upon Him because He cares for you!

Treasure God's Purpose in Discipline

Our fathers disciplined us for a little while as they thought best; but God disciplines us for our good, that we may share in his holiness. No discipline seems pleasant at the time, but painful. Later on, however, it produces a harvest of righteousness and peace for those who have been trained by it.

Therefore, strengthen your feeble arms and weak knees. "Make level paths for your feet," so that the lame may not be disabled, but rather healed. (Hebrews 12:10-13)

Notice that 12:10 says, "Our fathers disciplined us for a little while . . . but God disciplines us for our good, that we may share in his holiness." There's a difference in the quality of the discipline we have received from our fathers and that which comes from God above. Earthly fathers normally do what they believe best. But they operate on opinion, conjecture, supposition and preference.

In comparison, God's discipline is always for our good, and His discipline lasts and lasts and lasts. Much longer than the Energizer bunny! He doesn't quit disciplining us when we grow up and move out of home.

Part of the purpose is to create an opportunity for us to share in His holiness. Morris points out that this word "holiness" (*hagiotes*) points to *God's* holy character. The aim of divine discipline is *to produce in us a character like His own*. That's what we need, isn't it? Holiness. That's what we want! Holiness. It's our greatest need in the church today.

Furthermore, discipline deepens and enhances life. I must convince myself of that every time I have to apply "the board of education" to "the seat of understanding" with my children. When I discipline my kids I do it to arouse respect, not resentment. Verse 9 presents an analogy which compares submission to an earthly father with submission to the heavenly Father. "We have all had human fathers who disciplined us and we respected them for it. How much more should we submit to the Father of our spirits and live!" When we do that, the process deepens and enhances our walk with God.

"No discipline seems pleasant at the time, but painful. Later on, however, it produces a harvest of righteousness and peace for those who have been trained by it" (12:11). It is not a matter of accepting a minor chastisement or two with good grace; it is the habit of life that is meant. When that is present, the peace follows.

From July to October 1987, dozens of fires scorched more than 1.2 million acres of Yellowstone National Park, destroying forest land in approximately half the park. To many watching television, this was a total disaster. But not to former Yellowstone Park Superintendent Thomas Hobbs.

"Good things come out of seemingly bad things," he said. Even though the current scene was marked by ruined landscape, Hobbs explained that major fires can actually benefit the park in the long run. Burnouts rejuvenate park land. They purge it of insect and plant disease before the natural growth cycle starts again.[14] Like fires in a forest, discipline can actually benefit us in the long run.

Now we consider one more of God's purposes in discipline: Discipline can also lead to corporate healing. "Therefore, strengthen your feeble arms and weak knees. 'Make level paths for your feet,' so that the lame may not be disabled, but rather healed" (Hebrews 12:12-13).

Feeble arms and weak knees are typical of low spirits and discouraged believers. They portray persons who have become incapable of action through sheer exhaustion. We are told to make level paths for our feet, even in the midst of painful circumstances, in the midst of suffering and discomfort, so that spiritually lame people within the local fellowship who are watching our lives and the way we are responding to God's discipline will not be further disabled emotionally or morally. In other words, if we rightly respond to God's purposes in discipline, the spiritually lame people among us may be "healed."

We are not living in the "Twilight Zone." I don't care how vivid your imagination is, you can't live long in this world without coming to the conclusion that life is not a bowl of cherries. But if we can put into practice the advice given to us in Hebrews 12:4-13, we will make it.

Treasure God's Word in the midst of discipline. Don't run for cover; run to the Word. Dig for the gems that will feed you and instruct you in the way you should go. "All Scripture is God-breathed and is useful for teaching, rebuking, correcting and training in righteousness, so that the man of God may be thoroughly equipped for every good work" (2 Timothy 3:16-17). Look to the Lord and treasure His Word.

Treasure God's care for you in the discipline He brings. Echo the words of the psalmist: "I lift up my eyes to the hills—where does my help come from? My help comes from the LORD, the Maker of heaven and earth" (Psalm 121:1-2). "Cast your cares on the LORD and he will sustain you; he will never let the righteous fall" (Psalm 55:22). Amen and *amen*!

Treasure God's purposes in discipline. What the old man said one day is true: "God don't make no mistake." And there is no mistake about the reality of God's design. The place where you get everything you want is not heaven. For believers, a world without suffering is more like hell than like heaven.[15]

Yet unless suffering is accepted in the right spirit it does not produce the right result. The right spirit is the spirit of trust and submission to the Father above. Are you ready now to take that step? Willing to take the hand of the Father as He stoops gently to whisper in your ear?

> Under His wings I am safely abiding;
> Though the night deepens and tempests
>   are wild,
> Still I can trust Him, I know He will keep
>   me;
> He has redeemed me, and I am His child.
> Under His wings—what a refuge in
>   sorrow!

How the heart yearningly turns to His
    rest!
Often the earth has not balm for my
    healing,
There I find comfort, and there I am
    blest.

Making a Pit Stop

> *Make every effort to live in peace with all men and to
> be holy; without holiness no one will see the Lord. See to it
> that no one misses the grace of God and that no bitter root
> grows up to cause trouble and defile many. See that no one
> is sexually immoral, or is godless like Esau, who for a sin-
> gle meal sold his inheritance rights as the oldest son. After-
> ward, as you know, when he wanted to inherit this
> blessing, he was rejected. He could bring about no change
> of mind, though he sought the blessing with tears. (He-
> brews 12:14-17)*

The writer began this chapter with a strong appeal in the first verse. "Let us throw off everything that hinders and the sin that so easily entangles, and let us run with perseverance the race marked out for us." In verses 4-13 we discovered that the race includes those painful times of discipline and rebuke.

And why are we disciplined? Because discipline proves we're part of God's family. Discipline equips us for life. Stimulates holy living. Brings about restoration and healing. So, with those benefits in mind, let's run with perseverance the race marked out for us!

Hebrews 12:14-17 constitutes a pause in the middle of this race. Let me call it a "spiritual pit stop." And as we pull in for a checkup and more fuel, he quickly goes down the list, covering two major points we need to remember for the rest of the race: Be diligent (make every effort to live in peace) and be vigilant (see to it that no one misses God's grace).

The wrong attitude in a race like this can have serious consequences. Okay . . . ready for the flag?

Be Diligent During the Pit Stop!

> Make every effort to live in peace with all men and to be holy; without holiness no one will see the Lord. (Hebrews 12:14)

Hebrews 12:12-13 suggested that corporate healing is one of the purposes of the Lord's discipline in our lives. If we appropriately respond to God's purposes in discipline, the spiritually lame people among us may be healed. The word *may* is important. Spiritually lame people cannot become whole again if the family of faith is full of dissension and strife.

The link between verses 12-13 and verse 14 is that a rich sense of corporate unity in the local congregation will do more to create the right atmosphere for healing than almost anything else.[16] Bruised and battered believers cannot heal well unless they have an environment filled with peace.

I sometimes tease the folks in our church by quoting that little ditty: "To live above with saints we love, oh, that will be glory! But to live below, with saints we know, now that's another story!" But the New Testament will let us escape with nothing less than a fellowship where peace reigns.

Jesus wants His people to live in peace with one another and with people in general. There's no doubt that the author of Hebrews is especially interested in maintaining harmony among the saints in the church, but there seems to be no reason to take the words "all men" to mean anything but "all men," without any distinction regarding faith.

This idea is supported by other Scripture also. "Blessed are the peacemakers," Jesus said, "for they will be called sons of God" (Matthew 5:9). "Salt is good, but if it loses its saltiness, how can you make it salty again? Have salt in yourselves, and be at peace with each other" (Mark 9:50). "If it is possible, as far as it depends on you, live at peace with everyone" (Romans 12:18).

Between two farms near Valleyview, Alberta, not far from where I grew up, you can find two parallel fences, only two feet apart, running for a half mile.

Why two fences when one would do?

As the story goes, two farmers, Paul and Oscar, had a disagreement that erupted into a feud. Paul wanted to build a fence between their land and split the cost. Oscar was unwilling to contribute a red cent. Since he wanted to keep cattle on his land, Paul went ahead and built the fence anyway.

After the fence was completed Oscar said to Paul, "I see we have a fence."

"What do you mean 'we'?" Paul replied. "I got the property line surveyed and built the fence two feet into my land. That means that some of my land is outside the fence. And if any of your cows sets foot on my land, I'll shoot them."

Oscar knew Paul wasn't joking, so when he eventually decided to use the land adjoining Paul's for pasture, he was forced to build another fence, two feet away.[17]

Oscar and Paul are both dead now, but their double fence stands as a monument to the high price we pay for refusing to live in peace with all men.

We should be diligent in peace-filled living, and peace is a direct result of obedience, as indicated in Proverbs 3:1-2. "My son, forget not my law; but let thine heart keep my commandments: For length of days, and long life, *and peace*, shall they add to thee" (KJV, emphasis added). The word is clear: Obey the Lord and live in peace.

Coupled with peace is holiness. As Barclay puts it, although he lives in the world, the person who is holy must always in one sense be different from it and separate from it. His standards are not the world's standards. His conduct is not the world's conduct.[18]

"Without holiness no one will see the Lord" (Hebrews 12:14). The root meaning of holiness is always difference and separation. His speech and attitudes and thoughts are different. He is not consumed with pleasing men; his aim is to stand well with God (1 Thessalonians 2:4; 2 Timothy 2:4; 2 Corinthians 5:9).

We must understand that our goal as devoted followers of the Way is to seek what we can do to please God and be holy, not what He can do for us. Personal victories may come. But they are a fringe benefit not the object. True holiness is theocentric. So when I sin, I am not just "defeated" or in jeopardy of "losing the victory." I sin against a holy God and insult the character and person of the Almighty Holy One. Jerry Bridges puts it well:

> It is time for us Christians to face up to our responsibility for holiness. Too often we say we are defeated by this or that sin. No, we are not defeated; we are simply disobedient. It might be well if we stopped using the terms "victory" and "defeat" to describe our progress in holiness. Rather we should use the terms "obedience" and "disobedience."[19]

So far this pit stop has proven to be helpful, hasn't it? The crew captain has already cautioned us to be diligent. Live in peace and be holy. Keep listening. You don't want to be disqualified for the last few laps!

Be Vigilant During the Pit Stop!

> See to it that no one misses the grace of God and that no bitter root grows up to cause trouble and defile many. See that no one is sexually immoral, or is godless like Esau, who for a single meal sold his inheritance rights as the oldest son. Afterward, as you know, when he wanted to inherit this blessing, he was rejected. He could bring about no change of mind, though he sought the blessing with tears. (Hebrews 12:15-17)

If these believers are to follow holiness, then they must rely also on God's grace. It follows, then, that if the grace of God is missed, then holiness will cease to be a possibility. They began this life of faith by grace (Ephesians 2:8-9), and only by grace can it be continued. That's the reason for this call to be vigilant, guarded and watchful.

"The grace of God" stands here for all the benefits which God in His grace has provided for us, and we miss the grace of God when we fail to appropriate those benefits. When we don't keep pace with the movement of grace we fall behind. These words show how easy it is for believers to fall away from the grace of God. The tug of the world is so strong. We must guard ourselves and others as much as possible. Vigilance is needed if we want to persevere in the grace of God.

How can we prevent someone else from missing the grace of God? By living in peace, pursuing God, seeking holiness and living grace-filled lives. But far too many believers still operate in the realm of legalism, and as a consequence they become demanding, rigid, unbending, inflexible, harsh and judgmental.

New believers soon get a distorted picture of what church life is all about. They quit coming. Soon they return to their old ways. So every believer needs to model grace. Encourage grace. Talk about grace. Remind others of the importance of grace. Keep living in the sphere of grace, and don't let anyone miss the grace of God.

The writer of Hebrews demands vigilance in another area. He warns us not to allow bitterness to take root. "See to it that . . . no bitter root grows up to cause trouble . . ." (Hebrews 12:15). Root development is invisible. It takes place underground. Roots also take time to mature, but once bitterness sprouts, it soon bears fruit. Bitter roots always produce bitter fruit. Bitterness invariably corrupts and spoils.

Allowed to fester through carelessness or neglect, the toxic fumes of bitterness foam to a boil within the steamroom of the soul. Pressure mounts. Tension builds. Then it's only a matter of time—minutes, days, weeks maybe. Tragedy looms in the shadow: a battered child, a crime of passion, a ruined testimony, a domestic dispute. Don't let that bitter root grow. Forgive now and be forgiven. Cast all your anxiety and bitterness upon the Lord and He will care for you (1 Peter 5:7).

Finally, don't make the same mistake Esau made. "See that no one is sexually immoral, or is godless like Esau, who for a single meal sold his inheritance rights as the oldest son" (Hebrews 12:16).

"In Hebrew legend and in rabbinic elaboration Esau had come to be looked upon as the entirely sensual man, the man who put the needs of his body first."[20] Big problems kick into gear when you buy whatever you need to satisfy whatever you want—when you sell whatever's necessary to finance whatever's your pleasure. If you live that way—if you make those kinds of choices, you will also reap serious consequences.

After he sold his birthright to his brother for a single meal, Esau "could bring about no change of mind, though he sought the blessing with tears" (Hebrews 12:17). It was not that he was barred from the forgiveness of God; he could not reverse what he had done in frittering away his birthright.

The reference to "the blessing" is an allusion to the account in Genesis 27 where Isaac was tricked into giving his patriarchal blessing to Jacob and yet recognized that it could not be reversed even when he discovered his mistake. It's the grim fact that there are certain choices which cannot be unmade. There are certain consequences that even God cannot take away.

To take a very simple example—if a young man loses his purity or a young woman her virginity, nothing can ever bring it back. The choice has been made and it stands.

Hebrews 12:14-17 flagged us in for a pit stop in the middle of this race that has been marked out for us (Hebrews 12:1). We've been refueled. We've covered the list: Be diligent. Be vigilant. Are you ready to finish the race now?

Please keep in mind that the aftereffect of rejecting God is sobering. The results of doing this race by sight and not by faith are mournful. The repercussions of following the flesh instead of the Spirit of God can be disastrous. We do well to remember there is a certain finality in life. If, like Esau, we take the way of this world and make sensual things our goal, something will happen that cannot be reversed.

Belonging to the Kingdom of God

You have not come to a mountain that can be touched and that is burning with fire; to darkness, gloom and storm; to a trumpet blast or to such a voice speaking words that those who heard it begged that no further word be spoken to them, because they could not bear what was commanded: "If even an animal touches the mountain, it must be stoned." The sight was so terrifying that Moses said, "I am trembling with fear."

But you have come to Mount Zion, to the heavenly Jerusalem, the city of the living God. You have come to thousands upon thousands of angels in joyful assembly, to the church of the firstborn, whose names are written in heaven. You have come to God, the judge of all men, to the spirits of righteous men made perfect, to Jesus the mediator of a new covenant, and to the sprinkled blood that speaks a better word than the blood of Abel.

See to it that you do not refuse him who speaks. If they did not escape when they refused him who warned them on earth, how much less will we, if we turn away from him who warns us from heaven? At that time his voice shook the earth, but now he has promised, "Once more I will shake not only the earth but also the heavens." The words "once more" indicate the removing of what can be shaken—that is, created things—so that what cannot be shaken may remain.

Therefore, since we are receiving a kingdom that cannot be shaken, let us be thankful, and so worship God acceptably with reverence and awe, for our "God is a consuming fire." (Hebrews 12:18-29)

r. Rankin (not his real name) was eighty-three when we met. He had a sense of humor that kept him chuckling more than the people who listened to his jokes. When people asked how old he was, he'd tell them he was "a backward thirty-eight." He did not invite change openly. In 1987 he was still driving a 1963 Chevy with standard steering and standard brakes. No air conditioning, either. In his eighty-three years he never traveled more than fifty miles from his house. He didn't like the mountains even though he'd never been in them. And one of his oft-repeated sentiments was, "Things shore ain't the way they used t' be!"

You often hear people talk like that when they speak about "the good old days."

Things *aren't* the way they used to be, but I'm glad about that. Who wants to go back to black-and-white television, wringer washers and wearing ducktails? I'll bet there's not a single farmer alive today who would rather be using horses than a new diesel tractor with air conditioning.

What would we do without microwave ovens, dishwashers and remote control? It's true—things aren't what they used to be, but who wants to reverse progress? Yet that is precisely what the early believers were being tempted to do when the letter to the Hebrews was written.

They were probably being hassled by other Jewish people who wanted them to forsake the Christian way. *Come on back to the Jewish way of life! We miss ya! It's the good life. You remember, don't you, how we used to go to the temple together? So many good times. . . .*

To combat the possibility, the author makes several encouraging statements about our life in Christ and the position held by every believer in the kingdom of God. You belong to a spiritual, eternal and unshakable kingdom!

You Belong to a Spiritual Kingdom

You have not come to a mountain that can be touched and that is burning with fire; to darkness, gloom and storm; to a trumpet blast or to such a voice speaking words that those who heard it begged that no further word be spoken to them, because they could not bear what was commanded: "If even an animal touches the mountain, it must be stoned." The sight was so terrifying that Moses said, "I am trembling with fear."

But you have come to Mount Zion, to the heavenly Jerusalem, the city of the living God. . . ." (Hebrews 12:18-22)

In one commentary, this passage is handled under the subtitle "The Terror of the Old and the Glory of the New." There is an implied, but unmistakable, contrast in these verses between the Old Testament and the New, between the physical features of the Old Covenant and the spiritual aspects of the New.

There is a great difference between the physical mountain where the law was given to Moses, Mount Sinai, and the spiritual mountain where grace continues to flow to us. The phenomena of verse 18 are all associated with the Sinai event (see Deuteronomy 4:11). Elsewhere they are tied to the presence of God: fire (Judges 13:20; 1 Kings 18:38), darkness (1 Kings 8:12) and tempest (Nahum 1:3). Terror is right!

Under the old covenant the emphasis was on the infinite distance between God and man. The divine voice was frightful (Exodus 20:19; Deuteronomy 5:24-27) and the divine presence was inaccessible. But today, Jesus declares, "I no longer call you servants. . . . Instead, I have called you friends . . ." (John 15:15).

One bedtime story I remember telling our son Nathan was about the courageous Moravian missionaries who first went to the Eskimo people to tell them about the love of Jesus. Apparently, they could not find a word in the Eskimo language for "forgiveness," so they had to make one up. They had to compound one from existing words. This newly formed word for forgiveness turned out to be a formidable looking assembly with twenty-four letters: *issumagijou-jungnainermik*. It has a beautiful connotation. It means "not being able to think about it anymore."

I told Nathan that when we are forgiven by God, He removes our sins from us "as far as the east is from the west" (Psalm 103:12). He takes care of our sins so that we don't have to think about them anymore. Nathan smiled, a long, warm smile. So did I.

Jesus made us a part of His kingdom the moment we said, "I believe." Our King is the greatest phenomenon that has ever crossed the horizon of this world. He's God's Son; He's the sinner's Savior; He's the centerpiece of civilization; He's the loftiest idea in literature; He's the highest personality in philosophy; He's the only One to qualify as the Ruler of the spiritual kingdom to which you and I belong.

Can you see the kingdom paradox? As Solzhenitsyn wrote after his release from the Russian prison, "the meaning of earthly existence lies, not as we have grown used to thinking, in prospering, but in the development of the soul."[21]

We belong to a *spiritual* kingdom, thanks to Jesus Christ.

You Belong to an Everlasting Kingdom

> But you have come to Mount Zion, to the heavenly Jerusalem, the city of the living God. You have come to thousands upon thousands of angels in joyful assembly, to the church of the firstborn, whose names are written in heaven. You have come to God, the judge of all men, to the spirits of righteous men made perfect, to Jesus the mediator of a new covenant, and to the sprinkled blood that speaks a better word than the blood of Abel. (Hebrews 12:22-24)

"But" is the strong adversative conjunction (*alla*) which introduces this section. It emphasizes the fact that this is not a Sinai kind of experience. Instead, we have come to Mount Zion, which is the name of one of the hills on which the city of Jerusalem was built. Mount Zion sometimes stands for the city of Jerusalem. It is also called "the heavenly Jerusalem" and "the city of the living God."

In the Greek New Testament, verses 22-24 appear as one long sentence. It is an unparalleled, one-sentence account of the destiny of every genuine, born-again believer in Jesus Christ. You belong to an interminable kingdom! The new Jerusalem is waiting for you! The world with all of its fears and fighting will be gone and life will be made anew. On that day we'll hear the voice saying, "Now the dwelling of God is with men, and he will live with them. They will be his people, and God himself will be with them and be their God. He will wipe every tear from their eyes. There will be no more death or mourning or crying or pain, for the old order of things has passed away" (Revelation 21:3-4).

My little girl, who has a devastating disease, will have a new body and a new mind. Since the day she was born I have been waiting to hear her angelic voice call out to me. I would give anything to hear her call me "Daddy!" It hasn't happened yet. But one day she will call me "Daddy," the first day we're together in the new city that awaits us. She'll be able to walk and talk and run into the arms of Jesus who created her and filled our lives with love through her. On that day she'll be completely whole, and so will you. Praises to God above who reigns in majesty and glory and splendor. Hallelujah!

If you believe in Jesus, then you belong to an everlasting kingdom and thousands upon thousands of angels are waiting for you in joyful assembly (Hebrews 12:22). You belong to an eternal kingdom and God's elect, the church of the firstborn, those whose names are written in heaven are waiting for you over on the other side (Hebrews 12:23). If you believe in Jesus, you belong to an eternal kingdom and you have come to God, the Judge of all men. The glory is there; but the awe and the fear of God still remain (Hebrews 12:23).

You belong to an eternal kingdom, and that is possible only because of Jesus Christ, the Mediator of the new covenant through His blood.

You Belong to an Unshakable Kingdom

> See to it that you do not refuse him who speaks. If they did not escape when they refused him who warned them on earth, how much less will we, if we turn away from him who warns us from heaven? At that time his voice shook the earth, but now he has promised, "Once more I will shake not only the earth but also the heavens." The words "once more" indicate the removing of what can be shaken—that is, created things—so that what cannot be shaken may remain.
>
> Therefore, since we are receiving a kingdom that cannot be shaken, let us be thankful, and so worship God acceptably with reverence and awe, for our "God is a consuming fire." (Hebrews 12:25-29)

Another warning. "See to it that you do not refuse him who speaks." Several times the author has cautioned his readers. He does not miss this opportunity to remind them again. The human heart is prone to wander. Don't we feel it, all of us?

To say that we are operating under new management in no way suggests that God no longer speaks with authority. In fact, the opposite is true. When the law was given, the mountain shook. Exodus 19:18 says, "Mount Sinai was covered with smoke, because the LORD descended on it in fire. The smoke billowed up from it like smoke from a furnace, the whole mountain trembled violently. . . ." But in the coming great Day the entire earth and the heavens will be shaken and removed, and many people will face a real dilemma.

The Bible says that one day those who do not believe in the Lord will find trouble in the very place they run for safety (Amos 5:18-20). According to the prophet Amos, these people may be deeply religious. They may even long for the coming of the Lord. But they do not realize that His arrival will present for them the greatest problem of all—judgment. "It will be as though a man fled from a lion only to meet a bear" (Amos 5:19).

But there is good news. Jesus said, "I tell you the truth, whoever hears my word and believes him who sent me has eternal life and will not be condemned; he has crossed over from death to life" (John 5:24). Believers belong to the order of things that cannot be shaken.

The apostle Peter tells us in Second Peter 3:10, 12 that "the day of the Lord will come like a thief. The heavens will disappear with a roar; the elements will be destroyed by fire, and the earth and everything in it will be laid bare. . . . That day will bring about the destruction of the heavens by fire, and the elements will melt in the heat." In other words, all things that can be "shaken" will be shaken, so that which cannot be shaken will remain. The world as we know it will be uprooted, but there is one thing that cannot be destroyed—there is one thing that cannot be dissolved, decimated or obliterated—your relationship with God!

You belong to an unshakable kingdom. "For I am convinced that neither death nor life, neither angels nor demons, neither the present nor the future, nor any powers, neither height nor depth, nor anything else in all creation, will be able to separate us from the love of God that is in Christ Jesus our Lord" (Romans 8:38-39). Nothing's going to pry us loose from God's love because it's unshakable.

I would never want to return to the way things were when I was a kid. "Things shore ain't the way they used t' be," but I'm happy about that. Nothing appeals to me about black-and-white television. Not after my twenty-seven inch Panasonic color with remote control and external speaker jacks. *No sir!* And wringer washers? Ducktails? *You've got to be kidding me!*

Have you been moving forward in your walk with God? If you're not making progress you're probably in regress. Check the rearview mirror. Anybody behind you, or are you the last one in the lane and losing ground fast? Maybe you're being stalled by your friends or even someone in your family. *Come on back,* they say. *We miss ya back here in the spiritual desert. It's a pretty good life. You remember, don't you, how we used to go to all those parties? So many good times. . . .*

But you can't, can you? You know where you've come from. You're not going back. You abide in a spiritual kingdom now that is everlasting and more secure than the rock of Gibraltar!

The best conclusion? Since you are receiving a kingdom that cannot be shaken, be thankful. Worship God acceptably with reverence and awe, for our "God is a consuming fire" (Hebrews 12:29).

Endnotes

1. *Leadership* (Summer 1994): 49. Used by permission.

2. Leon Morris, *Hebrews, The Expositor's Bible Commentary,* Vol. 12, ed. Frank E. Gaebelein (Grand Rapids, MI: Zondervan Publishing House, 1981), 133.

3. F.F. Bruce, *The Epistle to the Hebrews* (Grand Rapids, MI: William B. Eerdmans Publishing Company, 1964), 352.

4. Ibid., 352, footnote.

5. Max Lucado, *In the Eye of the Storm: A Day in the Life of Jesus* (Dallas, TX: Word Publishing, 1991), 247-249.

6. Judson W. Van De Venter, 1855-1939, "I Surrender All."

7. Peter Kreeft, *Making Sense Out of Suffering* (Ann Arbor, MI: Servant Books, 1986), 97-98.

8. Ibid., 98.

9. Ibid., 100.

10. F.F. Bruce, 357.

11. Paul Lee Tan, *Encyclopedia of 7700 Illustrations* (Chicago, IL: Assurance Publishers, 1979), illustration number 408, 189-190.

12. William Barclay, *The Letter to the Hebrews* (Philadelphia, PA: The Westminster Press, 1976, revised edition), 175.

13. Leon Morris, 136.

14. *Leadership* (Winter 1992): 48. Used by permission.

15. Ibid., 100.

16. Raymond Brown, 237.

17. *Leadership* (Winter 1995): 38. Used by permission.

18. William Barclay, 183.

19. Jerry Bridges, *Pursuit of Holiness* (Colorado Springs. CO: NavPress, 1982).

20. William Barclay, 183.

21. Alexander Solzhenitsyn, *Gulag Archipelago II* (New York, NY: Harper & Row, 1974), 613-15.

Discussion Questions for Further Study

1. From Abel to Zechariah (A-Z), the Old Testament saints testified to their faith in hardship, persecution and death (Hebrews 11:1-40). How should this "cloud of witnesses" affect what we do now?

2. What are some of the things that might be included in "everything that hinders" (12:1)? Are any of these things operative in your life right now?

3. Practically speaking, what do you think it means to "fix our eyes" on Jesus (12:2)? How can fixing your eyes on Jesus help you to resist the temptation to grow weary and lose heart?

4. Jesus' motivation for enduring the cross and its shame was "the joy set before him" (12:2). What joy is set before you that can motivate you to endure and persevere?

5. What state might your life be in today if God chose not to discipline you when you went astray? Take a few minutes to thank Him for his love.

6. Are there any bitter roots in your heart defiling you and others (12:15)? If so, confess them to God and ask Him to forgive you and cleanse you. If the bitter root is unforgiveness of someone else, forgive that person.

7. Is there a connection between suffering and the deeper life?

13

Hebrews 13:1-21

Final Exhortations

Keep on loving each other as brothers. Do not forget to entertain strangers, for by so doing some people have entertained angels without knowing it. Remember those in prison as if you were their fellow prisoners, and those who are mistreated as if you yourselves were suffering.

Marriage should be honored by all, and the marriage bed kept pure, for God will judge the adulterer and all the sexually immoral. Keep your lives free from the love of money and be content with what you have, because God has said,

> *"Never will I leave you;*
> *never will I forsake you."*

So we say with confidence,

> *"The Lord is my helper; I will not be afraid*
> *What can man do to me?"*

Remember your leaders, who spoke the word of God to you. Consider the outcome of their way of life and imitate their faith. (Hebrews 13:1-7)

This closing chapter comes almost as an abrupt intrusion, says commentator Raymond Brown. This final chapter in the letter leaves no stone unturned. It's not a series of pious platitudes praising the prudence of a lifestyle marked by fantasy or perfection or unattainable spirituality.

Here we see some straightforward, discriminating advice on several topics for people living in an age of indifference and compromise. We are faced with pastoral appeals about love, hospitality, visiting prisoners, martial fidelity, financial contentment and loyalty to the leaders God has given to the Church.

Love Each Other

> Keep on loving each other as brothers.
>   (Hebrews 13:1)

Brotherly love is an essential virtue for every believer in Christ. "This is the message you heard from the beginning: We should love one another" (1 John 3:11).

The apostle Paul penned the most eloquent chapter on love recorded in the Scriptures. "If I speak in the tongues of men and of angels, but have not love, I am only a resounding gong or a clanging cymbal. If I have the gift of prophecy and can fathom all mysteries and all knowledge, and if I have a faith that can move mountains, but have not love, I am nothing" (1 Corinthians 13:1-2). What Paul spent an entire chapter saying in First Corinthians 13, this writer says in just a few words: "Keep on loving each other as brothers."

The milieu of evangelical churches sometimes threatens brotherly love. The very fact that we take our faith so sincerely is a danger in one sense. In a church that is endangered from the outside and seriously earnest on the inside, there are always two dangers. First, there is the danger of the "doctrinal witch hunt." Heresy-hunting. Keeping the faith pure. That passion tends to make men eager to track down the heretic. Dislodge the person whose faith has gone adrift. Extricate the dissenter.

Second, there is the danger of stern and unsympathetic treatment of the person whose nerve and faith have failed. The indispensability of unswerving loyalty to Christ in the midst of an antagonistic world tends to add sharpness to the treatment of the person who in some crisis had not the courage to stand for his or her faith.

It is a desirable thing to keep the faith pure; but when the desire to do so makes us censorious, harsh and unsympathetic, brotherly love is overturned, and we are left with a situation which may be worse than the one we tried to avoid. Somehow or other we have to combine two things—an earnestness in the faith and a kindness to the man who has strayed from it.[1] Thus, the exhortation to "keep on loving each other as brothers."

We build many fences in the church, some to keep people in and others to keep them out. Restrictions, rules and silly preferences that demonstrate a lack of brotherly love. Comedian Emo Philips illustrates how ridiculous it can become:

> In conversation with a person I had recently met, I asked, "Are you Protestant or Catholic?"
>
> My new acquaintance replied, "Protestant."
>
> I said, "Me too! What franchise?"
>
> He answered, "Baptist."
>
> "Me too!" I said. "Northern Baptist or Southern Baptist?"
>
> "Northern Baptist," he replied.
>
> "Me too!" I shouted.
>
> We continued to go back and forth. Finally I asked, "Northern conservative fundamentalist Baptist, Great Lakes Region, Council of 1879 or Northern conservative fundamentalist Baptist, Great Lakes Region, Council of 1912?"

He replied, "Northern conservative fundamentalist
Baptist, Great Lakes Region, Council of 1912."
I said, *"Die, heretic!"*[2]

What did we say this verse was about? Loving each other as
brothers, in spite of denominational idiosyncrasies? Not allowing trifling differences to become major issues? Brotherly love
stands out like the silhouette of a lonely tree against a crimson
sunset. Do we care enough about our brothers and sisters in
Christ to keep loving them and to demonstrate that we do?

Entertain Strangers

Do not forget to entertain strangers, for by so doing
some people have entertained angels without knowing it. (Hebrews 13:2)

This is the second concise statement concerning our responsibility as brothers in the same family. In my reading
recently I came across an interesting observation. Kent
Hughes wrote:

There has been an interesting development in sub-
urban architecture. Long gone are the days when
homes all had large front porches, with easy access to
the front door, enabling one to become quickly acquainted with others in the neighborhood. In the
1990s we have architecture which speaks more directly to our current values. The most prominent part
of a house seems to be the two- or three-car garage.
Modern architecture employs small living and dining
rooms and now smaller kitchens as well, because entertaining is no longer a priority.[3]

Entertaining is no longer a priority, and entertaining
strangers is almost extinct. In the days of the New Testament, most public accommodations were not always safe,

and often they were morally offensive to believers. So the writer to the Hebrews tells them to open their homes and open their hearts to people who need a place to eat or a place to stay—even if they are strangers!

Galatians 6:10 says, "As we have opportunity, let us do good to all people, especially to those who belong to the family of believers." So, our first responsibility is to our brothers and sisters in Christ, but it does not end there. We are to show compassion and Christian love to strangers. To encourage open hospitality, reference is made to the fact that by welcoming visitors some have entertained angels without knowing it. That's exactly what happened to Abraham, Lot and Gideon (Genesis 18:1-3; 19:1-2; Judges 6:11-24).

However you look at this text, and however you try to justify not obeying it because of the times in which we live, there is no way around this command from God's Word: Do not forget to entertain strangers. In our cold, scary, surreal, sequestered, super-independent experience, this kind of counsel and compassion is not only rare, but virtually extinct (cf. Matthew 25:32-40). Entertaining is no longer a priority in our society. But it should be a priority in our church. Christianity was, and still should be, a religion of the open door.

Remember the Prisoners

> Remember those in prison as if you were their fellow prisoners, and those who are mistreated as if you yourselves were suffering. (Hebrews 13:3)

Christians were persecuted for their faith. Some were under considerable pressure and others had been imprisoned. But prisoners are out of sight and apt to be forgotten, hence the exhortation to "remember." Out of sight—out of mind. It's easy to forget about the plight of fellow believers in places like Lebanon, Poland, Cambodia, China, Rwanda, Bosnia and Zaire. The Iron Curtain is down in Eastern Europe and Russia, but the suffering is not over.

From 1986 to 1990, Frank Reed was held hostage in a Lebanon cell. For months at a time, Reed was blindfolded, living in complete darkness or chained to a wall and kept in absolute silence. On one occasion, he was moved to another room, and, although blindfolded, he could sense others in the room. Yet it was three weeks before he dared peek out to discover he was chained next to Terry Anderson and Tom Sutherland.

Although he was beaten, made ill and tormented, Reed felt most the lack of anyone caring. He said in an interview with *Time*, "Nothing I did mattered to anyone. I began to realize how withering it is to exist with not a single expression of caring around [me]. . . . I learned one overriding fact: caring is a powerful force. If no one cares, you are truly alone."[4]

"Remember . . . those who are mistreated as if you yourselves were suffering." *If no one cares, you are truly alone.* Sensitive, sympathetic and responsive believers should feel concern for others who live in places far and near and who suffer painful conditions of all sorts. Let's not wait for someone else to heed the call of God and take action. *If no one cares, you are truly alone.*

Keep Your Marriage Pure

> Marriage should be honored by all, and the marriage bed kept pure, for God will judge the adulterer and all the sexually immoral. (Hebrews 13:4)

The writer's exposition of "brotherly love" (13:1) leads naturally to married love. This first-century letter calls for the marriage bed to be kept pure, for moral uprightness and eternal accountability. The church was being troubled by advocates of extreme asceticism. These people regarded marriage as defiling and insisted on celibacy for the consummation of piety. "They forbid people to marry and order them to abstain from certain foods, which God created to be received with thanksgiving by those who believe and who know the truth. For everything God created is good, and nothing is to be rejected if it is received with thanksgiving . . ." (1 Timothy 4:3-4). But the author clearly renounces the position of asceticism. He's not advocating celibacy. He's preaching purity. Honor the marriage bed. Keep it uncontaminated.

"The marriage bed" is probably a euphemism for sexual intercourse and the Greek word translated "pure" means "free from contamination."[5] What is it that contaminates the marriage bed? The writer names two things: adultery and sexual immorality. The first is specific, referring to extra-marital relations. The second is more general, pointing to all kinds of impurities, unnatural vices and sex outside of marriage.

Adultery and sexual immorality are perversions of God's plan for you and me, and the Bible says, "Run away from it." "Flee from sexual immorality" (1 Corinthians 6:18). If you don't, you'll face the judgment of God. Hebrews 13:4 says, "God will judge the adulterer and all the sexually immoral." This judgment likely includes some kind of final reckoning with God at the end of life, but I think there is more to it. It's a judgment which produces *a deterioration in the quality of life*.

In Psalm 32:3-4, David said, "When I kept silent (about my sin), my bones wasted away through my groaning all day long. For day and night your hand (O God) was heavy upon me; my strength was sapped as in the heat of summer. . . ." God's judgment for sexual sin often includes intense mental pressure produced by guilt, which often leads to mental and emotional failure, and a general deterioration in the quality of life.

The pastor in prison in Cuba may seem rather remote from our immediate concern. But almost everyone in the church today is in touch with someone who's had a marriage breakdown due to sexual unfaithfulness. Sexual escapades and extra-marital affairs are no longer hidden from view. We are assured that marital unfaithfulness is just part of living.

"The most powerful force in the physical world is not the nuclear bomb—but sex!" states Dr. Archibald Hart. "Addictions to alcohol and cocaine may be major problems for our age, but they pale into insignificance when compared to the ravages of sex gone wrong."[6] Full-length books have been written on how to have an affair without getting caught. Television, movies and talk shows promote this kind of thing. Our senses have become dull to it.

Be Content with What You Have

> Keep your lives free from the love of money and be content with what you have, because God has said,
>
> "Never will I leave you;
>   never will I forsake you."
>
> So we say with confidence,
>
> "The Lord is my helper; I will not be afraid.
>   What can man do to me?" (Hebrews 13:5-6).

Marital infidelity is coupled with material idolatry, and we may assume that love of money was just one more temptation to which the recipients of this letter were showing signs of giving in. Many commentators have remarked on the close connection between marital unfaithfulness and covetousness.[7]

One is just as serious as the other in the homes and hearts of believers in Jesus. Not only does the culture-at-large teach us to pursue prosperity and success at any cost, but that message is being repeated from a growing number of pulpits in North America.

In *Success, Motivation, and the Scriptures* William H. Cook describes a meeting in 1923 of a group of business tycoons. Together these men controlled unthinkable sums of wealth, and for years the media had trumpeted their success stories.

On this day in Chicago they assembled to enjoy their mutual success. Dr. Cook relays what happened to these men in the years that followed:

> Charles Schwab, the president of the largest independent steel company, lived on borrowed money the last five years of his life and died penniless.
> Richard Whitney, the president of the New York Stock Exchange, served time in Sing Sing Prison.
> Albert Fall, a former member of the President's Cabinet, was pardoned from prison so he could die at home.
> Jesse Livermore, the greatest bear on Wall Street, committed suicide.
> Leon Fraser, the president of the Bank of International Settlement, committed suicide.
> Ivar Krueger, head of the world's greatest monopoly, committed suicide.[8]

The success they celebrated proved illusory. Yet today we are made to feel that we need to get more, have more, want more, and if we don't then something's wrong with our motivation and we're missing out on God's plan. But Hebrews advises us to "keep your lives free from the love of money and be content with what you have" (Hebrews 13:5).

The avaricious man is never content. He's ungenerous and grasping. Always wanting more. Always afraid of losing what he has. How different from the sweet Christian who knows that in Christ he lacks nothing. "The LORD is my shepherd, *I shall not be in want*" (Psalm 23:1, italics added for emphasis).

Not unlike us today, the recipients of this letter were no doubt anxious about the ability of their heavenly Father to adequately care for them in this time of difficulty. Maybe they had recessions back then too? Black Monday in October? Consequently the author assures them with this promise that has been proven over the centuries: "Never will I leave you; never will I forsake you." No matter how limited our earthly resources may be, we can say with confidence, "The Lord is my helper; I will not be afraid!"

Be Loyal to Your Leaders

Remember your leaders, who spoke the word of God to you. Consider the outcome of their way of life and imitate their faith. Jesus Christ is the same yesterday and today and forever. . . . Obey your leaders and submit to their authority. They keep watch over you as men who must give an account. Obey them so that their work will be a joy, not a burden, for that would be of no advantage to you. (Hebrews 13:7-8, 17)

From writing about love in 13:4-5 the author moves to leadership. Not much is found in the New Testament about the way Christians should treat their leaders, so this is important material. Three times in this chapter the word "leaders" is used (7, 17, 24). It's a general term used of religious leaders, military leaders and princes, among others. They may have been "elders," but that word is not specifically used here.[9]

Regarding the leaders of the past we are told to do two things: first, remember them; and second, imitate their faith (Hebrews 13:7). A closer look at these men and women reveals that they led the people of God properly, and they spoke the Word of God faithfully and they lived the life of faith consistently (Hebrews 13:17).

"*Consider* the outcome of their way of life" suggests that we make a careful study of individuals of the past who have led people in faith. People like Abraham, Isaac and Jacob. Moses, Joshua and David. Such reflection will make a positive impact on our lives and thinking.

Then, in a profound and wonderfully succinct verse, the writer turns us again to Christ. He is "the same yesterday and today and forever." Earthly leaders come and go. Political leaders vanish with the vote. Committee chairmen replaced. CEOs sent packing. But Jesus Christ is always there. This verse expresses the unfailing reliability of Him who is our Savior. And while it is a truth that can be applied to many situations, it belongs first to the context in which it appears.

So, the same Christ who was with leaders like Abraham, Moses and Joshua is with you, and He will be with those who come after us, even to the end of the age. The one who "yesterday" did not fail to help His appointed leaders, as He had promised, "today" helps them, and will continue to help His faithful ones "forever." Hallelujah!

Regarding today's model leaders, Hebrews 13:17 says, "Obey your leaders and submit to their authority. They keep watch over you as men who must give an account. Obey them so that their work will be a joy, not a burden, for that would be of no advantage to you."

It's more difficult for us to "obey" spiritual leaders than it is to "remember" them. But the Holy Spirit wants us to recognize that our God-appointed leaders occupy positions of spiritual authority in spite of their flaws. Bear in mind that He does not have in mind self-seeking, deceptive, carnal leaders, but those who do their jobs the best they know how from a pure heart.

Hebrews 13:1-8, like earlier passages, is not a series of pious platitudes praising the prudence of a lifestyle marked by fantasy or perfection or unattainable spirituality. Rather, it gives the reader some straightforward, discriminating advice on brotherly love, entertaining strangers, remembering the prisoners, marriage, money and leadership. Advice for people like us who are living in an age of indifference and compromise.

What does it take for men and women in touch with the real world to survive the swelling torrent of deceitful information that tells them that they owe it to themselves to traffic in sexual immorality? It takes *commitment*. What does it take to stay free from the love of money? It takes *contentment*. What does it take to obey local church leadership? It takes *loyalty*.

Commitment declares, "I don't need a secret, intimate alliance outside my present marriage to give me joy and satisfaction. I will find pleasure and delight in the spouse God has given to me. I am not looking for a way out. No greener pastures exist. This is it!"

Contentment proclaims, "I don't need more things outside my current situation to make me happy or fulfilled. Life does not consist of the abundance of things. I will not let myself be confused by the cacophony of voices that keep telling me I need more, bigger, better. My contentment is in Christ. He is all—and all I need."

Loyalty asserts, "I don't need perfect leaders in the church in order to obey and submit to their authority. God has given me this command and I will obey it. I will not let myself become critical, bitter or resentful. If I hear others gossiping about the leaders, I will state only the truth and hastily dismantle the rumors. When I'm needed for ministry, I'll volunteer of my own accord without waiting to be prodded or cuddled. I'll do whatever I can so that the work of our leaders will not become a burden."

Maybe you need a minute or two for personal surrender. I do.

"Lord, You are the Head of the church. I'm determined to follow You and obey those who are over me in the Lord. When self hinders Your will in this regard, please remind me that "I have been crucified with Christ and I no longer live, but Christ lives in me. The life I live in the body, I live by faith in the Son of God, who loved me and gave himself for me" (Galatians 2:20). I present myself in service and obedience to You and to the godly leaders in my church who are under Your supervision."

Unchanging Truth in a Changing World

Jesus Christ is the same yesterday and today and forever.
Do not be carried away by all kinds of strange teach-
ings. It is good for our hearts to be strengthened by grace,

*not by ceremonial foods, which are of no value to those who
eat them. We have an altar from which those who minister at the tabernacle have no right to eat.*

*The high priest carries the blood of animals into the
Most Holy Place as a sin offering, but the bodies are
burned outside the camp. And so Jesus also suffered outside
the city gate to make the people holy through his own
blood. Let us, then, go to him outside the camp, bearing the
disgrace he bore. For here we do not have an enduring
city, but we are looking for the city that is to come.*

*Through Jesus, therefore, let us continually offer to God
a sacrifice of praise—the fruit of lips that confess his name.
And do not forget to do good and to share with others, for
with such sacrifices God is pleased. (Hebrews 13:8-16)*

Change is everywhere. At a given point in time the
Democrats may be in power on Capitol Hill. An
election is held and the tide turns to the Republi-
cans. Some rejoice with the change, while others scowl.

At one time you could buy more goods with one Canadian dollar than you could with one American dollar. But
times change. So does the financial stability of the money
markets.

We change our calendars once a month, and we become
conscious as we change the calendar that we ourselves have
changed. The creamy smooth complexion you used to have
now displays a few wrinkles. That's change, however painful it may be. The slim physique of twenty years ago? Only
a wishful thought. Some men now have more hair on their
faces than on the top of their heads!

This afternoon I had an appointment with my doctor.
Thought I had a bone chip floating on my knee. Did it ever
hurt when I knelt down in the garden to pull weeds! "Well,
Garth, I think it has more to do with the fact that you're getting older," she said carefully. I'm aging. Just like the rest of
the baby-boomer population I represent, and I need to be
more careful. Thanks a lot! Just what I wanted to hear!

Modifications of one form or another seem to pounce upon us when we least expect it. And in light of all this change in the economy, our health, the government, the social climate, the educational system and even the family structure today, we long for a center of permanence in our lives. Yet where shall we find it? Only in the Word of God.

In Hebrews 13:8-16, for example, we witness several unchanging truths that produce a nucleus of continuity in this world of secular superficiality and rapid-fire change.

Christ Does Not Change

Jesus Christ is the same yesterday and today and forever.

Do not be carried away by all kinds of strange teachings. It is good for our hearts to be strengthened by grace, not by ceremonial foods, which are of no value to those who eat them. We have an altar from which those who minister at the tabernacle have no right to eat. (Hebrews 13:8-10)

Clearly there was some false teaching in the church to which the letter was written. We may never know exactly what it was, but we can start with one basic fact: The writer knew that real strength comes to a person's heart only from the grace of God and that what people eat and drink has nothing to do with spiritual power. The regulations concerning food had changed from the rigid laws first laid down for Israel in Leviticus 11. You can't please God by eating Kosher. *Things have changed since the new covenant was established*, the writer says, *and we need to change with them.*

Nevertheless, the human heart needs to know a center of permanence, a place that is familiar and unchanging. And there's only one place to find that. "Jesus Christ is the same yesterday and today and forever." He never changes. He's our center of permanence and stability and dependability.

This is followed in verse 9 by a warning against heresy.

"Do not be carried away by all kinds of strange teachings." The writer is warning his readers: Although the doctrines of others may be appealing, they may be fake. Be careful. Don't be carried away. Many of our contemporaries are beginning to acknowledge some form of spiritual need in their lives. Unfortunately many of them are looking in all the wrong places. There has scarcely been any other time in this century when so many cults have been present and active.

When Jehovah's Witnesses come knocking on your door, they often sound like Christians, but be careful. They teach that Jesus Christ is not really God. In a publication called *Let God Be True*, Jehovah's Witnesses teach that "At baptism Jesus was anointed to become the Messiah, or Jesus the Christ."[10] That's heresy.

Mormons say that "by obedience and devotion (Jesus) attained to the pinnacle of intelligence which ranked him as a God . . . ."[11] That's heresy also.

The authors of *Plain Truth* magazine, which is the official publication of the Worldwide Church of God, long recognized as a leading cult (but currently making some positive theological modifications), say that before Jesus Christ was conceived by Mary He was not the Son of God.[12] Heresy again.

When you consider the doctrine of immutability you discover that Jesus Christ is the same yesterday and today and forever. If *any* group teaches something contrary to that biblical truth for *any* reason, then they should be considered armed and dangerous.

Jesus Is Your Substitute

> The high priest carries the blood of animals into the Most Holy Place as a sin offering, but the bodies are burned outside the camp. And so Jesus also suffered outside the city gate to make the people holy through his own blood. Let us, then, go to him outside the camp, bearing the disgrace he bore. (Hebrews 13:11-13)

The writer makes reference to the fact that under the Old Testament sacrificial system, the bodies of sacrificial animals were carried outside the camp of Israel. And so, Christ's death outside the city of Jerusalem also represented the removal of sin. Through His suffering, people are made holy. His blood removes our sin.

Jesus died for our sake and on our behalf. But is it proper to speak of His death as substitutionary? Did He actually die in our place? Was He really our substitute? According to God's Word, He was, and He continues to be the substitute for all who express their faith in Him.

The most prominent proof is a passage found in Isaiah 53:6: "We all, like sheep, have gone astray, each of us has turned to his own way; and the LORD has laid on him the iniquity of us all."

Paul said, "God made (Jesus Christ) who had no sin to be sin for us, so that in him we might become the righteousness of God" (2 Corinthians 5:21). Earlier in Hebrews we read, "so Christ was sacrificed once to take away the sins of many people; and he will appear a second time, not to bear sin, but to bring salvation to those who are waiting for him" (9:28). Peter wrote, "He himself bore our sins in his body on the tree, so that we might die to sins and live for righteousness; by his wounds you have been healed" (1 Peter 2:24).

Jesus bore our sins. They were laid on Him or transferred from us to Him. He has become sin so that we could cease to be sin. The idea of substitution is unmistakable, and the doctrine of substitutionary atonement is an unchanging truth for us who believe.

"Let us, then, go to him outside the camp, bearing the disgrace he bore" (Hebrews 13:13). Christ died for us, and to flirt with other religious movements would be grievous.

Heaven Is a Real Place

For here we do not have an enduring city, but we are looking for the city that is to come. (Hebrews 13:14)

We have no stake in any earthly city. New York, Hong Kong, Toronto, Lima, Los Angeles, Kinchasa, São Paulo. No city on earth is "an enduring city". They're all passing away in decay, temporal. Therefore we should pursue what is lasting, immortal and eternal.

Heaven plays an important role in the Word of God, as it does in our own personal theology. For example, Jesus taught His disciples to pray, "Our Father who art in heaven." He often spoke of "your Father in heaven" (Matthew 6:1; 7:11; 18:14).

Jesus came from heaven (John 3:13, 31). It is from heaven that Christ is to be revealed (2 Thessalonians 1:7). He has gone away to heaven to prepare an eternal dwelling for believers (John 14:1-4). We are told to make preparations for heaven (Matthew 6:19-20). Peter tells us that true believers have been born again "into an inheritance that can never perish, spoil or fade—kept in heaven for you, who through faith are shielded by God's power until the coming of the salvation that is ready to be revealed in the last time" (1 Peter 1:4-5). In Colossians 1:5 Paul speaks of the hope laid up for us in heaven.

So, you see, nothing can change the truth about heaven, and because we have eternity in our hearts, "we have a divine discontent, a lover's quarrel with the world."[13] This is not our home.

A changing world emphasizes our need for a changeless Christ. A changeless Christ underscores the necessity of a personal relationship with God. A personal relationship with God strengthens our hope in a glorious future.[14]

But that's not all. The writer of Hebrews leaves us with a very practical conclusion to the consideration of unchanging truth: Unchanging truth calls for practical living. Doctrine without application is dead orthodoxy. "Through Jesus, therefore, let us continually offer to God a sacrifice of praise—the fruit of lips that confess his name. And do not forget to do good and to share with others, for with such sacrifices God is pleased" (Hebrews 13:15-16).

Animal offerings are now obsolete. But because of the wonderful things God has done for us, we desire to offer up some kind of sacrifice. How can we say thanks for the things God has done for us? The Bible says to offer a continual sacrifice of praise, lifting your voices in thanksgiving to God. And we should not forget to do good and to share with others, for with such sacrifices God is pleased.

Change is everywhere. And in light of all this change in the economy, the government, the social climate, the educational system and even the family structure today, we long for a center of permanence in our lives. But where shall we find it? In Jesus Christ who is the same yesterday and today and forever. In the death of Christ, for He paid the price we owed. And in the hope of heaven and our eternal home.

Prayer in Two Directions

> *Pray for us. We are sure that we have a clear conscience and desire to live honorably in every way. I particularly urge you to pray so that I may be restored to you soon.*
>
> *May the God of peace, who through the blood of the eternal covenant brought back from the dead our Lord Jesus, that great Shepherd of the sheep, equip you with everything good for doing his will, and may he work in us what is pleasing to him, through Jesus Christ, to whom be glory for ever and ever. Amen. (Hebrews 13:18-21)*

Once a woman asked Brennan Manning to come and pray with her father, who was dying of cancer. When Brennan arrived, he found the man lying in bed with his head propped up on two pillows and an empty chair beside his bed. He assumed the old fellow had been informed of this visit. "I guess you were expecting me," Manning said.

"No, who are you?"

"I'm the new associate at your parish," I replied. "When I

saw the empty chair, I figured you knew I was going to show up."

"Oh yeah, the chair," said the bedridden man. "Would you mind closing the door?"

Puzzled, Manning shut the door.

"I've never told anyone this, not even my daughter," said the man, "but all my life I have never known how to pray. At the Sunday service I used to hear the pastor talk about prayer, but it always went right over my head."

"I abandoned any attempt at prayer," he continued, "until one day about four years ago my best friend said to me, 'Joe, prayer is just a simple matter of having a conversation with Jesus. Here's what I suggest. Sit down on a chair, place an empty chair in front of you, and in faith see Jesus on the chair. It's not spooky because He promised, *I'll be with you all days*. Then just speak to Him and listen in the same way you're doing with me right now.' "

"So, Padre, I tried it, and I liked it so much that I do it a couple of hours every day. I'm careful though. If my daughter saw me talking to an empty chair, she'd send me off to the funny farm."

Manning said he was deeply moved by the story and encouraged the old guy to continue on the journey. Then he prayed with him, anointed him with oil and returned to the rectory.

Two nights later the daughter called to say that her daddy had died that afternoon.

"Did he seem to die in peace?" asked Manning.

"Yes. But there was something strange. In fact, beyond strange—kinda weird. Apparently just before Daddy died, he leaned over and rested his head on a chair beside his bed."[15]

The promised presence of our Lord will not only help us die well, but it also helps us live well and pray effectively for each other. And that's what Hebrews 13:18-21 is about. Prayer. People praying for their leaders and leaders praying for their people. Each prayer reveals something about those who pray and the God who listens.

People Praying for Their Leaders

> Pray for us. We are sure that we have a clear con-
> science and desire to live honorably in every way. I
> particularly urge you to pray so that I may be re-
> stored to you soon. (Hebrews 13:18-19)

The author makes a personal request for prayer. It's clear
that the identity of the author was no secret to the readers,
even though his name and his colleagues (if we should understand the plural "us" as more than a literary device) are
unknown to us. He has come down hard on his readers from
time to time throughout the epistle. After all, this letter is a
"word of exhortation" (Hebrews 13:22), warning them about
their conduct and their theology. But now he needs their
prayers.

"We are sure that we have a clear conscience and desire to
live honorably in every way," so pray for us. He's not aware
of any sin that he committed. His heart is right before God.
He wants to live a life pleasing to the Lord. His desire to live
honorably in every way is firm. For that reason he asks for
their fellowship and support in prayer.

By way of special emphasis, he repeats his request for
prayer. "I particularly urge you to pray so that I may be
restored to you soon." The adverb *perissoteros* (which the
NIV renders "particularly") means something like "more
abundantly," "beyond measure."[16] Circumstances must be
preventing a reunion between him and his readers, but we
have no indication what these were. He's desperate for
prayer.

John Piper wrote a book on missions, and one of the chapters carries the title "The Supremacy of God in Missions
Through Prayer." He says, in part:

> Not only has God made the accomplishment of his
> purposes hang on the preaching of the word; he has
> also made the success of that preaching hang on

prayer. God's goal to be glorified will not succeed without the powerful proclamation of the gospel. And that gospel will not be proclaimed in power to all the nations without the prevailing, earnest, faith-filled prayers of God's people. This is the awesome place of prayer in the purpose of God for the world. That purpose won't happen without prayer.[17]

Without prayer the gospel cannot advance. Nor will the leaders be encouraged. Leaders need the encouragement that comes through intercessory prayer. That's what the writer is asking for: support and encouragement that comes through intercessory prayer.

Leaders Praying for Their People

May the God of peace, who through the blood of the eternal covenant brought back from the dead our Lord Jesus, that great Shepherd of the sheep, equip you with everything good for doing his will, and may he work in us what is pleasing to him, through Jesus Christ, to whom be glory for ever and ever. Amen. (Hebrews 13:20-21)

As we review these words, we must realize that suffering, persecuted Christians were the first to read them. Many had lost their homes and their businesses. Scattered about because of their faith in Jesus, they wondered what the future held for them. Likely most were wondering what kind of God would allow them to go through such horrific experiences. "Why doesn't God protect us from this danger?"

So, the author of Hebrews writes to reassure them and encourage them in their faith. He brings this majestic letter to an inspiring conclusion by praying for his readers, and in that prayer reveals more of the nature and character of God. His great longing is that the Lord will equip us with everything good for doing His will—especially during difficult times.

First of all, he suggests that only a *saving God* can equip His people with everything good. This saving God, the God of peace, is the only one who can equip us with everything that we need to do what is pleasing in His sight.[18] He not only exemplifies peace, but promotes peace among His people. All our prosperity is centered in Him. There is no well-rounded life that does not depend on Him.

Through this prayer for the people, the author presents the Father as our *mighty God*. He brought the Lord Jesus back from the dead (Hebrews 13:20) after He was put to death by men who nailed Him to the cross. "But God raised him from the dead, freeing him from the agony of death, because it was impossible for death to keep its hold on him" (Acts 2:24). And if God the Father is mighty enough to raise Jesus from the dead, He's competent to carry your burdens and handle your problems as well.

Furthermore, when the writer of Hebrews 13:20 refers to our Lord Jesus Christ as the great Shepherd of the sheep, he invokes the image of a *compassionate God*. Throughout His lifetime Jesus exercised the caring, compassionate ministry of a good shepherd. As the great Shepherd of the sheep, nothing escapes His watchful eye and no matter of concern, no problem, no worry in our lives is too small—or too large—for Him.

When this leader prayed for his people, he addressed a God who is *faithful*, for this great work of redemption was accomplished through the blood of the eternal covenant. When God makes a covenant with His people, He's faithful to fulfill it. Psalm 145:13 says, "The LORD is faithful to all his promises and loving toward all he has made." He is the Maker of heaven and earth "who remains faithful forever" (146:6).

Moreover, this pastoral prayer is addressed to a *resourceful God*. The Lord knows what is best for us, and He has all the spiritual gifts necessary, says Hebrews 13:21, "to equip you with everything good for doing his will, and may he work in us what is pleasing to him. . . ." The word used here for equip literally means "to put into a proper condition," or "to make complete." You may be aware of what you need in your Christian life in order to be complete. But notice who does the equipping. *God* equips you with everything good for doing His will, so that He may work in us what is pleasing to Him. Our Father is extremely resourceful. Conferences and seminars help, but only God can supply the missing ingredients for your life and ministry. Don't ever underestimate what God can do in your life.

The verb "equip" (*katartizo*) can also mean "restore," "repair" or "mend."[19] It is the word used in the gospels to describe the work of the disciples when they were mending (*katartizontas*) their fishing nets. So in equipping His people with everything good, our God supplies not only what's necessary, but also repairs any damage along the way.

You may feel that your compromises in the past have destroyed your witness for Christ today. But God wants to repair the broken pieces and equip you with everything good to do His will again. You may sense that your devotion has grown cold and you don't have the fire burning in your heart that you once did. The God of peace can restore what has been lost.

Perhaps your life has been torn and divided by strife or rejection or bitterness or divorce or death, and you're beginning to wonder if you can ever be made whole again. I want you to know that the saving God, the mighty, compassionate, faithful, resourceful God can take the broken pieces and craft something that is even better than the original.

A certain cathedral in Europe was famous for the large, magnificent, stained-glass window that was located behind the altar and high above the sanctuary. One day a violent windstorm shattered the beautiful window into a thousand tiny pieces. The church custodian was somewhat hesitant to discard the precious fragments, so he put them in an old wooden box and stored them in the cathedral basement.

A man who heard about the damage asked for the broken pieces of glass. About two years later the same man invited the custodian to visit him. When the caretaker arrived, the man unveiled a stained-glass window that he had crafted from the broken pieces. It was even more beautiful than the original.

That's often the way it is with God. When we offer our broken lives to Jesus Christ in faith, He always crafts a work of art that is more beautiful than what we started with.

May the God of peace, who through the blood of the eternal covenant brought back from the dead our Lord Jesus, that great Shepherd of the sheep, equip you with everything good for doing his will, and may he work in us what is pleasing to him, through Jesus Christ, to whom be glory for ever and ever. Amen.

Endnotes

1. Adapted from William Barclay, *The Letter to the Hebrews*, revised edition (Philadelphia, PA: Westminster Press, 1976), 190.

2. *Leadership* (Fall 1992): 47. Used by permission.

3. Kent Hughes, *Disciplines of a Godly Man* (Wheaton, IL: Crossway Books, 1991), 59.

4. *Leadership* (Winter 1991): 49. Used by permission.

5. Leon Morris, *Hebrews, The Expositor's Bible Commentary*, vol. 12, ed. Frank E. Gaebelein (Grand Rapids, MI: Zondervan, 1981), 146.

6. Archibald D. Hart, *Healing Life's Hidden Addictions* (Ann Arbor, MI: Servant Publications, 1990), 145.

7. I suggest reading Philip Edgcumbe Hughes, *A Commentary on the Epistle to the Hebrews* (Grand Rapids, MI: William B. Eerdmans Publishing Company, 1977), 567-568.

8. *Leadership* (Fall 1991): 45. Used by permission.

9. Leon Morris, 148.

10. *Let God Be True*, 32.

11. McConkie, *Mormon Doctrine*, p. 670.

12. "Just What Do You Mean—Born Again?" p. 43 in *Tomorrow's World*.

13. Peter Kreeft, in Making Sense Out of Suffering (Ann Arbor, MI: Servant Books, 1986) goes on to say, "To have a quarrel with her, to criticize her, you need to know there is a standard. If the only world we ever knew or remembered was here, we would feel at home here. We do not" (page 94).

14. Charles Swindoll, *Hebrews Bible Study Guide*, Vol. II (Fullerton, CA: Insight for Living, 1983), 60.

15. Brennan Manning, "The One Jesus Loves," *Discipleship Journal* 82 (July/August 1994): 17-18.

16. Leon Morris, 154.

17. John Piper, *Let the Nations Be Glad! The Supremacy of God in Missions* (Grand Rapids, MI: Baker Book House, 1993), 66.

18. See also Romans 15:33, 16:20; 2 Corinthians 13:11; Philippians 4:9; 1 Thessalonians 5:23.

19. Raymond Brown, *The Message of Hebrews* (Leicester, England: InterVarsity Press, 1982), 268-269.

Discussion Questions for Further Study

1. Do you have trouble being peacefully content with your level of income and possessions?

2. Do you have a settled confidence that the Lord will always be there to protect you from financial disaster if you are walking obediently with Him?

3. Examine your financial attitudes and practices in light of 13:5-6. Do you need to make any changes?

4. Why is it so important to honor marriage and keep the marriage bed pure (13:4)?

5. Do you try to make your leaders' work joyful and not burdensome (13:17)? How can you do this better?

6. What picture is given of God in the benediction of 13:20-21?

7. Prayerfully evaluate your current life in the following areas. Ask God to make clear where you are fruitful and where you are falling short: hospitality, remembering the prisoners, purity in marriage, proper attitude on material wealth, offering praise to God, doing good and sharing with others, obedience to spiritual leaders, prayer. If you feel that you are below God's desires for you in any of these areas, what action can you take?

CONCLUSION

After twenty years of thinking of preaching as my attempts to close the gap, I now conceive of preaching—faithful evangelical preaching—as opening up the gap. For it is in the gaps, the great big frightening, invigorating gaps, that we can wander, reenvision, reform, be reborn. When preachers try to fill all the gaps with our suggestions for better living, our solutions to the world's problems, there is no space left for God to come and save us. God must have room.[1]

I have purposely avoided trying to fill all the gaps in the book of Hebrews. There is still plenty of room for God to work through His Word. If you have received the Word of God, which you read in the biblical text of Hebrews, and you accepted it not as the word of men, but as it actually is, the Word of God, then that Word is at work in you who believe (1 Thessalonians 2:13). God declared that His Word would be effective: "As the rain and the snow come down from heaven, and do not return to it without watering the earth and making it bud and flourish, so that it yields seed for the sower and bread for the eater, so is my word that goes out from my mouth: It will not return to me empty, but will accomplish what I desire and achieve the purpose for which I sent it" (Isaiah 55:10-11). If any good comes from reading *this* book, it's because of the power of God's Word that was activated in you through the ministry of the Holy Spirit.

Let's not strive to fill all the gaps created by this marvelous and magnificent book of the Bible. Give God the room He needs to do what He does best. Allow the Holy Spirit to convince you of the supremacy and superiority of Jesus Christ in a fresh form.

The first readers of this great epistle were Jewish Christians under severe pressure to turn back to Judaism. Fierce persecution from orthodox Jewish leaders had undermined their commitment to Jesus Christ. They paused on their spiritual journey and even slipped back. They made little progress, and they were not experiencing the deeper Christian life, the abundant life, that Jesus promised. The writer consequently appeals to them to follow the Lord, to make Jesus the supreme Master of their lives.

You may not be facing the same kind of persecution, but you understand what pressure is, don't you? You know the hassles, the temptations, the pain, the strain of life in the fast lane. And maybe you're starting to slip back also. You've got that faraway look in your eye, and you hear the sounds of Egypt. Do you smell the leeks and garlic, too?

Don't do it! Don't you turn around. Don't you go back to the world you left behind. The world is not worthy of you now that you belong to the King of kings and Lord of lords (Hebrews 11:38). Keep your eyes fixed on Christ. Stay focused. Persevere. Refuse the pull of earthly kingdoms and their pseudo-rulers, and keep moving toward the cross: "If anyone would come after me, he must deny himself and take up his cross daily and follow me" (Luke 9:23). That's the message of Hebrews, too. Pay attention, persevere, enter His rest, approach with confidence, show diligence to the very end, draw near to God, provoke one another, maintain faith, endure hardship, hold fast in discipline. Make Jesus Christ the Lord of all because He is incomparably superior to anything this world has to offer!

In the first part of the book the author passionately argues that Christ is superior to all the Old Testament characters and institutions. Superior to the prophets (1:1-4), the angels (1:5-2:18), Moses (3:1-6) and Melchizedek (7:1-28). Therefore, we must avoid unbelief because the consequences are tragic (3:7-4:16).

Christ has superior priestly functions (5:1-10), and He is worthy of our trust, for His promise is sure (6:13-20). "We have this hope as an anchor for the soul, firm and secure" (Hebrews 6:19). His covenant is superior to the old agreement (8:1-13), and His sacrifice superior to anything offered in the old order (9:1-10:18).

That provides the doctrinal foundation upon which the second part of the letter, the practical section, stands. Straightforward, practical advice. Persevere (10:19-39). Maintain faith in Christ (11:1-40). Remember that the ancients were commended for being sure of what they hoped for and certain of what they did not see. Accept God's discipline and stay committed to Him, no matter what (12:1-29). Exercise love (13:1-21).

We need knowledge, and we cannot understand spiritual things apart from special divine illumination of our minds. Jesus meets this need by revealing God to us. Hebrews presents Christ as the superior Prophet-Teacher. He does this through His own person, in whom the Father is fully revealed (Hebrews 1:1-4); through the gift to us of the written Word of God (John 20:31); and by the particular illumination of our minds by the Holy Spirit (John 16:13). "The man without the Spirit does not accept the things that come from the Spirit of God, for they are foolishness to him, and he cannot understand them, because they are spiritually discerned" (1 Corinthians 2:14). The Holy Spirit communicates the person of Christ to our minds and hearts through the Scriptures and thus provides for our salvation and sanctification.

Christ is also named the superior Priest in the book of Hebrews. A priest is a man appointed to act for others in things pertaining to God. He is a bridge-builder—closing the gap between sinful mankind and a holy, transcendent God—a mediator. We all have need of salvation. We are not merely ignorant of God and of spiritual things; we are also sinful. We have rebelled against God and like sheep have all gone our own way. Jesus meets this need as our Priest (Hebrews 3:1, 4:14). He offers Himself up as a sacrifice, thereby pro-

viding the perfect atonement for our sin (Hebrews 2:17). He
also intercedes for us at the right hand of the Father in
heaven, thereby guaranteeing our right to be heard (Hebrews 1:3, 7:25, 8:1, 10:12, 12:2).

Finally, we need spiritual discipline, guidance and rule.
We are not autonomous, even after our conversion. We do
not have the right to rule ourselves, nor can we rule ourselves successfully. Christ meets our need by His proper and
loving rule over us within the church. He is our Com-
mander-in-chief, Master and King. The apostle Paul made
that clear as he prayed for the Ephesians:

> I pray also that the eyes of your heart may be enlight-
> ened in order that you may know the hope to which
> he has called you, the riches of his glorious inheri-
> tance in the saints, and his incomparably great power
> for us who believe. That power is like the working of
> his mighty strength, which he exerted in Christ when
> he raised him from the dead and seated him at his
> right hand in the heavenly realms, *far above all rule*
> and authority, power and dominion, and every title
> that can be given, not only in the present age but also
> in the one to come. And God placed *all things* under
> his feet and appointed him to be head over *everything*
> for the church, which is his body, the fullness of him
> who fills everything in every way. (Ephesians 1:18-
> 23, italics added)

Hebrews also describes Jesus Christ as the supreme Head
of the Church and King of our lives. Have you given Him
His proper place on the throne of your life? Have you ac-
knowledged the superiority of Jesus in your heart and mind?
If not, why don't you do it now? Take a few minutes to re-
sign as landlord and give Jesus the keys to your heart.

> King of my life, I crown Thee now, Thine shall
>   the glory be;

> Lest I forget Thy thorn–crowned brow,
>   Lead me to Calvary.
> Lest I forget Gethsemane; Lest I forget Thine
>   agony;
> Lest I forget Thy love for me, Lead me to
>   Calvary.
>
> May I be willing, Lord, to bear daily my cross
>   for Thee;
> Even Thy cup of grief to share, Thou hast borne
>   all for me.
> Lest I forget Gethsemane; Lest I forget
>   thine agony;
> Lest I forget Thy love for me, Lead me to
>   Calvary.

Become engrossed with the superiority of Jesus Christ. Honor Him with your body, soul and spirit (1 Corinthians 6:20). If you dedicate yourself to the preeminence of Jesus Christ in all things, the Holy Spirit will exalt you and fill you and bless you. Honoring Jesus means doing what Jesus told you to do. Trusting Him as your all in all. Following Him as the Way. Believing Him as the Truth. Living with Him as the Life.

When you honor Jesus as the superior Prophet, Priest and King, the Spirit of God becomes glad within you. "The LORD your God is with you, he is mighty to save. He will take great delight in you, he will quiet you with his love, *he will rejoice over you with singing*" (Zephaniah 3:17, emphasis added). What an awesome thought. God, rejoicing over us with singing!

The sun comes up and heaven comes near as Jesus Christ, the superior One of all the ages, becomes Lord of your life.

Tozer said the man who preaches truth and applies it to the lives of his hearers "will feel the nails and the thorns. He will lead a hard life, but a glorious one."[2] May God raise up many such preachers and teachers among us. The church needs them badly.

> May the God of peace, who through the blood of the eternal covenant brought back from the dead our Lord Jesus, that great Shepherd of the sheep, equip you with everything good for doing his will, and may he work in us what is pleasing to him, through Jesus Christ, to whom be glory for ever and ever. Amen. (Hebrews 13:20-21)

Endnotes

1. William H. Willimon, *The Intrusive Word* (Grand Rapids, MI: William B. Eerdmans Publishing, 1994), 64

2. A.W. Tozer, *The Best of A.W. Tozer*, compiled by Warren W. Wiersbe (Harrisburg, PA: Christian Publications, 1978), 142.

APPENDIX

Summary of Views
on Hebrews 6:4-6

A listing and brief explanation of current interpretations may be helpful. No attempt is made to be exhaustive nor to include rare interpretations.

A Hypothetical Case

Defenders of this view hold that the author has described a supposed case, an imaginary scenario, assuming for the moment the presuppositions of some of his confused and wavering readers.[1]

They say, "*If* anyone would become apostate, it would be impossible to restore him," with an implication that a defection of this sort would actually never take place. The warning is seen as a kind of "straw man" for the purpose of frightening the first-century readers into being better Christians.

Saved People Who Lose Their Salvation

This view sees the description in verses 4-5 to be none other than full salvation. People who have once been enlightened, who have tasted the heavenly gift, etc., are seen as having experienced the fullness of salvation by grace through faith; they are fully regenerated by the Spirit of God, but then lose their salvation through deliberate apostasy. The

361

well-known Lutheran commentator, R.C.H. Lenski, holds to
this view, as do Arminians generally.

Professed Believers Who Have Never Been Saved

Proponents of this view say that the sin of apostasy is a
grim possibility for people who through identification with
the people of God have been brought within the sphere of
divine blessing.[2] They may be baptized as Simon Magus
was, occupied in Christians labors, as Demas was, endowed
with charismatic gifts, healers of the sick and casters out of
demons and privileged to belong to the inner circle of disciples like Judas was, and yet their hearts may be far from the
One they profess to serve.

People are frequently immunized against a disease by being inoculated with a mild form of it or with a related but
milder disease. And in the spiritual realm experience suggests that it is possible to be "immunized" against Christianity by being inoculated with something which, for the time
being, looks so like the real thing that it is generally mistaken
for it.[3]

In other words, some of the people addressed in this letter had the appearance of believers: They had professed repentance, been enlightened and so on, but despite all this,
it is doubtful whether they had grasped even the first principles of faith outlined in Hebrews 5:11-6:3. Perhaps these
people had identified with the people of God, and they had
been brought within the sphere of divine blessing, but
they failed to enter into a personal faith relationship with
Christ.

Therefore, people who hold this view say that it is quite
possible for some people to look like they are Christians for
a while. They have come within the sphere of divine blessing, but they show their true colors when they deliberately
and knowingly turn away from the gospel and the grace of
God.

Christians Who Backslide Too Far

To put this viewpoint in a sentence, the believer, in falling away so far, is disqualified from turning around in repentance. A Christian may go far enough into the depths of a carnal lifestyle, embracing the world's beliefs and behavior, that he can ultimately come to the place where God doesn't permit repentance. His life becomes worthless fruit.

The Bible does acknowledge that believers can drift into moral sin and theological error, they can backslide into carnality and worldliness. Most of the letters of the New Testament were written to correct moral or theological error. In First Corinthians we hear about a man who is sleeping with his father's wife. In Second Corinthians 6 readers are encouraged not to be yoked together with unbelievers. For what fellowship can light have with darkness? In Galatians, the apostle Paul shares his heart about the fallacy of observing the law.

In Philippians there is a veiled reference to the lack of unity between Euodia and Syntyche. In Colossians you have rules for husbands and wives. Thessalonians was written to correct some misunderstanding about the second coming of Christ. First John says if you love the world, the love of the Father is not in you. The Bible does acknowledge that believers can drift into moral and theological error; they can backslide into carnality and worldliness.

Endnotes

1. Warren W. Wiersbe and Homer A. Kent, Jr. take this view to be the correct approach to this passage. K.S. Wuest minimizes the warning when he assures us that "having fallen away" is "a conditional participle here presenting a hypothetical case, a straw man" and that the sin in question cannot be committed today. Hughes states: "The danger of apostasy, it must be emphasized, is real, not imaginary; otherwise this epistle with its high-sounding admonitions must be dismissed as trifling, worthless, and ridiculous" (p. 206).

2. John MacArthur, Jr. supports this position in his commentary on *Hebrews* (Chicago, IL: Moody Press, 1983), 142-149. F.F. Bruce says, "It is a question of people who see clearly where the truth lies, and perhaps for a period conform to it, but then, for one reason or another, renounce it" (p. 119).

3. F.F. Bruce, 118-119.

SELECTED BIBLIOGRAPHY

Barclay, William. *The Letter to the Hebrews*. Edinburgh, Scotland: The Saint Andrew Press, 1955; revised, Philadelphia, PA: The Westminster Press, 1976.

Bauer, Walter. *A Greek-English Lexicon of the New Testament and Other Early Christian Literature*. A translation and adaptation of the fourth revised and augmented edition of Walter Bauer's *Griechisch-Deutsches Worterbuch zu den Schriften des Neuen Testaments und der ubrigen urchristlichen Literatur*. Second edition, Chicago, IL: The University of Chicago Press, 1979.

Bridges, Jerry. *Pursuit of Holiness*. Colorado Springs, CO: NavPress, 1982.

Brown, Raymond. *The Message of Hebrews*. Downers Grove, IL: InterVarsity Press, 1982.

Bruce, F.F. *The Epistle to the Hebrews. The International Commentary on the New Testament*. Grand Rapids, MI: William. B. Eerdmans Publishing Co., 1964.

Calvin, John. *Hebrews and I and II Peter*. Translated by W.B. Johnston. Edited by David W. Torrance and Thomas F. Torrance. Grand Rapids, MI: William B. Eerdmans Publishing Company, 1963.

Campolo, Tony. "Just a Kid with Cerebral Palsy." *Discipleship Journal*, Issue 84 (November/December, 1994).

Chambers, Oswald. *My Utmost for His Highest*. Edited by James Reitmann, Grand Rapids, MI: Discovery House Publishers, reprint, 1992.

Colson, Charles. *Loving God*. Grand Rapids, MI: Zondervan Publishing House, 1983.

Crockett, William V. and James G. Sigountos, eds. *Through No Fault of Their Own?* Grand Rapids, MI: Baker Book House, 1991.

Erickson, Millard J. *Christian Theology*. Grand Rapids, MI: Baker Book House, 1985.

Gire, Ken. *Incredible Moments with the Savior: Learning to See*. Grand Rapids, MI: Daybreak Books, Zondervan Publishing House, 1990.

Guthrie, Donald. *Hebrews*. Grand Rapids, MI: William B. Eerdmans Publishing Company, 1983.

Hart, Archibald D. *Healing Life's Hidden Addictions*. Ann Arbor, MI: Servant Publications, 1990.

Hughes, Kent. *Disciplines of a Godly Man*. Wheaton, IL: Crossway Books, 1991.

Hughes, Philip Edgcumbe. *A Commentary on the Epistle to the Hebrews*. Grand Rapids, MI: William B. Eerdmans Publishing Company, 1977.

Kent, Homer. *The Epistle to the Hebrews: A Commentary*. Grand Rapids, MI: Baker Book House, 1972.

Kreeft, Peter. *Making Sense Out of Suffering*. Ann Arbor, MI: Servant Books, 1986.

Leno, Garth E. "Real Security." *Alliance Life* (June 15, 1994): 32.

Lenski, R.C.H. *The Interpretation of the Epistle to the Hebrews and the Epistle of James*. Minneapolis, MN: Augsburg Publishing House, 1966.

Lucado, Max. *God Came Near: Chronicles of the Christ*. Portland, OR: Multnomah Press, 1987.

_____. *In the Eye of the Storm: A Day in the Life of Jesus*. Dallas, TX: Word Publishing , 1991.

MacArthur, John, Jr. *The MacArthur New Testament Commentary: Hebrews*. Chicago, IL: Moody Press, 1983.

MacDonald, Gordon. *Ordering Your Private World*. Nashville, TN: Thomas Nelson Publishers, 1984.

Manning, Brennan. "The One Jesus Loves." *Discipleship Journal* 82 (July/August 1994).

McGinnis, Alan Loy, *Bringing Out the Best in People: How to Enjoy Helping Others Excel*. Minneapolis, MN: Augsburg Publishing House, 1985.

Morris, Leon. *Hebrews, The Expositor's Bible Commentary*, vol. 12. ed. Frank E. Gaebelein. Grand Rapids, MI: Zondervan Publishing House, 1981.

Newell, William R. *Hebrews: Verse by Verse*. Chicago, IL: Moody Press, 1947.

Peterson, Eugene H. *Under the Unpredictable Plant: An Exploration in Vocational Holiness*. Grand Rapids, MI: William B. Eerdmans Publishing House, 1992.

Pink, Arthur W. *An Exposition of Hebrews*. Grand Rapids, MI: Baker Book House, 1954.

Piper, John. *Let the Nations Be Glad! The Supremacy of God in Missions*. Grand Rapids, MI: Baker Book House, 1993.

Richmond, Gary. *A View from the Zoo*. Waco, TX: Word Books Publisher, 1987.

Seamands, David A. *Healing for Damaged Emotions*. Wheaton, IL: Victor Books, 1981.

Simpson, A.B. *The Fourfold Gospel*. Harrisburg, PA: Christian Publications.

Smalley, Gary and John Trent. *The Blessing*. New York, NY: Pocket Books, 1990.

Solzhenitsyn, Alexander. *Gulag Archipelago II*. New York, NY: Harper & Row, 1974.

Swindoll, Charles R. *Hebrews Bible Study Guide, Vol. I & II*. Fullerton, CA: Insight for Living, 1983.

Tan, Paul Lee. *Encyclopedia of 7700 Illustrations*. Chicago, IL: Assurance Publishers, 1979.

Thomas, W.H. Griffith. *Hebrews: A Devotional Commentary*. Grand Rapids, MI: William B. Eerdmans Publishing Company, reprint, 1982.

Tozer, A.W. *The Best of A.W. Tozer*, Harrisburg, PA: Christian Publications Inc., 1978.

_____. *The Knowledge of the Holy*. San Francisco, CA: Harper & Row Publishers, 1961.

_____. *The Pursuit of God*. Harrisburg, PA: Christian Publications, 1948, Mass Market Edition assigned 1976 to Horizon House Publishers, 46.

_____. *Who Put Jesus on the Cross?* Harrisburg, PA: Christian Publications, 1975.

Wiersbe, Warren W. *Be Confident*. Wheaton, IL: Victor Books, 1982.

_____. *Run with the Winners: A Study of the Champions of Hebrews 11*. Wheaton, IL: Tyndale House Publishers, Inc., 1985.

Zimmerman, Carle C. *Family and Civilization*. New York, NY: Harper & Brothers, 1947.

Studies in Hebrews

Barclay, William. *The Letter to the Hebrews*. Edinburgh: The Saint Andrew Press, 1955; revised, Philadelphia, PA: The Westminster Press, 1976.

Brown, Raymond. *The Message of Hebrews*. Downers Grove, IL: InterVarsity Press, 1982.

Bruce, F.F. *The Epistle to the Hebrews. The International Commentary on the New Testament*. Grand Rapids, MI: William. B. Eerdmans Publishing Company, 1964.

Calvin, John. *Hebrews and I and II Peter*. Translated by W. B. Johnston. Edited by David W. Torrance and Thomas F. Torrance. Grand Rapids, IL: William B. Eerdmans Publishing Company, 1963.

Guthrie, Donald. *Hebrews*. Grand Rapids, MI: William B. Eerdmans Publishing Company, 1983.

Hughes, Philip Edgcumbe. *A Commentary on the Epistle to the Hebrews*. Grand Rapids, MI: William B. Eerdmans Publishing Company, 1977.

Kent, Homer. *The Epistle to the Hebrews: A Commentary*. Grand Rapids, MI: Baker Book House, 1972.

Lenski, R.C.H. *The Interpretation of the Epistle to the Hebrews and the Epistle of James*. Minneapolis, MN: Augsburg Publishing House, 1966.

MacArthur, John, Jr. *The MacArthur New Testament Commentary: Hebrews*. Chicago, IL: Moody Press, 1983.

Morris, Leon. *Hebrews. The Expositor's Bible Commentary*, Vol. 12, ed. Frank E. Gaebelein. Grand Rapids, MI: Zondervan Publishing House, 1981.

Newell, William R. *Hebrews: Verse by Verse*. Chicago, IL: Moody Press, 1947.

Pink, Arthur W. *An Exposition of Hebrews*. Grand Rapids, MI: Baker Book House, 1954.

Swindoll, Charles R. *Hebrews Bible Study Guide, Vol. I & II*. Fullerton, CA: Insight for Living, 1983.

Thomas, W.H. Griffith. *Hebrews: A Devotional Commentary*. Grand Rapids: William B. Eerdmans Publishing Company, rep., 1982.

Wiersbe, Warren W. *Be Confident*. Wheaton, IL: Victor Books, 1982.